MW00395874

# THE TREATISE DE SPIRITU SANCTO

# SANCTO

## AND THE NINE HOMILIES
## OF THE HEXÆMERON

OF

# SAINT BASIL THE GREAT

# ARCHBISHOP OF CÆSARIA,

TRANSLATED WITH NOTES

BY

# THE REV. BLOMFIELD JACKSON, M.A.

Edited by
Paul A. Böer, Sr.

**VERITATIS SPLENDOR PUBLICATIONS**
*et cognoscetis veritatem et veritas liberabit vos (Jn 8:32)*

**MMXII**

This is a re-publication of a work found in:

*A Select Library of the Nicene and Post-Nicene Fathers of the Christian Church,* ed. Philip Schaff, LL.D. (Buffalo: The Christian Literature Co., 1886). Vol. 8 Basil: Letters and Select Works.

. The contents of which is in the public domain.

However, this excerpted version is copyrighted.

ALL RIGHTS RESERVED.

This publication may not be reproduced, stored in a retrieval system, or transmitted in any form or by any means, in whole or in part, without written permission from the Publisher, except as permitted by United States and International copyright law.

Copyright © 2012. Veritatis Splendor Publications.

# AD MAJOREM DEI GLORIAM

# A SELECT LIBRARY

OF THE

# NICENE AND
# POST-NICENE FATHERS

OF

# THE CHRISTIAN CHURCH.

## SECOND SERIES

TRANSLATED INTO ENGLISH WITH PROLEGOMENA AND
EXPLANATORY NOTES.

*Edited by*
PHILIP SCHAFF, D.D., LL.D.,
PROFESSOR OF CHURCH HISTORY IN THE UNION
THEOLOGICAL SEMINARY, NEW YORK.
AND
HENRY WACE, D.D.,
PRINCIPAL OF KING'S COLLEGE, LONDON.

## VOLUME VIII
## BASIL: LETTERS AND SELECT WORKS

T&T CLARK

EDINBURGH

WM. B. EERDMANS PUBLISHING COMPANY

GRAND RAPIDS, MICHIGAN

# TABLE OF CONTENTS

# St. Basil the Great*

Bishop of Caesarea, and one of the most distinguished Doctors of the Church. Born probably 329; died 1 January, 379. He ranks after Athanasius as a defender of the Oriental Church against the heresies of the fourth century. With his friend Gregory of Nazianzus and his brother Gregory of Nyssa, he makes up the trio known as "The Three Cappadocians", far outclassing the other two in practical genius and actual achievement.

## Life

St. Basil the Elder, father of St. Basil the Great, was the son of a Christian of good birth and his wife, Macrina (Acta SS., January, II), both of whom suffered for the faith during the persecution of Maximinus Galerius (305-314), spending several years of hardship in the wild mountains of Pontus. St. Basil the Elder was noted for his virtue (Acta SS, May, VII) and also won considerable reputation as a teacher in Caesarea. He was not a priest (Cf. Cave, Hist. Lit., I, 239). He married Emmelia, the daughter of a martyr and became the father of ten children. Three of these, Macrina, Basil, and Gregory are honoured as saints; and of the sons, Peter, Gregory, and Basil attained the dignity of the episcopate.

Under the care of his father and his grandmother, the elder Macrina, who preserved the traditions of their countryman, St. Gregory Thaumaturgus (c. 213-275) Basil was formed in habits of piety and study. He was still young when his father died and the family moved to the estate of the elder Macrina at Annesi in Pontus, on the banks of the Iris. As a boy, he was sent to school at Caesarea, then "a metropolis of letters", and conceived a fervent admiration for the local bishop, Dianius. Later, he went to

11

Constantinople, at that time "distinguished for its teachers of philosophy and rhetoric", and thence to Athens. Here he became the inseparable companion of Gregory of Nazianzus, who, in his famous panegyric on Basil (Or. xliii), gives a most interesting description of their academic experiences. According to him, Basil was already distinguished for brilliancy of mind and seriousness of character and associated only with the most earnest students. He was able, grave, industrious, and well advanced in rhetoric, grammar, philosophy, astronomy, geometry, and medicine. (As to his not knowing Latin, see Fialon, Etude historique et littéraire sur St. Basile, Paris, 1869). We know the names of two of Basil's teachers at Athens — Prohaeresius, possibly a Christian, and Himerius, a pagan. It has been affirmed, though probably incorrectly, that Basil spent some time under Libanius. He tells us himself that he endeavoured without success to attach himself as a pupil to Eustathius (Ep., I). At the end of his sojourn at Athens, Basil being laden, says St. Gregory of Nazianzus "with all the learning attainable by the nature of man", was well equipped to be a teacher. Caesarea took possession of him gladly "as a founder and second patron" (Or. xliii), and as he tells us (ccx), he refused the splendid offers of the citizens of Neo-Caesarea, who wished him to undertake the education of the youth of their city.

To the successful student and distinguished professor, "there now remained", says Gregory (Or. xliii), "no other need than that of spiritual perfection". Gregory of Nyssa, in his life of Macrina, gives us to understand that Basil's brilliant success both as a university student and a professor had left traces of worldliness and self-sufficiency on the soul of the young man. Fortunately, Basil came again in contact with Dianius, Bishop of Caesarea, the object of his boyish affection, and Dianius seems to have baptized him, and ordained him Reader soon after his return to Caesarea. It was at the same time also that he fell under the influence of that very remarkable woman, his sister Macrina, who had meanwhile founded a religious community on the family estate at Annesi. Basil himself tells us how, like a man roused from deep sleep, he turned his eyes to the marvellous truth of the Gospel, wept many tears over his miserable life, and prayed for guidance from God: "Then I read the Gospel, and saw there that a great means of reaching perfection was the selling of one's goods, the sharing of them with the poor, the giving up of all care for this life, and the refusal to allow the soul to be turned by any sympathy towards things of earth" (Ep. ccxxiii). To learn the ways of perfection, Basil now visited the monasteries of Egypt, Palestine, Coele-Syria, and Mesopotamia. He returned, filled with admiration for the austerity and piety of the monks, and founded a monastery in his native Pontus, on the banks of the Iris, nearly opposite Annesi. (Cf. Ramsay, Hist. Geog. of Asia Minor, London, 1890, p. 326). Eustathius of Sebaste had already introduced the eremitical life into Asia Minor; Basil added the cenobitic or community form, and the new feature was imitated by many companies of men and women. (Cf. Sozomen, Church History VI.27; Epiphanius, Haer., lxxv, 1; Basil, Ep. ccxxiii; Tillemont, Mém., IX, Art. XXI, and note XXVI.) Basil became known as the father of Oriental monasticism, the forerunner of St. Benedict. How well he deserved the title, how seriously and in what spirit he undertook the systematizing of the religious life, may be seen by the study of his Rule. He seems to have read Origen's writings very systematically about this time, for in union with Gregory of Nazianzus, he published a selection of them called the "Philocalia".

Basil was drawn from his retreat into the area of theological controversy in 360 when he accompanied two delegates from Seleucia to the emperor at Constantinople, and supported his namesake of Ancyra. There is some dispute as to his courage and his perfect orthodoxy on this occasion (cf. Philostorgius, Hist. Eccl., IV, xii; answered by Gregory of Nyssa, Answer to Eunomius' Second Book I, and Maran, Proleg., vii; Tillemont, Mém., note XVIII). A little later, however, both qualities seem to have been sufficiently in evidence, as Basil forsook Dianius for having signed the heretical creed of Rimini. To this time (c. 361) may be referred the "Moralia"; and a little later came two books against Eunomius (363) and some correspondence with Athanasius. It is possible, also, that Basil wrote his monastic rules in the briefer forms while in Pontus, and enlarged them later at Caesarea. There is an account of an invitation from Julian for Basil to present himself a court and of Basil's refusal, coupled with an admonition that angered the emperor and endangered Basil's safety. Both incident and correspondence however are questioned by some critics.

Basil still retained considerable influence in Caesarea, and it is regarded as fairly probable that he had a hand in the election of the successor of Dianius who died in 362, after having been reconciled to Basil. In any case the new bishop, Eusebius, was practically placed in his office by the elder Gregory of Nazianzus. Eusebius having persuaded the reluctant Basil to be ordained priest, gave him a prominent place in the administration of the diocese (363). In ability for the management of affairs Basil so far eclipsed the bishop that ill-feeling rose between the two. "All the more eminent and wiser portion of the church was roused against the bishop" (Greg. Naz., Or. xliii; Ep. x), and to avoid trouble Basil again withdrew into the solitude of Pontus. A little later (365) when the attempt of Valens to impose Arianism on the clergy and the people necessitated the presence of a strong personality, Basil was restored to his former position, being reconciled to the bishop by St. Gregory of Nazianzus. There seems to have been no further disagreement between Eusebius and Basil and the latter soon became the real head of the diocese. "The one", says Gregory of Nazianzus (Or. xliii), "led the people the other led their leader". During the five years spent in this most important office, Basil gave evidence of being a man of very unusual powers. He laid down the law to the leading citizens and the imperial governors, settled disputes with wisdom and finality, assisted the spiritually needy, looked after "the support of the poor, the entertainment of strangers, the care of maidens, legislation written and unwritten for the monastic life, arrangements of prayers, (liturgy?), adornment of the sanctuary" (op. cit.). In time of famine, he was the saviour of the poor.

In 370 Basil succeeded to the See of Caesarea, being consecrated according to tradition on 14 June. Caesarea was then a powerful and wealthy city (Sozomen, Church History V.5). Its bishop was Metropolitan of Cappadocia and Exarch of Pontus which embraced more than half of Asia Minor and comprised eleven provinces. The see of Caesarea ranked with Ephesus immediately after the patriarchal sees in the councils, and the bishop was the superior of fifty chorepiscopi (Baert). Basil's actual influence, says Jackson (Prolegomena, XXXII) covered the whole stretch of country "from the Balkans to the Mediterranean and from the Aegean to the Euphrates". The need of a man like Basil in such a see as Caesarea was most pressing, and he must have known this well. Some think that he set about procuring his own election; others (e.g. Maran, Baronius, Ceillier) say that he made no attempt on his own behalf. In any event, he became Bishop of Caesarea largely by the influence of the elder Gregory of Nazianzus. His election, says the younger Gregory (loc. cit.), was followed by disaffection on the part of several suffragan bishops "on whose side were found the greatest scoundrels in the city". During his previous administration of the diocese Basil had so clearly defined his ideas of discipline and orthodoxy, that no one could doubt the direction and the vigour of his policy. St. Athanasius was greatly pleased at Basil's election (Ad Pallad., 953; Ad Joann. et Ant., 951); but the Arianizing Emperor Valens, displayed considerably annoyance and the defeated minority of bishops became consistently hostile to the new metropolitan. By years of tactful conduct, however, "blending his correction with consideration and his gentleness with firmness" (Greg. Naz., Or. xliii), he finally overcame most of his opponents.

Basil's letters tell the story of his tremendous and varied activity; how he worked for the exclusion of unfit candidates from the sacred ministry and the deliverance of the bishops from the temptation of simony; how he required exact discipline and the faithful observance of the canons from both laymen and clerics; how he rebuked the sinful, followed up the offending, and held out hope of pardon to the penitent. (Cf. Epp. xliv, xlv, and xlvi, the beautiful letter to a fallen virgin, as well as Epp. liii, liv, lv, clxxxviii, cxcix, ccxvii, and Ep. clxix, on the strange incident of Glycerius, whose story is well filled out by Ramsay, The Church in the Roman Empire, New York, 1893, p. 443 sqq.) If on the one hand he strenuously defended clerical rights and immunities (Ep. civ), on the other he trained his clergy so strictly that they grew famous as the type of all that a priest should be (Epp. cii, ciii). Basil did not confine his activity to diocesan affairs, but threw himself vigorously into the troublesome theological disputes then rending the unity of Christendom. He drew up a summary of the orthodox faith; he attacked by word of mouth the heretics near at hand and wrote tellingly against those afar. His correspondence shows that he paid visits, sent messages, gave interviews, instructed, reproved, rebuked, threatened, reproached, undertook the protection of nations, cities, individuals great and small. There was very little chance of opposing him successfully, for he was a cool, persistent, fearless fighter in defence both of doctrine and of principles. His bold stand against Valens parallels the meeting of Ambrose with Theodosius. The emperor was dumbfounded at the archbishop's calm indifference to his presence and his wishes. The incident, as narrated by Gregory of Nazianzus, not only tells much concerning Basil's character but throws a clear light on the type of Christian bishop with which the emperors had to deal and goes far to explain why Arianism, with little court behind it, could make so little impression on the ultimate history of Catholicism.

While assisting Eusebius in the care of his diocese, Basil had shown a marked interest in the poor and afflicted; that interest now displayed itself in the erection of a magnificent institution, the Ptochoptopheion, or Basileiad, a house for the care of friendless strangers, the medical treatment of the sick poor, and the industrial training of the unskilled. Built in the suburbs, it attained such importance as to become practically the centre of a new city with the name of he kaine polis or "Newtown". It was the motherhouse of like institutions erected in other dioceses and stood as a constant reminder to the rich of their privilege of spending wealth in a truly Christian way. It may be mentioned here that the social obligations of the wealthy were so plainly and forcibly preached by St. Basil that modern sociologists have ventured to claim him as one of their own, though with no more foundation than would exist in the case of any other consistent teacher of the principles of Catholic ethics. The truth is that St. Basil was a practical lover of Christian poverty, and even in his exalted position preserved that simplicity in food and clothing and that austerity of life for which he had been remarked at his first renunciation of the world.

In the midst of his labours, Basil underwent suffering of many kinds. Athanasius died in 373 and the elder Gregory in 374, both of them leaving gaps never to be filled. In 373 began the painful estrangement from Gregory of Nazianzus. Anthimus, Bishop of Tyana, became an open enemy, Apollinaris "a cause of sorrow to the churches" (Ep. cclxiii), Eustathius of Sebaste a traitor to the Faith and a personal foe as well. Eusebius of Samosata was banished, Gregory of Nyssa condemned and deposed. When Emperor Valentinian died and the Arians recovered their influence, all Basil's efforts must have seemed in vain. His health was breaking, the Goths were at the door of the empire, Antioch was in schism, Rome doubted his sincerity, the bishops refused to be brought together as he wished. "The notes of the church were obscured in his part of Christendom, and he had to fare on as best he might,--admiring, courting, yet coldly treated by the Latin world, desiring the friendship of Rome, yet wounded by her reserve,-- suspected of heresy by Damasus, and accused by Jerome of pride" (Newman, The Church of the Fathers). Had he lived a little longer and attended the Council of Constantinople (381), he would have seen the death of its first president, his friend Meletius, and the forced resignation of its second, Gregory of Nazianzus. Basil died 1 January, 379. His death was regarded as a public bereavement; Jews, pagans, and foreigners vied with his own flock in doing him honour. The earlier Latin martyrologies (Hieronymian and Bede) make no mention of a feast of St. Basil. The first mention is by Usuard and Ado who place it on 14 June, the supposed date of Basil's consecration to the episcopate. In the Greek "Menaea" he is commemorated on 1 January, the day of his death. In 1081, John, Patriarch of Constantinople, in consequence of a vision, established a feast in common honour of St. Basil, Gregory of Nazianzus, and John Chrysostom, to be celebrated on 30 January. The Bollandists give an account of the origin of this feast; they also record as

18

worthy of note that no relics of St. Basil are mentioned before the twelfth century, at which time parts of his body, together with some other very extraordinary relics were reputed to have been brought to Bruges by a returning Crusader. Baronius (c. 1599) gave to the Naples Oratory a relic of St. Basil sent from Constantinople to the pope. The Bollandists and Baronius print descriptions of Basil's personal appearance and the former reproduce two icons, the older copied from a codex presented to Basil, Emperor of the East (877-886).

By common consent, Basil ranks among the greatest figures in church history and the rather extravagant panegyric by Gregory of Nazianzus has been all but equalled by a host of other eulogists. Physically delicate and occupying his exalted position but a few years, Basil did magnificent and enduring work in an age of more violent world convulsions than Christianity has since experienced. (Cf. Newman, The Church of the Fathers). By personal virtue he attained distinction in an age of saints; and his purity, his monastic fervour, his stern simplicity, his friendship for the poor became traditional in the history of Christian asceticism. In fact, the impress of his genius was stamped indelibly on the Oriental conception of religious life. In his hands the great metropolitan see of Caesarea took shape as the sort of model of the Christian diocese; there was hardly any detail of episcopal activity in which he failed to mark out guiding lines and to give splendid example. Not the least of his glories is the fact that toward the officials of the State he maintained that fearless dignity and independence which later history has shown to be an indispensable condition of healthy life in the Catholic episcopate.

Some difficulty has arisen out of the correspondence of St. Basil with the Roman See. That he was in communion with the Western bishops and that he wrote repeatedly to Rome asking that steps be taken to assist the Eastern Church in her struggle with schismatics and heretics is undoubted; but the disappointing result of his appeals drew from him certain words which require explanation. Evidently he was deeply chagrined that Pope Damasus on the one hand hesitated to condemn Marcellus and the Eustathians, and on the other preferred Paulinus to Meletius in whose right to the See of Antioch St. Basil most firmly believed. At the best it must be admitted that St. Basil criticized the pope freely in a private letter to Eusebius of Samosata (Ep. ccxxxix) and that he was indignant as well as hurt at the failure of his attempt to obtain help from the West. Later on, however, he must have recognized that in some respects he had been hasty; in any event, his strong emphasis of the influence which the Roman See could exercise over the Eastern bishops, and his abstaining from a charge of anything like usurpation are great facts that stand out obviously in the story of the disagreement. With regard to the question of his association with the Semi-Arians, Philostorgius speaks of him as championing the Semi-Arian cause, and Newman says he seems unavoidably to have Arianized the first thirty years of his life. The explanation of this, as well as of the disagreement with the Holy See, must be sought in a careful study of the times, with due reference to the unsettled and changeable condition of theological distinctions, the lack of anything like a final pronouncement by the Church's defining power, the "lingering imperfections of the Saints" (Newman), the substantial orthodoxy of many of the so-called Semi-Arians, and above all the great plan which Basil was steadily pursuing of effecting unity in a disturbed and divided Christendom.

## Writings

## Dogmatic

Of the five books against Eunomius (c. 364) the last two are classed as spurious by some critics. The work assails the equivalent Arianism of Eunomius and defends the Divinity of the Three Persons of the Trinity; it is well summarized by Jackson (Nicene and Post Nicene Fathers, Series II, VIII). The work On the Holy Spirit, or treatise on the Holy Spirit (c. 375) was evoked in part by the Macedonian denial of the Divinity of the Third Person and in part by charges that Basil himself had "slurred over the Spirit" (Gregory Naz., Ep. lviii), that he had advocated communion with all such a should admit simply that the Holy Ghost was not a creature (Basil, Ep. cxiii), and that he had sanctioned the use of a novel doxology, namely, "Glory be to the Father with the Son together with the Holy Ghost" (De Sp. S., I, i) The treatise teaches the doctrine of the Divinity of the Holy Ghost, while avoiding the phrase "God, the Holy Ghost" for prudential reasons (Greg. Naz., Or. xliii). Wuilcknis and Swete affirm the necessity of some such reticence on Basil's part. (Cf. Jackson, op. cit., p. XXIII, note.) With regard to Basil's teaching on the Third Person, as expressed in his work against Eunomius (III, i), a controversy arose at the Council of Florence between the Latins and the Greeks; but strong arguments both external and internal, availed to place Basil on the side of the "Filioque". The dogmatic writings were edited separately by Goldhorn, in his "S. Basilii Opera Dogmatica Selecta" (Leipzig, 1854). The On the Holy Spirit, was translated into English by Johnston (Oxford, 1892); by Lewis in the Christian Classic Series (1888); and by Jackson (op. cit.).

## Exegetical

These include nine homilies "On the Hexaemeron" and thirteen (Maran) genuine homilies on particular Psalms. A lengthy commentary on the first sixteen chapters of Isaias is of doubtful authenticity (Jackson), though by a contemporary hand. A commentary on Job has disappeared. "The Hexaemeron" was highly admired by Gregory of Nazianzus (Or. xliii, no. 67). It is translated entire by Jackson (op. cit.). The homilies on the Psalms are moral and hortatory rather than strictly exegetical. In interpreting the Scripture, Basil uses both the literal and the allegorical methods, but favours the literal system of Antioch. His second homily contains a denunciation of usury which has become famous.

## Homiletical

Twenty-four sermons, doctrinal, moral, and panegyrical in character, are looked upon as generally genuine, certain critical difficulties, however, remaining still unsolved. Eight of these sermons were translated into Latin by Rufinus. The discourses place Basil among the very greatest of Christian preachers and evince his special gift for preaching upon the responsibilities of wealth. The most noteworthy in the collection are the homilies on the rich (vi and vii) copied by St. Ambrose (De Nabuthe Jez., v, 21-24), and the homily (xxii) on the study of pagan literature. The latter was edited by Fremion (Paris, 1819, with French translation), Sommer (Paris, 1894), Bach (Münster, 1900), and Maloney (New York, 1901). With regard to Basil's style and his success as a preacher much has been written. (Cf. Villemain, "Tableau d'éloq. Chrét. au IVe siècle", Paris, 1891; Fialon, "Etude Litt. sur St. B.", Paris, 1861); Roux, "Etude sur la prédication de B. le Grand", Strasburg, 1867; Croiset, "Hist. de la litt. Grecque", Paris, 1899.)

## Moral and ascetical

This group contains much of spurious or doubtful origin. Probably authentic are the latter two of the three prefatory treatises, and the five treatises: "Morals", "On the Judgment of God", "On Faith", "The Longer Monastic Rules", "The Shorter Monastic Rules". The twenty-four sermons on morals are a cento of extracts from the writings of Basil made by Simeon Metaphrastes. Concerning the authenticity of the Rules there has been a good deal of discussion. As is plain from these treatises and from the homilies that touch upon ascetical or moral subjects, St. Basil was particularly felicitous in the field of spiritual instruction.

## Correspondence

The extant letters of Basil are 366 in number, two-thirds of them belonging to the period of his episcopate. The so-called "Canonical Epistles" have been assailed as spurious, but are almost surely genuine. The correspondence with Julian and with Libanius is probably apocryphal; the correspondence with Apollinarus is uncertain. All of the 366 letters are translated in the "Nicene and Post-Nicene Fathers". Some of the letters are really dogmatic treatises, and others are apologetic replies to personal attacks. In general they are very useful for their revelation of the saint's character and for the pictures of his age which they offer.

## Liturgical

A so-called "Liturgy of St. Basil" exists in Greek and in Coptic. It goes back at least to the sixth century, but its connexion with Basil has been a matter of critical discussion (Brightman, "Liturgies, Eastern and Western", Oxford, 1896, I; Probst, "Die Liturgie des vierten Jahrhunderts und deren Reform", Münster, 1893, 377-412).

## Editions of St. Basil

The editio princeps of the original text of the extant works of Basil appeared at Basle, 1551, and the first complete Latin translation at Rome, 1515 (autograph manuscript in the British Museum). The best edition is that of the Maurist Benedictines, Garnier and Maran (Paris, 1721-30), republished with appendixes by Migne (P.G., XXIX-XXXII). For fragments attributed to Basil with more or less certainty, and edited by Matthaei, Mai, Pitra, and others, see Bardenhewer, "Patrologie" (Freiburg, 1901), 247. Portions of letters recently discovered in Egyptian papyri were published by H. Landwehr, "Grieschische Handschriften aus Fayûm", in "Philologus", XLIII (1884).

## Sources

GREG. NAZ., Prationes, especially xliii; IDEM, Epistolae; Carm. de vitá suâ; GREG. NYSS., Vita Macrinae; IDEM, Or. in laudem fratris Basilii; IDEM, Answer to Eunomius' Second Book I; SOCRATES, Church History IV.26 and VI.3; SOZOMEN, Church History VI.26 and VII.15-17, 22; RUFINUS, Hist. Eccl., II, ix; THEODORET, Church History IV.19; PHILOSTORGIUS, Hist. Eccl., VIII, xi-xiii; EPHILEM SYRUS, Encomium in Bas., ap. COTELIER, Mon. Eccl. Gr., II; JEROME, De Vir. Illust., cxvi. The Vita Basilii by AMPHILOCHIUS is a forgery of about the ninth century. NEWMAN, Church of the Fathers, I-III

*McSorley, J. (1907). St. Basil the Great. In The Catholic Encyclopedia. New York: Robert Appleton Company.

# De Spiritu Sancto

## Chapter 1
## Prefatory remarks on the need of exact investigation of the most minute portions of theology.

1. Your desire for information, my right well-beloved and most deeply respected brother Amphilochius, I highly commend, and not less your industrious energy. I have been exceedingly delighted at the care and watchfulness shown in the expression of your opinion that of all the terms concerning God in every mode of speech, not one ought to be left without exact investigation. You have turned to good account your reading of the exhortation of the Lord, "Every one that asks receives, and he that seeks finds," Luke 11:10 and by your diligence in asking might, I ween, stir even the most reluctant to give you a share of what they possess. And this in you yet further moves my admiration, that you do not, according to the manners of the most part of the men of our time, propose your questions by way of mere test, but with the honest desire to arrive at the actual truth. There is no lack in these days of captious listeners and questioners; but to find a character desirous of information, and seeking the truth as a remedy for ignorance, is very difficult. Just as in the hunter's snare, or in the soldier's ambush, the trick is generally ingeniously concealed, so it is with the inquiries of the majority of the questioners who advance arguments, not so much with the view of getting any good out of them, as in order that, in the event of their failing to elicit answers which chime in with their own desires, they may seem to have fair ground for controversy.

2. If "To the fool on his asking for wisdom, wisdom shall be reckoned," at how high a price shall we value "the wise hearer" who is quoted by the Prophet in the same verse with "the admirable counsellor"? It is right, I ween, to hold him worthy of all approbation, and to urge him on to further progress, sharing his enthusiasm, and in all things toiling at his side as he presses onwards to perfection. To count the terms used in theology as of primary importance, and to endeavour to trace out the hidden meaning in every phrase and in every syllable, is a characteristic wanting in those who are idle in the pursuit of true religion, but distinguishing all who get knowledge of "the mark" "of our calling;" Philippians 3:14 for what is set before us is, so far as is possible with human nature, to be made like God. Now without knowledge there can be no making like; and knowledge is not got without lessons. The beginning of teaching is speech, and syllables and words are parts of speech. It follows then that to investigate syllables is not to shoot wide of the mark, nor, because the questions raised are what might seem to some insignificant, are they on that account to be held unworthy of heed. Truth is always a quarry hard to hunt, and therefore we must look everywhere for its tracks. The acquisition of true religion is just like that of crafts; both grow bit by bit; apprentices must despise nothing. If a man despise the first elements as small and insignificant, he will never reach the perfection of wisdom.

Yea and Nay are but two syllables, yet there is often involved in these little words at once the best of all good things, Truth, and that beyond which wickedness cannot go, a Lie. But why mention Yea and Nay? Before now, a martyr bearing witness for Christ has been judged to have paid in full the claim of true religion by merely nodding his head. If, then, this be so, what term in theology is so small but that the effect of its weight in the scales according as it be rightly or wrongly used is not great? Of the law we are told "not one jot nor one tittle shall pass away;" Matthew 5:18 how then could it be safe for us to leave even the least unnoticed? The very points which you yourself have sought to have thoroughly sifted by us are at the same time both small and great. Their use is the matter of a moment, and perhaps they are therefore made of small account; but, when we reckon the force of their meaning, they are great. They may be likened to the mustard plant which, though it be the least of shrub-seeds, yet when properly cultivated and the forces latent in its germs unfolded, rises to its own sufficient height.

If any one laughs when he sees our subtlety, to use the Psalmist's words, about syllables, let him know that he reaps laughter's fruitless fruit; and let us, neither giving in to men's reproaches, nor yet vanquished by their disparagement, continue our investigation. So far, indeed, am I from feeling ashamed of these things because they are small, that, even if I could attain to ever so minute a fraction of their dignity, I should both congratulate myself on having won high honour, and should tell my brother and fellow-investigator that no small gain had accrued to him therefrom.

While, then, I am aware that the controversy contained in little words is a very great one, in hope of the prize I do not shrink from toil, with the conviction that the discussion will both prove profitable to myself, and that my hearers will be rewarded with no small benefit. Wherefore now with the help, if I may so say, of the Holy Spirit Himself, I will approach the exposition of the subject, and, if you will, that I may be put in the way of the discussion, I will for a moment revert to the origin of the question before us.

3. Lately when praying with the people, and using the full doxology to God the Father in both forms, at one time "with the Son together with the Holy Ghost," and at another "through the Son in

the Holy Ghost," I was attacked by some of those present on the ground that I was introducing novel and at the same time mutually contradictory terms. You, however, chiefly with the view of benefiting them, or, if they are wholly incurable, for the security of such as may fall in with them, have expressed the opinion that some clear instruction ought to be published concerning the force underlying the syllables employed. I will therefore write as concisely as possible, in the endeavour to lay down some admitted principle for the discussion.

## Chapter 2
## The origin of the heretics' close observation of syllables.

4. The petty exactitude of these men about syllables and words is not, as might be supposed, simple and straightforward; nor is the mischief to which it tends a small one. There is involved a deep and covert design against true religion. Their pertinacious contention is to show that the mention of Father, Son, and Holy Ghost is unlike, as though they will thence find it easy to demonstrate that there is a variation in nature. They have an old sophism, invented by Aetius, the champion of this heresy, in one of whose Letters there is a passage to the effect that things naturally unlike are expressed in unlike terms, and, conversely, that things expressed in unlike terms are naturally unlike. In proof of this statement he drags in the words of the Apostle, "One God and Father of whom are all things,...and one Lord Jesus Christ by whom are all things." 1 Corinthians 8:6 "Whatever, then," he goes on, "is the relation of these terms to one another, such will be the relation of the natures indicated by them; and as the term 'of whom' is unlike the term 'by whom,' so is the Father unlike the Son." On this heresy depends the idle subtlety of these men about the phrases in question. They accordingly assign to God the Father, as though it were His distinctive portion and lot, the phrase "of Whom;" to God the Son

they confine the phrase "by Whom," to the Holy Spirit that of "in Whom," and say that this use of the syllables is never in terchanged, in order that, as I have already said, the variation of language may indicate the variation of nature. Verily it is sufficiently obvious that in their quibbling about the words they are endeavouring to maintain the force of their impious argument.

By the term "of whom" they wish to indicate the Creator; by the term "through whom," the subordinate agent or instrument; by the term "in whom," or "in which," they mean to show the time or place. The object of all this is that the Creator of the universe may be regarded as of no higher dignity than an instrument, and that the Holy Spirit may appear to be adding to existing things nothing more than the contribution derived from place or time.

## Chapter 3
## The systematic discussion of syllables is derived from heathen philosophy.

5. They have, however, been led into this error by their close study of heathen writers, who have respectively applied the terms "of whom" and "through whom" to things which are by nature distinct. These writers suppose that by the term "of whom" or "of which" the matter is indicated, while the term "through whom" or "through which" represents the instrument, or, generally speaking, subordinate agency. Or rather— for there seems no reason why we should not take up their whole argument, and briefly expose at once its incompatibility with the truth and its inconsistency with their own teaching— the students of vain philosophy, while expounding the manifold nature of cause and distinguishing its peculiar significations, define some causes as principal, some as cooperative or con-causal, while others are of the character of "sine qua non," or indispensable.

For every one of these they have a distinct and peculiar use of terms, so that the maker is indicated in a different way from the instrument. For the maker they think the proper expression is "by whom," maintaining that the bench is produced "by" the carpenter; and for the instrument "through which," in that it is produced "through" or by means of adze and gimlet and the rest. Similarly they appropriate "of which" to the material, in that the thing made is "of" wood, while "according to which" shows the design, or pattern put before the craftsman. For he either first makes a mental sketch, and so brings his fancy to bear upon what he is about, or else he looks at a pattern previously put before him, and arranges his work accordingly. The phrase "on account of which" they wish to be confined to the end or purpose, the bench, as they say, being produced for, or on account of, the use of man. "In which" is supposed to indicate time and place. When was it produced? In this time. And where? In this place. And though place and time contribute nothing to what is being produced, yet without these the production of anything is impossible, for efficient agents must have both place and time. It is these careful distinctions, derived from unpractical philosophy and vain delusion, which our opponents have first studied and admired, and then transferred to the simple and unsophisticated doctrine of the Spirit, to the belittling of God the Word, and the setting at naught of the Divine Spirit. Even the phrase set apart by non-Christian writers for the case of lifeless instruments or of manual service of the meanest kind, I mean the expression "through or by means of which," they do not shrink from transferring to the Lord of all, and Christians feel no shame in applying to the Creator of the universe language belonging to a hammer or a saw.

## Chapter 4
## That there is no distinction in the scriptural use of these syllables.

6. We acknowledge that the word of truth has in many places made use of these expressions; yet we absolutely deny that the freedom of the Spirit is in bondage to the pettiness of Paganism. On the contrary, we maintain that Scripture varies its expressions as occasion requires, according to the circumstances of the case. For instance, the phrase "of which" does not always and absolutely, as they suppose, indicate the material, but it is more in accordance with the usage of Scripture to apply this term in the case of the Supreme Cause, as in the words "One God, of whom are all things," 1 Corinthians 8:6 and again, "All things of God." 1 Corinthians 11:12 The word of truth has, however, frequently used this term in the case of the material, as when it says "You shall make an ark of incorruptible wood;" and "You shall make the candlestick of pure gold;" Exodus 25:31 and "The first man is of the earth, earthy;" 1 Corinthians 15:47 and "You are formed out of clay as I am." But these men, to the end, as we have already remarked, that they may establish the difference of nature, have laid down the law that this phrase befits the Father alone. This distinction they have originally derived from heathen authorities, but here they have shown no faithful accuracy of limitation. To the Son they have in conformity with the teaching of their masters given the title of instrument, and to the Spirit that of place, for they say in the Spirit, and through the Son. But when they apply "of whom" to God they no longer follow heathen example, but go over, as they say, to apostolic usage, as it is said, "But of him are you in Christ Jesus," 1 Corinthians 1:30 and "All things of God." 1 Corinthians 11:12 What, then, is the result of this systematic discussion? There is one nature of Cause; another of Instrument;

another of Place. So the Son is by nature distinct from the Father, as the tool from the craftsman; and the Spirit is distinct in so far as place or time is distinguished from the nature of tools or from that of them that handle them.

## Chapter 5
## That "through whom" is said also in the case of the Father, and "of whom" in the case of the Son and of the Spirit.

7. After thus describing the outcome of our adversaries' arguments, we shall now proceed to show, as we have proposed, that the Father does not first take "of whom" and then abandon "through whom" to the Son; and that there is no truth in these men's ruling that the Son refuses to admit the Holy Spirit to a share in "of whom" or in "through whom," according to the limitation of their new-fangled allotment of phrases. "There is one God and Father of whom are all things, and one Lord Jesus Christ through whom are all things." 1 Corinthians 8:6

Yes; but these are the words of a writer not laying down a rule, but carefully distinguishing the hypostases.

The object of the apostle in thus writing was not to introduce the diversity of nature, but to exhibit the notion of Father and of Son as unconfounded. That the phrases are not opposed to one another and do not, like squadrons in war marshalled one against another, bring the natures to which they are applied into mutual conflict, is perfectly plain from the passage in question. The blessed Paul brings both phrases to bear upon one and the same subject, in the words "of him and through him and to him are all things." Romans 11:36 That this plainly refers to the Lord will be admitted even by a reader paying but small attention to the meaning of the words. The apostle has just quoted from the prophecy of Isaiah, "Who has known the mind of the Lord, or who has been his counsellor," and then goes on, "For of him and from him and to him are all things." That the prophet is speaking about God the Word, the Maker of all creation, may be learned from what immediately precedes: "Who has measured the waters in the hollow of his hand, and meted out heaven with the span, and comprehended the dust of the earth in a measure, and weighed the mountains in scales, and the hills in a balance? Who has directed the Spirit of the Lord, or being his counsellor has taught him?" Isaiah 40:12-13 Now the word "who" in this passage does not mean absolute impossibility, but rarity, as in the passage "Who will rise up for me against the evil doers?" and "What man is he that desires life?" and "Who shall ascend into the hill of the Lord?" So is it in the passage in question, "Who has directed [lxx., known] the Spirit of the Lord, or being his counsellor has known him?" "For the Father loves the Son and shows him all things." John 5:20 This is He who holds the earth, and has grasped it with His hand, who brought all things to order and adornment, who poised the hills in their places, and measured the waters, and gave to all things in the universe their proper rank, who encompasses the whole of heaven with but a small portion of His power, which, in a figure, the prophet calls a span. Well then did the apostle add "Of him and through him and to him are all things." Romans 11:38 For of Him, to all things that are, comes the cause of their being, according to the will of God the Father. Through Him all things have their continuance and constitution, for He created all things, and metes out to each severally what is necessary for its health and preservation. Wherefore to Him all things are turned, looking with irresistible longing and unspeakable affection to "the author" Acts 3:15 and maintainer "of" their "life," as it is written "The eyes of all wait upon you," and again, "These wait all upon you," and "You open your hand, and satisfiest the desire of every living thing."

8. But if our adversaries oppose this our interpretation, what argument will save them from being caught in their own trap?

For if they will not grant that the three expressions "of him" and "through him" and "to him" are spoken of the Lord, they cannot but be applied to God the Father. Then without question their rule will fall through, for we find not only "of whom," but also "through whom" applied to the Father. And if this latter phrase indicates nothing derogatory, why in the world should it be confined, as though conveying the sense of inferiority, to the Son? If it always and everywhere implies ministry, let them tell us to what superior the God of glory and Father of the Christ is subordinate.

They are thus overthrown by their own selves, while our position will be on both sides made sure. Suppose it proved that the passage refers to the Son, "of whom" will be found applicable to the Son. Suppose on the other hand it be insisted that the prophet's words relate to God, then it will be granted that "through whom" is properly used of God, and both phrases have equal value, in that both are used with equal force of God. Under either alternative both terms, being employed of one and the same Person, will be shown to be equivalent. But let us revert to our subject.

9. In his Epistle to the Ephesians the apostle says, "But speaking the truth in love, may grow up into him in all things, which is the head, even Christ; from whom the whole body fitly joined together and compacted by that which every joint supplies, according to the effectual working in the measure of every part, makes increase of the body." Ephesians 4:15-16

And again in the Epistle to the Colossians, to them that have not the knowledge of the Only Begotten, there is mention of him that holds "the head," that is, Christ, "from which all the body by joints

and bands having nourishment ministered increases with the
increase of God." Colossians 2:19 And that Christ is the head of
the Church we have learned in another passage, when the apostle
says "gave him to be the head over all things to the Church,"
Ephesians 1:22 and "of his fullness have all we received." John 1:16
And the Lord Himself says "He shall take of mine, and shall show
it unto you." will perceive that "of whom" is used in diverse
manners. For instance, the Lord says, "I perceive that virtue is gone
out of me." Similarly we have frequently observed "of whom" used
of the Spirit. "He that sows to the spirit," it is said, "shall of the
spirit reap life everlasting." Galatians 6:8 John too writes, "Hereby
we know that he abides in us by (ἐκ) the spirit which he has given
us." 1 John 3:24 "That which is conceived in her," says the angel,
"is of the Holy Ghost," Matthew 1:20 and the Lord says "that
which is born of the spirit is spirit." John 3:6 Such then is the case
so far.

10. It must now be pointed out that the phrase "through whom" is
admitted by Scripture in the case of the Father and of the Son and
of the Holy Ghost alike. It would indeed be tedious to bring
forward evidence of this in the case of the Son, not only because it
is perfectly well known, but because this very point is made by our
opponents. We now show that "through whom" is used also in the
case of the Father. "God is faithful," it is said, "by whom (δι' οὗ)
you were called unto the fellowship of his Son," 1 Corinthians 1:9
and "Paul an apostle of Jesus Christ by (διά) the will of God;" and
again, "Wherefore you are no more a servant, but a son; and if a
son, then an heir through God." And "like as Christ was raised up
from the dead by (διά) the glory of God the Father." Isaiah,
moreover, says, "Woe unto them that make deep counsel and not
through the Lord;" and many proofs of the use of this phrase in
the case of the Spirit might be adduced. "God has revealed him to

35

us," it is said, "by (διά) the spirit;" 1 Corinthians 2:10 and in another place, "That good thing which was committed unto you keep by (διά) the Holy Ghost;" 2 Timothy 1:14 and again, "To one is given by (διά) the spirit the word of wisdom." 1 Corinthians 12:8

11. In the same manner it may also be said of the word "in," that Scripture admits its use in the case of God the Father. In the Old Testament it is said through (ἐν) God we shall do valiantly, and, "My praise shall be continually of (ἐν) you;" and again, "In your name will I rejoice." In Paul we read, "In God who created all things," Ephesians 3:9 and, "Paul and Silvanus and Timotheus unto the church of the Thessalonians in God our Father;" 2 Thessalonians 1:1 and "if now at length I might have a prosperous journey by (ἐν) the will of God to come to you;" Romans 1:10 and, "You make your boast of God." Romans 2:17 Instances are indeed too numerous to reckon; but what we want is not so much to exhibit an abundance of evidence as to prove that the conclusions of our opponents are unsound. I shall, therefore, omit any proof of this usage in the case of our Lord and of the Holy Ghost, in that it is notorious. But I cannot forbear to remark that "the wise hearer" will find sufficient proof of the proposition before him by following the method of contraries. For if the difference of language indicates, as we are told, that the nature has been changed, then let identity of language compel our adversaries to confess with shame that the essence is unchanged.

12. And it is not only in the case of the theology that the use of the terms varies, but whenever one of the terms takes the meaning of the other we find them frequently transferred from the one subject to the other. As, for instance, Adam says, "I have gotten a man through God," meaning to say the same as from God; and in another passage "Moses commanded . . . Israel through the word

of the Lord," and, again, "Is not the interpretation through God?" Joseph, discoursing about dreams to the prisoners, instead of saying "from God" says plainly "through God." Inversely Paul uses the term "from whom" instead of "through whom," when he says "made from a woman" (A.V., "of" instead of "through a woman"). Galatians 4:4 And this he has plainly distinguished in another passage, where he says that it is proper to a woman to be made of the man, and to a man to be made through the woman, in the words "For as the woman is from [A.V., of] the man, even so is the man also through [A.V., by] the woman." 1 Corinthians 11:12 Nevertheless in the passage in question the apostle, while illustrating the variety of usage, at the same time corrects obiter the error of those who supposed that the body of the Lord was a spiritual body, and, to show that the God-bearing flesh was formed out of the com mon lump of human nature, gave precedence to the more emphatic preposition.

The phrase "through a woman" would be likely to give rise to the suspicion of mere transit in the generation, while the phrase "of the woman" would satisfactorily indicate that the nature was shared by the mother and the offspring. The apostle was in no wise contradicting himself, but he showed that the words can without difficulty be interchanged. Since, therefore, the term "from whom" is transferred to the identical subjects in the case of which "through whom" is decided to be properly used, with what consistency can these phrases be invariably distinguished one from the other, in order that fault may be falsely found with true religion?

## Chapter 6
## Issue joined with those who assert that the Son is not with the Father, but after the Father. Also concerning the equal glory.

13. Our opponents, while they thus artfully and perversely encounter our argument, cannot even have recourse to the plea of ignorance. It is obvious that they are annoyed with us for completing the doxology to the Only Begotten together with the Father, and for not separating the Holy Spirit from the Son. On this account they style us innovators, revolutionizers, phrase-coiners, and every other possible name of insult. But so far am I from being irritated at their abuse, that, were it not for the fact that their loss causes me "heaviness and continual sorrow," I could almost have said that I was grateful to them for the blasphemy, as though they were agents for providing me with blessing. For "blessed are you," it is said, "when men shall revile you for my sake." Matthew 5:11 The grounds of their indignation are these: The Son, according to them, is not together with the Father, but after the Father. Hence it follows that glory should be ascribed to the Father "through him," but not "with him;" inasmuch as "with him" expresses equality of dignity, while "through him" denotes subordination. They further assert that the Spirit is not to be ranked along with the Father and the Son, but under the Son and the Father; not coordinated, but subordinated; not connumerated, but subnumerated.

With technical terminology of this kind they pervert the simplicity and artlessness of the faith, and thus by their ingenuity, suffering no one else to remain in ignorance, they cut off from themselves the plea that ignorance might demand.

14. Let us first ask them this question: In what sense do they say that the Son is "after the Father;" later in time, or in order, or in

dignity? But in time no one is so devoid of sense as to assert that the Maker of the ages holds a second place, when no interval intervenes in the natural conjunction of the Father with the Son. And indeed so far as our conception of human relations goes, it is impossible to think of the Son as being later than the Father, not only from the fact that Father and Son are mutually conceived of in accordance with the relationship subsisting between them, but because posteriority in time is predicated of subjects separated by a less interval from the present, and priority of subjects farther off. For instance, what happened in Noah's time is prior to what happened to the men of Sodom, inasmuch as Noah is more remote from our own day; and, again, the events of the history of the men of Sodom are posterior, because they seem in a sense to approach nearer to our own day. But, in addition to its being a breach of true religion, is it not really the extremest folly to measure the existence of the life which transcends all time and all the ages by its distance from the present? Is it not as though God the Father could be compared with, and be made superior to, God the Son, who exists before the ages, precisely in the same way in which things liable to beginning and corruption are described as prior to one another?

The superior remoteness of the Father is really inconceivable, in that thought and intelligence are wholly impotent to go beyond the generation of the Lord; and St. John has admirably confined the conception within circumscribed boundaries by two words, "In the beginning was the Word." For thought cannot travel outside "was," nor imagination beyond "beginning." Let your thought travel ever so far backward you cannot get beyond the "was," and however you may strain and strive to see what is beyond the Son, you will find it impossible to get further than the "beginning." True religion, therefore, thus teaches us to think of the Son together with the Father.

15. If they really conceive of a kind of degradation of the Son in relation to the Father, as though He were in a lower place, so that the Father sits above, and the Son is thrust off to the next seat below, let them confess what they mean. We shall have no more to say. A plain statement of the view will at once expose its absurdity. They who refuse to allow that the Father pervades all things do not so much as maintain the logical sequence of thought in their argument. The faith of the sound is that God fills all things; Ephesians 4:10 but they who divide their up and down between the Father and the Son do not remember even the word of the Prophet: "If I climb up into heaven you are there; if I go down to hell you are there also." Now, to omit all proof of the ignorance of those who predicate place of incorporeal things, what excuse can be found for their attack upon Scripture, shameless as their antagonism is, in the passages "Sit on my right hand" and "Sat down on the right hand of the majesty of God"? The expression "right hand" does not, as they contend, indicate the lower place, but equality of relation; it is not understood physically, in which case there might be something sinister about God, but Scripture puts before us the magnificence of the dignity of the Son by the use of dignified language indicating the seat of honour. It is left then for our opponents to allege that this expression signifies inferiority of rank. Let them learn that "Christ is the power of God and wisdom of God," 1 Corinthians 1:24 and that "He is the image of the invisible God" Colossians 1:15 and "brightness of his glory," Hebrews 1:3 and that "Him has God the Father sealed," John 6:27 by engraving Himself on Him.

Now are we to call these passages, and others like them, throughout the whole of Holy Scripture, proofs of humiliation, or rather public proclamations of the majesty of the Only Begotten, and of the equality of His glory with the Father? We ask them to listen to the Lord Himself, distinctly setting forth the equal dignity of His glory with the Father, in His words, "He that has seen me has seen the Father;" John 14:9 and again, "When the Son comes in the glory of his Father;" Mark 8:38 that they "should honour the Son even as they honour the Father;" John 5:23 and, "We beheld his glory, the glory as of the only begotten of the Father;" John 1:14 and "the only begotten God which is in the bosom of the Father." Of all these passages they take no account, and then assign to the Son the place set apart for His foes. A father's bosom is a fit and becoming seat for a son, but the place of the footstool is for them that have to be forced to fall.

We have only touched cursorily on these proofs, because our object is to pass on to other points. You at your leisure can put together the items of the evidence, and then contemplate the height of the glory and the preeminence of the power of the Only Begotten. However, to the well-disposed hearer, even these are not insignificant, unless the terms "right hand" and "bosom" be accepted in a physical and derogatory sense, so as at once to circumscribe God in local limits, and invent form, mould, and bodily position, all of which are totally distinct from the idea of the absolute, the infinite, and the incorporeal. There is moreover the fact that what is derogatory in the idea of it is the same in the case both of the Father and the Son; so that whoever repeats these arguments does not take away the dignity of the Son, but does incur the charge of blaspheming the Father; for whatever audacity a man be guilty of against the Son he cannot but transfer to the Father. If he assigns to the Father the upper place by way of precedence, and asserts that the only begotten Son sits below, he will find that to the creature of his imagination attach all the consequent conditions of body. And if these are the imaginations of drunken delusion and phrensied insanity, can it be consistent with true religion for men taught by the Lord himself that "He that honours not the Son honours not the Father" John 5:23 to refuse to worship and glorify with the Father him who in nature, in glory, and in dignity is conjoined with him? What shall we say? What just defence shall we have in the day of the awful universal judgment of all-creation, if, when the Lord clearly announces that He will come "in the glory of his Father;" Matthew 16:27 when Stephen beheld Jesus standing at the right hand of God; Acts 7:55 when Paul testified in the spirit concerning Christ "that he is at the right hand of God;" Romans 8:34 when the Father says, "Sit on my right hand;" when the Holy Spirit bears witness that he has sat down on "the right hand of the majesty" Hebrews 8:1 of God; we attempt to degrade him who shares the honour and the throne, from his condition of equality, to a lower state? Standing and sitting, I apprehend, indicate the fixity and entire stability of the nature, as Baruch, when he wishes to exhibit the immutability and immobility of the Divine mode of existence, says, "For you sit for ever and we perish utterly." Moreover, the place on the right hand indicates in my judgment equality of honour. Rash, then, is the attempt to deprive the Son of participation in the doxology, as though worthy only to be ranked in a lower place of honour.

## Chapter 7
**Against those who assert that it is not proper for "with whom" to be said of the Son, and that the proper phrase is "through whom."**

16. But their contention is that to use the phrase "with him" is altogether strange and unusual, while "through him" is at once most familiar in Holy Scripture, and very common in the language of the brotherhood. What is our answer to this? We say, Blessed are the ears that have not heard you and the hearts that have been kept from the wounds of your words. To you, on the other hand,

who are lovers of Christ, I say that the Church recognizes both uses, and deprecates neither as subversive of the other. For whenever we are contemplating the majesty of the nature of the Only Begotten, and the excellence of His dignity, we bear witness that the glory is with the Father; while on the other hand, whenever we bethink us of His bestowal on us of good gifts, and of our access to, and admission into, the household of God, we confess that this grace is effected for us through Him and by Him.

It follows that the one phrase "with whom" is the proper one to be used in the ascription of glory, while the other, "through whom," is specially appropriate in giving of thanks. It is also quite untrue to allege that the phrase "with whom" is unfamiliar in the usage of the devout. All those whose soundness of character leads them to hold the dignity of antiquity to be more honourable than mere new-fangled novelty, and who have preserved the tradition of their fathers unadulterated, alike in town and in country, have employed this phrase. It is, on the contrary, they who are surfeited with the familiar and the customary, and arrogantly assail the old as stale, who welcome innovation, just as in dress your lovers of display always prefer some utter novelty to what is generally worn. So you may even still see that the language of country folk preserves the ancient fashion, while of these, our cunning experts in logomachy, the language bears the brand of the new philosophy.

What our fathers said, the same say we, that the glory of the Father and of the Son is common; wherefore we offer the doxology to the Father with the Son. But we do not rest only on the fact that such is the tradition of the Fathers; for they too followed the sense of Scripture, and started from the evidence which, a few sentences back, I deduced from Scripture and laid before you. For "the brightness" is always thought of with "the glory," "the image" with the archetype, 2 Corinthians 4:4 and the Son always and everywhere together with the Father; nor does even the close connection of the names, much less the nature of the things, admit of separation.

## Chapter 8
**In how many ways "Through whom" is used; and in what sense "with whom" is more suitable. Explanation of how the Son receives a commandment, and how He is sent.**

17. When, then, the apostle "thanks God through Jesus Christ," Romans 1:8 and again says that "through Him" we have "received grace and apostleship for obedience to the faith among all nations," Romans 1:5 or "through Him have access unto this grace wherein we stand and rejoice," Romans 5:2 he sets forth the boons conferred on us by the Son, at one time making the grace of the good gifts pass through from the Father to us, and at another bringing us to the Father through Himself. For by saying "through whom we have received grace and apostleship," Romans 1:5 he declares the supply of the good gifts to proceed from that source; and again in saying "through whom we have had access," Romans 5:2 he sets forth our acceptance and being made "of the household of God" through Christ. Is then the confession of the grace wrought by Him to usward a detraction from His glory? Is it not truer to say that the recital of His benefits is a proper argument for glorifying Him? It is on this account that we have not found Scripture describing the Lord to us by one name, nor even by such terms alone as are indicative of His godhead and majesty. At one time it uses terms descriptive of His nature, for it recognises the "name which is above every name," Philippians 2:9 the name of Son, and speaks of true Son, and only begotten God, and Power of God, and Wisdom, 1 Corinthians 1:24 and Word. Then again, on account of the various manners wherein grace is given to us, which, because of the riches of His goodness, according to his manifold

Ephesians 3:10 wisdom, he bestows on them that need, Scripture designates Him by innumerable other titles, calling Him Shepherd, King, Physician, Bridegroom, Way, Door, Fountain, Bread, Axe, and Rock. And these titles do not set forth His nature, but, as I have remarked, the variety of the effectual working which, out of His tender-heartedness to His own creation, according to the peculiar necessity of each, He bestows upon them that need. Them that have fled for refuge to His ruling care, and through patient endurance have mended their wayward ways, He calls "sheep," and confesses Himself to be, to them that hear His voice and refuse to give heed to strange teaching, a "shepherd." For "my sheep," He says, "hear my voice." To them that have now reached a higher stage and stand in need of righteous royalty, He is a King. And in that, through the straight way of His commandments, He leads men to good actions, and again because He safely shuts in all who through faith in Him betake themselves for shelter to the blessing of the higher wisdom, He is a Door.

So He says, "By me if any man enter in, he shall go in and out and shall find pastare." John 10:9 Again, because to the faithful He is a defence strong, unshaken, and harder to break than any bulwark, He is a Rock. Among these titles, it is when He is styled Door, or Way, that the phrase "through Him" is very appropriate and plain. As, however, God and Son, He is glorified with and together with the Father, in that "at, the name of Jesus every knee should bow, of things in heaven, and things in earth, and things under the earth; and that every tongue should confess that Jesus Christ is Lord, to the glory of God the Father." Philippians 2:10-11 Wherefore we use both terms, expressing by the one His own proper dignity, and by the other His grace to usward.

18. For "through Him" comes every succour to our souls, and it is in accordance with each kind of care that an appropriate title has

been devised. So when He presents to Himself the blameless soul, not having spot or wrinkle, Ephesians 5:29 like a pure maiden, He is called Bridegroom, but whenever He receives one in sore plight from the devil's evil strokes, healing it in the heavy infirmity of its sins, He is named Physician. And shall this His care for us degrade to meanness our thoughts of Him? Or, on the contrary, shall it smite us with amazement at once at the mighty power and love to man of the Saviour, in that He both endured to suffer with us in our infirmities, and was able to come down to our weakness? For not heaven and earth and the great seas, not the creatures that live in the water and on dry land, not plants, and stars, and air, and seasons, not the vast variety in the order of the universe, so well sets forth the excellency of His might as that God, being incomprehensible, should have been able, impassibly, through flesh, to have come into close conflict with death, to the end that by His own suffering He might give us the boon of freedom from suffering. The apostle, it is true, says, "In all these things we are more than conquerors through him that loved us." Romans 8:37 But in a phrase of this kind there is no suggestion of any lowly and subordinate ministry, but rather of the succour rendered "in the power of his might." Ephesians 6:10 For He Himself has bound the strong man and spoiled his goods, that is, us men, whom our enemy had abused in every evil activity, and made "vessels meet for the Master's use" 2 Timothy 2:21 us who have been perfected for every work through the making ready of that part of us which is in our own control. Thus we have had our approach to the Father through Him, being translated from "the power of darkness to be partakers of the inheritance of the saints in light." Colossians 1:12-13 We must not, however, regard the œconomy through the Son as a compulsory and subordinate ministration resulting from the low estate of a slave, but rather the voluntary solicitude working effectually for His own creation in goodness and in pity, according to the will of God the Father. For we shall be consistent with true religion if in all that was and is from time to time perfected by Him, we both bear witness to the perfection of His power, and in no case put it asunder from the Father's will. For instance, whenever the Lord is called the Way, we are carried on to a higher meaning, and not to that which is derived from the vulgar sense of the word. We understand by Way that advance to perfection which is made stage by stage, and in regular order, through the works of righteousness and "the illumination of knowledge;" ever longing after what is before, and reaching forth unto those things which remain, until we shall have reached the blessed end, the knowledge of God, which the Lord through Himself bestows on them that have trusted in Him. For our Lord is an essentially good Way, where erring and straying are unknown, to that which is essentially good, to the Father. For "no one," He says, comes to the Father but ["by" A.V.] through me. John 14:6 Such is our way up to God "through the Son."

19. It will follow that we should next in order point out the character of the provision of blessings bestowed on us by the Father "through him." Inasmuch as all created nature, both this visible world and all that is conceived of in the mind, cannot hold together without the care and providence of God, the Creator Word, the Only begotten God, apportioning His succour according to the measure of the needs of each, distributes mercies various and manifold on account of the many kinds and characters of the recipients of His bounty, but appropriate to the necessities of individual requirements. Those that are confined in the darkness of ignorance He enlightens: for this reason He is true Light. John 1:9 Portioning requital in accordance with the desert of deeds, He judges: for this reason He is righteous Judge. 2 Timothy 4:8 "For the Father judges no man, but has committed all judgment to the

Son." John 5:22 Those that have lapsed from the lofty height of life into sin He raises from their fall: for this reason He is Resurrection. John 11:25 Effectually working by the touch of His power and the will of His goodness He does all things. He shepherds; He enlightens; He nourishes; He heals; He guides; He raises up; He calls into being things that were not; He upholds what has been created. Thus the good things that come from God reach us "through the Son," who works in each case with greater speed than speech can utter. For not lightnings, not light's course in air, is so swift; not eyes' sharp turn, not the movements of our very thought. Nay, by the divine energy is each one of these in speed further surpassed than is the slowest of all living creatures outdone in motion by birds, or even winds, or the rush of the heavenly bodies: or, not to mention these, by our very thought itself. For what extent of time is needed by Him who "upholds all things by the word of His power," Hebrews 1:3 and works not by bodily agency, nor requires the help of hands to form and fashion, but holds in obedient following and unforced consent the nature of all things that are? So as Judith says, "You have thought, and what things you determined were ready at hand." On the other hand, and lest we should ever be drawn away by the greatness of the works wrought to imagine that the Lord is without beginning, what says the Self-Existent? "I live through [by, A.V.] the Father," John 6:57 and the power of God; "The Son has power [can, A.V.] to do nothing of himself." John 5:19 And the self-complete Wisdom? I received "a commandment what I should say and what I should speak." John 12:49 Through all these words He is guiding us to the knowledge of the Father, and referring our wonder at all that is brought into existence to Him, to the end that "through Him" we may know the Father. For the Father is not regarded from the difference of the operations, by the exhibition of a separate and peculiar energy; for whatsoever things He sees the Father doing, "these also does the

Son likewise;" John 5:19 but He enjoys our wonder at all that comes to pass out of the glory which comes to Him from the Only Begotten, rejoicing in the Doer Himself as well as in the greatness of the deeds, and exalted by all who acknowledge Him as Father of our Lord Jesus Christ, "through whom [by whom, A.V.] are all things, and for whom are all things." Wherefore, says the Lord, "All mine are yours," John 17:10 as though the sovereignty over created things were conferred on Him, and "Yours are mine," as though the creating Cause came thence to Him. We are not to suppose that He used assistance in His action, or yet was entrusted with the ministry of each individual work by detailed commission, a condition distinctly menial and quite inadequate to the divine dignity. Rather was the Word full of His Father's excellences; He shines forth from the Father, and does all things according to the likeness of Him that begot Him. For if in essence He is without variation, so also is He without variation in power. And of those whose power is equal, the operation also is in all ways equal. And Christ is the power of God, and the wisdom of God. 1 Corinthians 1:24 And so "all things are made through [by, A.V.] him," John 1:3 and "all things were created through [by, A.V.] him and for him," Colossians 1:16 not in the discharge of any slavish service, but in the fulfilment of the Father's will as Creator.

20. When then He says, "I have not spoken of myself," John 12:49 and again, "As the Father said unto me, so I speak," John 12:50 and "The word which you hear is not mine, but [the Father's] which sent me," John 14:24 and in another place, "As the Father gave me commandment, even so I do," John 14:31 it is not because He lacks deliberate purpose or power of initiation, nor yet because He has to wait for the preconcerted key-note, that he employs language of this kind. His object is to make it plain that His own will is connected in indissoluble union with the Father. Do not

then let us understand by what is called a "commandment" a peremptory mandate delivered by organs of speech, and giving orders to the Son, as to a subordinate, concerning what He ought to do. Let us rather, in a sense befitting the Godhead, perceive a transmission of will, like the reflexion of an object in a mirror, passing without note of time from Father to Son. "For the Father loves the Son and shows him all things," John 5:20 so that "all things that the Father has" belong to the Son, not gradually accruing to Him little by little, but with Him all together and at once. Among men, the workman who has been thoroughly taught his craft, and, through long training, has sure and established experience in it, is able, in accordance with the scientific methods which now he has in store, to work for the future by himself. And are we to suppose that the wisdom of God, the Maker of all creation, He who is eternally perfect, who is wise, without a teacher, the Power of God, "in whom are hid all the treasures of wisdom and knowledge," needs piecemeal instruction to mark out the manner and measure of His operations? I presume that in the vanity of your calculations, you mean to open a school; you will make the one take His seat in the teacher's place, and the other stand by in a scholar's ignorance, gradually learning wisdom and advancing to perfection, by lessons given Him bit by bit. Hence, if you have sense to abide by what logically follows, you will find the Son being eternally taught, nor yet ever able to reach the end of perfection, inasmuch as the wisdom of the Father is infinite, and the end of the infinite is beyond apprehension. It results that whoever refuses to grant that the Son has all things from the beginning will never grant that He will reach perfection. But I am ashamed at the degraded conception to which, by the course of the argument, I have been brought down. Let us therefore revert to the loftier themes of our discussion.

21. He that has seen me has seen the Father; John 14:9 not the express image, nor yet the form, for the divine nature does not admit of combination; but the goodness of the will, which, being concurrent with the essence, is beheld as like and equal, or rather the same, in the Father as in the Son.

What then is meant by "became subject"? Philippians 2:8 What by "delivered him up for us all"? Romans 8:32 It is meant that the Son has it of the Father that He works in goodness on behalf of men. But you must hear too the words, "Christ has redeemed us from the curse of the law;" Galatians 3:13 and "while we were yet sinners, Christ died for us." Romans 5:8

Give careful heed, too, to the words of the Lord, and note how, whenever He instructs us about His Father, He is in the habit of using terms of personal authority, saying, "I will; be clean;" Matthew 8:3 and "Peace, be still;" Mark 4:39 and "But I say unto you;" and "Thou dumb and deaf spirit, I charge you;" Mark 9:25 and all other expressions of the same kind, in order that by these we may recognise our Master and Maker, and by the former may be taught the Father of our Master and Creator. Thus on all sides is demonstrated the true doctrine that the fact that the Father creates through the Son neither constitutes the creation of the Father imperfect nor exhibits the active energy of the Son as feeble, but indicates the unity of the will; so the expression "through whom" contains a confession of an antecedent Cause, and is not adopted in objection to the efficient Cause.

## Chapter 9
## Definitive conceptions about the Spirit which conform to the teaching of the Scriptures.

22. Let us now investigate what are our common conceptions concerning the Spirit, as well those which have been gathered by us

from Holy Scripture concerning It as those which we have received
from the unwritten tradition of the Fathers. First of all we ask, who
on hearing the titles of the Spirit is not lifted up in soul, who does
not raise his conception to the supreme nature? It is called "Spirit
of God," "Spirit of truth which proceeds from the Father," John
15:26 "right Spirit," "a leading Spirit." Its proper and peculiar title
is "Holy Spirit;" which is a name specially appropriate to everything
that is incorporeal, purely immaterial, and indivisible. So our Lord,
when teaching the woman who thought God to be an object of
local worship that the incorporeal is incomprehensible, said "God
is a spirit." John 4:24 On our hearing, then, of a spirit, it is
impossible to form the idea of a nature circumscribed, subject to
change and variation, or at all like the creature. We are compelled
to advance in our conceptions to the highest, and to think of an
intelligent essence, in power infinite, in magnitude unlimited,
unmeasured by times or ages, generous of Its good gifts, to whom
turn all things needing sanctification, after whom reach all things
that live in virtue, as being watered by Its inspiration and helped on
toward their natural and proper end; perfecting all other things, but
Itself in nothing lacking; living not as needing restoration, but as
Supplier of life; not growing by additions; but straightway full, self-
established, omnipresent, origin of sanctification, light perceptible
to the mind, supplying, as it were, through Itself, illumination to
every faculty in the search for truth; by nature unapproachable,
apprehended by reason of goodness, filling all things with Its
power, but communicated only to the worthy; not shared in one
measure, but distributing Its energy according to "the proportion
of faith;" Romans 12:6 in essence simple, in powers various, wholly
present in each and being wholly everywhere; impassively divided,
shared without loss of ceasing to be entire, after the likeness of the
sunbeam, whose kindly light falls on him who enjoys it as though it
shone for him alone, yet illumines land and sea and mingles with

the air. So, too, is the Spirit to every one who receives it, as though given to him alone, and yet It sends forth grace sufficient and full for all mankind, and is enjoyed by all who share It, according to the capacity, not of Its power, but of their nature.

23. Now the Spirit is not brought into intimate association with the soul by local approximation. How indeed could there be a corporeal approach to the incorporeal? This association results from the withdrawal of the passions which, coming afterwards gradually on the soul from its friendship to the flesh, have alienated it from its close relationship with God. Only then after a man is purified from the shame whose stain he took through his wickedness, and has come back again to his natural beauty, and as it were cleaning the Royal Image and restoring its ancient form, only thus is it possible for him to draw near to the Paraclete. And He, like the sun, will by the aid of your purified eye show you in Himself the image of the invisible, and in the blessed spectacle of the image you shall behold the unspeakable beauty of the archetype. Through His aid hearts are lifted up, the weak are held by the hand, and they who are advancing are brought to perfection. Shining upon those that are cleansed from every spot, He makes them spiritual by fellowship with Himself. Just as when a sunbeam falls on bright and transparent bodies, they themselves become brilliant too, and shed forth a fresh brightness from themselves, so souls wherein the Spirit dwells, illuminated by the Spirit, themselves become spiritual, and send forth their grace to others. Hence comes foreknowledge of the future, understanding of mysteries, apprehension of what is hidden, distribution of good gifts, the heavenly citizenship, a place in the chorus of angels, joy without end, abiding in God, the being made like to God, and, highest of all, the being made God. Such, then, to instance a few out of many, are the conceptions concerning the Holy Spirit, which we have

been taught to hold concerning His greatness, His dignity, and His operations, by the oracles of the Spirit themselves.

## Chapter 10
## Against those who say that it is not right to rank the Holy Spirit with the Father and the Son.

24. But we must proceed to attack our opponents, in the endeavour to confute those "oppositions" advanced against us which are derived from "knowledge falsely so-called."

It is not permissible, they assert, for the Holy Spirit to be ranked with the Father and Son, on account of the difference of His nature and the inferiority of His dignity. Against them it is right to reply in the words of the apostles, "We ought to obey God rather than men." Acts 5:29

For if our Lord, when enjoining the baptism of salvation, charged His disciples to baptize all nations in the name "of the Father and of the Son and of the Holy Ghost," Matthew 28:19 not disdaining fellowship with Him, and these men allege that we must not rank Him with the Father and the Son, is it not clear that they openly withstand the commandment of God? If they deny that coordination of this kind is declaratory of any fellowship and conjunction, let them tell us why it behooves us to hold this opinion, and what more intimate mode of conjunction they have.

If the Lord did not indeed conjoin the Spirit with the Father and Himself in baptism, do not let them lay the blame of conjunction upon us, for we neither hold nor say anything different. If on the contrary the Spirit is there conjoined with the Father and the Son, and no one is so shameless as to say anything else, then let them not lay blame on us for following the words of Scripture.

25. But all the apparatus of war has been got ready against us; every intellectual missile is aimed at us; and now blasphemers' tongues shoot and hit and hit again, yet harder than Stephen of old was smitten by the killers of the Christ. And do not let them succeed in concealing the fact that, while an attack on us serves for a pretext for the war, the real aim of these proceedings is higher. It is against us, they say, that they are preparing their engines and their snares; against us that they are shouting to one another, according to each one's strength or cunning, to come on. But the object of attack is faith. The one aim of the whole band of opponents and enemies of "sound doctrine" 1 Timothy 1:10 is to shake down the foundation of the faith of Christ by levelling apostolic tradition with the ground, and utterly destroying it. So like the debtors,— of course bona fide debtors— they clamour for written proof, and reject as worthless the unwritten tradition of the Fathers. But we will not slacken in our defence of the truth. We will not cowardly abandon the cause. The Lord has delivered to us as a necessary and saving doctrine that the Holy Spirit is to be ranked with the Father. Our opponents think differently, and see fit to divide and rend asunder, and relegate Him to the nature of a ministering spirit. Is it not then indisputable that they make their own blasphemy more authoritative than the law prescribed by the Lord? Come, then, set aside mere contention. Let us consider the points before us, as follows:

26. Whence is it that we are Christians? Through our faith, would be the universal answer. And in what way are we saved? Plainly because we were regenerate through the grace given in our baptism. How else could we be? And after recognising that this salvation is established through the Father and the Son and the Holy Ghost, shall we fling away "that form of doctrine" Romans 6:17 which we received? Would it not rather be ground for great groaning if we

are found now further off from our salvation "than when we first believed," and deny now what we then received? Whether a man have departed this life without baptism, or have received a baptism lacking in some of the requirements of the tradition, his loss is equal. And whoever does not always and everywhere keep to and hold fast as a sure protection the confession which we recorded at our first admission, when, being delivered "from the idols," we came "to the living God," 1 Thessalonians 1:9 constitutes himself a "stranger" from the "promises" Ephesians 2:12 of God, fighting against his own handwriting, which he put on record when he professed the faith. For if to me my baptism was the beginning of life, and that day of regeneration the first of days, it is plain that the utterance uttered in the grace of adoption was the most honourable of all. Can I then, perverted by these men's seductive words, abandon the tradition which guided me to the light, which bestowed on me the boon of the knowledge of God, whereby I, so long a foe by reason of sin, was made a child of God? But, for myself, I pray that with this confession I may depart hence to the Lord, and them I charge to preserve the faith secure until the day of Christ, and to keep the Spirit undivided from the Father and the Son, preserving, both in the confession of faith and in the doxology, the doctrine taught them at their baptism.

## Chapter 11
## That they who deny the Spirit are transgressors.

27. "Who has woe? Who has sorrow?" Proverbs 23:29 For whom is distress and darkness? For whom eternal doom? Is it not for the transgressors? For them that deny the faith? And what is the proof of their denial? Is it not that they have set at naught their own confessions? And when and what did they confess? Belief in the Father and in the Son and in the Holy Ghost, when they renounced the devil and his angels, and uttered those saving words. What fit

title then for them has been discovered, for the children of light to use? Are they not addressed as transgressors, as having violated the covenant of their salvation? What am I to call the denial of God? What the denial of Christ? What but transgressions? And to him who denies the Spirit, what title do you wish me to apply? Must it not be the same, inasmuch as he has broken his covenant with God? And when the confession of faith in Him secures the blessing of true religion. and its denial subjects men to the doom of godlessness, is it not a fearful thing for them to set the confession at naught, not through fear of fire, or sword, or cross, or scourge, or wheel, or rack, but merely led astray by the sophistry and seductions of the pneumatomachi? I testify to every man who is confessing Christ and denying God, that Christ will profit him nothing; to every man that calls upon God but rejects the Son, that his faith is vain; to every man that sets aside the Spirit, that his faith in the Father and the Son will be useless, for he cannot even hold it without the presence of the Spirit. For he who does not believe the Spirit does not believe in the Son, and he who has not believed in the Son does not believe in the Father. For none "can say that Jesus is the Lord but by the Holy Ghost," 1 Corinthians 12:3 and "No man has seen God at any time, but the only begotten God which is in the bosom of the Father, he has declared him."

Such an one has neither part nor lot in the true worship; for it is impossible to worship the Son, save by the Holy Ghost; impossible to call upon the Father, save by the Spirit of adoption.

## Chapter 12
### Against those who assert that the baptism in the name of the Father alone is sufficient.

28. Let no one be misled by the fact of the apostle's frequently omitting the name of the Father and of the Holy Spirit when

57

making mention of baptism, or on this account imagine that the invocation of the names is not observed. "As many of you," he says, "as were baptized into Christ have put on Christ;" and again, "As many of you as were baptized into Christ were baptized into his death." For the naming of Christ is the confession of the whole, showing forth as it does the God who gave, the Son who received, and the Spirit who is, the unction. So we have learned from Peter, in the Acts, of "Jesus of Nazareth whom God anointed with the Holy Ghost;" Acts 10:38 and in Isaiah, "The Spirit of the Lord is upon me, because the Lord has anointed me;" Isaiah 60:1 and the Psalmist, "Therefore God, even your God, has anointed you with the oil of gladness above your fellows." Scripture, however, in the case of baptism, sometimes plainly mentions the Spirit alone.

"For into one Spirit," it says, "we were all baptized in one body." And in harmony with this are the passages: "You shall be baptized with the Holy Ghost," Acts 1:5 and "He shall baptize you with the Holy Ghost." Luke 3:16 But no one on this account would be justified in calling that baptism a perfect baptism wherein only the name of the Spirit was invoked. For the tradition that has been given us by the quickening grace must remain for ever inviolate. He who redeemed our life from destruction gave us power of renewal, whereof the cause is ineffable and hidden in mystery, but bringing great salvation to our souls, so that to add or to take away anything involves manifestly a falling away from the life everlasting. If then in baptism the separation of the Spirit from the Father and the Son is perilous to the baptizer, and of no advantage to the baptized, how can the rending asunder of the Spirit from Father and from Son be safe for us? Faith and baptism are two kindred and inseparable ways of salvation: faith is perfected through baptism, baptism is established through faith, and both are completed by the same names. For as we believe in the Father and the Son and the

Holy Ghost, so are we also baptized in the name of the Father and of the Son and of the Holy Ghost; first comes the confession, introducing us to salvation, and baptism follows, setting the seal upon our assent.

## Chapter 13
## Statement of the reason why in the writings of Paul the angels are associated with the Father and the Son.

29. It is, however, objected that other beings which are enumerated with the Father and the Son are certainly not always glorified together with them. The apostle, for instance, in his charge to Timothy, associates the angels with them in the words, "I charge you before God and the Lord Jesus Christ and the elect angels." 1 Timothy 5:21 We are not for alienating the angels from the rest of creation, and yet, it is argued, we do not allow of their being reckoned with the Father and the Son. To this I reply, although the argument, so obviously absurd is it, does not really deserve a reply, that possibly before a mild and gentle judge, and especially before One who by His leniency to those arraigned before Him demonstrates the unimpeachable equity of His decisions, one might be willing to offer as witness even a fellow-slave; but for a slave to be made free and called a son of God and quickened from death can only be brought about by Him who has acquired natural kinship with us, and has been changed from the rank of a slave. For how can we be made kin with God by one who is an alien? How can we be freed by one who is himself under the yoke of slavery? It follows that the mention of the Spirit and that of angels are not made under like conditions. The Spirit is called on as Lord of life, and the angels as allies of their fellow-slaves and faithful witnesses of the truth. It is customary for the saints to deliver the commandments of God in the presence of witnesses, as also the apostle himself says to Timothy, "The things which you have heard

of me among many witnesses, the same commit thou to faithful men;" 2 Timothy 2:2 and now he calls the angels to witness, for he knows that angels shall be present with the Lord when He shall come in the glory of His Father to judge the world in righteousness. For He says, "Whoever shall confess me before men, him shall the Son of Man also confess before the angels of God, but he that denies Me before men shall be denied before the angels of God;" Luke 12:8-9 and Paul in another place says, "When the Lord Jesus shall be revealed from heaven with his angels." 2 Thessalonians 1:7 Thus he already testifies before the angels, preparing good proofs for himself at the great tribunal.

30. And not only Paul, but generally all those to whom is committed any ministry of the word, never cease from testifying, but call heaven and earth to witness on the ground that now every deed that is done is done within them, and that in the examination of all the actions of life they will be present with the judged. So it is said, "He shall call to the heavens above and to earth, that he may judge his people." And so Moses when about to deliver his oracles to the people says, "I call heaven and earth to witness this day;" Deuteronomy 4:26 and again in his song he says, "Give ear, O you heavens, and I will speak, and hear, O earth, the words of my mouth;" Deuteronomy 32:1 and Isaiah, "Hear, O heavens, and give ear, O earth;" Isaiah 1:2 and Jeremiah describes astonishment in heaven at the tidings of the unholy deeds of the people: "The heaven was astonished at this, and was horribly afraid, because my people committed two evils." And so the apostle, knowing the angels to be set over men as tutors and guardians, calls them to witness. Moreover, Joshua, the son of Nun, even set up a stone as witness of his words (already a heap somewhere had been called a witness by Jacob), Genesis 31:47 for he says, "Behold this stone shall be a witness unto you this day to the end of days, when you lie

to the Lord our God," perhaps believing that by God's power even the stones would speak to the conviction of the transgressors; or, if not, that at least each man's conscience would be wounded by the force of the reminder. In this manner they who have been entrusted with the stewardship of souls provide witnesses, whatever they may be, so as to produce them at some future day. But the Spirit is ranked together with God, not on account of the emergency of the moment, but on account of the natural fellowship; is not dragged in by us, but invited by the Lord.

## Chapter 14
## Objection that some were baptized unto Moses and believed in him, and an answer to it; with remarks upon types.

31. But even if some are baptized unto the Spirit, it is not, it is urged, on this account right for the Spirit to be ranked with God. Some "were baptized unto Moses in the cloud and in the sea." 1 Corinthians 10:2 And it is admitted that faith even before now has been put in men; for "The people believed God and his servant Moses." Why then, it is asked, do we, on account of faith and of baptism, exalt and magnify the Holy Spirit so far above creation, when there is evidence that the same things have before now been said of men? What, then, shall we reply? Our answer is that the faith in the Spirit is the same as the faith in the Father and the Son; and in like manner, too, the baptism. But the faith in Moses and in the cloud is, as it were, in a shadow and type. The nature of the divine is very frequently represented by the rough and shadowy outlines of the types; but because divine things are prefigured by small and human things, it is obvious that we must not therefore conclude the divine nature to be small. The type is an exhibition of things expected, and gives an imitative anticipation of the future. So Adam was a type of "Him that was to come." Romans 5:14 Typically, "That rock was Christ;" 1 Corinthians 10:4 and the water

a type of the living power of the word; as He says, "If any man thirst, let him come unto me and drink." John 7:37 The manna is a type of the living bread that came down from heaven; John 6:49, 51 and the serpent on the standard, of the passion of salvation accomplished by means of the cross, wherefore they who even looked thereon were preserved. So in like manner, the history of the exodus of Israel is recorded to show forth those who are being saved through baptism. For the firstborn of the Israelites were preserved, like the bodies of the baptized, by the giving of grace to them that were marked with blood. For the blood of the sheep is a type of the blood of Christ; and the firstborn, a type of the first-formed. And inasmuch as the first-formed of necessity exists in us, and, in sequence of succession, is transmitted till the end, it follows that "in Adam" we "all die," 1 Corinthians 15:22 and that "death reigned" Romans 5:17 until the fulfilling of the law and the coming of Christ. And the firstborn were preserved by God from being touched by the destroyer, to show that we who were made alive in Christ no longer die in Adam. The sea and the cloud for the time being led on through amazement to faith, but for the time to come they typically prefigured the grace to be. "Who is wise and he shall understand these things?" Hosea 14:9 — how the sea is typically a baptism bringing about the departure of Pharaoh, in like manner as this washing causes the departure of the tyranny of the devil. The sea slew the enemy in itself: and in baptism too dies our enmity towards God. From the sea the people came out unharmed: we too, as it were, alive from the dead, step up from the water "saved" by the "grace" of Him who called us. Ephesians 2:5 And the cloud is a shadow of the gift of the Spirit, who cools the flame of our passions by the "mortification" of our "members." Colossians 3:5

32. What then? Because they were typically baptized unto Moses, is the grace of baptism therefore small? Were it so, and if we were in

each case to prejudice the dignity of our privileges by comparing them with their types, not even one of these privileges could be reckoned great; then not the love of God, who gave His only begotten Son for our sins, would be great and extraordinary, because Abraham did not spare his own son; then even the passion of the Lord would not be glorious, because a sheep typified the offering instead of Isaac; then the descent into hell was not fearful, because Jonah had previously typified the death in three days and three nights. The same prejudicial comparison is made also in the case of baptism by all who judge of the reality by the shadow, and, comparing the typified with the type, attempt by means of Moses and the sea to disparage at once the whole dispensation of the Gospel. What remission of sins, what renewal of life, is there in the sea? What spiritual gift is there through Moses? What dying of sins is there? Those men did not die with Christ; wherefore they were not raised with Him. They did not "bear the image of the heavenly;" 1 Corinthians 15:49 they did "bear about in the body the dying of Jesus;" 2 Corinthians 4:10 they did not "put off the old man;" they did not "put on the new man which is renewed in knowledge after the image of Him which created him." Colossians 3:9-10 Why then do you compare baptisms which have only the name in common, while the distinction between the things themselves is as great as might be that of dream and reality, that of shadow and figures with substantial existence?

33. But belief in Moses not only does not show our belief in the Spirit to be worthless, but, if we adopt our opponents' line of argument, it rather weakens our confession in the God of the universe. "The people," it is written, "believed the Lord and his servant Moses." Exodus 14:31 Moses then is joined with God, not with the Spirit; and he was a type not of the Spirit, but of Christ. For at that time in the ministry of the law, he by means of himself

typified "the Mediator between God and men." 1 Timothy 2:5
Moses, when mediating for the people in things pertaining to God,
was not a minister of the Spirit; for the law was given, "ordained by
angels in the hand of a mediator," Galatians 3:19 namely Moses, in
accordance with the summons of the people, "Speak thou with
us,...but let not God speak with us." Exodus 20:19 Thus faith in
Moses is referred to the Lord, the Mediator between God and men,
who said, "Had ye believed Moses, you would have believed me."
John 5:46 Is then our faith in the Lord a trifle, because it was
signified beforehand through Moses? So then, even if men were
baptized unto Moses, it does not follow that the grace given of the
Spirit in baptism is small. I may point out, too, that it is usual in
Scripture to say Moses and the law, as in the passage, "They have
Moses and the prophets." Luke 16:29 When therefore it is meant to
speak of the baptism of the law, the words are, "They were
baptized unto Moses." 1 Corinthians 10:2 Why then do these
calumniators of the truth, by means of the shadow and the types,
endeavour to bring contempt and ridicule on the "rejoicing" of our
"hope," Hebrews 3:6 and the rich gift of our God and Saviour,
who through regeneration renews our youth like the eagle's? Surely
it is altogether childish, and like a babe who must needs be fed on
milk, to be ignorant of the great mystery of our salvation; inasmuch
as, in accordance with the gradual progress of our education, while
being brought to perfection in our training for godliness, we were
first taught elementary and easier lessons, suited to our intelligence,
while the Dispenser of our lots was ever leading us up, by gradually
accustoming us, like eyes brought up in the dark, to the great light
of truth. For He spares our weakness, and in the depth of the
riches Romans 11:33 of His wisdom, and the inscrutable judgments
of His intelligence, used this gentle treatment, fitted for our needs,
gradually accustoming us to see first the shadows of objects, and to
look at the sun in water, to save us from dashing against the

spectacle of pure unadulterated light, and being blinded. Just so the Law, having a shadow of things to come, and the typical teaching of the prophets, which is a dark utterance of the truth, have been devised means to train the eyes of the heart, in that hence the transition to the wisdom hidden in mystery 1 Corinthians 2:7 will be made easy. Enough so far concerning types; nor indeed would it be possible to linger longer on this topic, or the incidental discussion would become many times bulkier than the main argument.

## Chapter 15
**Reply to the suggested objection that we are baptized "into water." Also concerning baptism.**

34. What more? Verily, our opponents are well equipped with arguments. We are baptized, they urge, into water, and of course we shall not honour the water above all creation, or give it a share of the honour of the Father and of the Son. The arguments of these men are such as might be expected from angry disputants, leaving no means untried in their attack on him who has offended them, because their reason is clouded over by their feelings. We will not, however, shrink from the discussion even of these points. If we do not teach the ignorant, at least we shall not turn away before evil doers. But let us for a moment retrace our steps.

35. The dispensation of our God and Saviour concerning man is a recall from the fall and a return from the alienation caused by disobedience to close communion with God. This is the reason for the sojourn of Christ in the flesh, the pattern life described in the Gospels, the sufferings, the cross, the tomb, the resurrection; so that the man who is being saved through imitation of Christ receives that old adoption. For perfection of life the imitation of Christ is necessary, not only in the example of gentleness,

lowliness, and long suffering set us in His life, but also of His actual death. So Paul, the imitator of Christ, says, "being made conformable unto his death; if by any means I might attain unto the resurrection of the dead." Philippians 3:10-11 How then are we made in the likeness of His death? Romans 6:4-5 In that we were buried with Him by baptism. What then is the manner of the burial? And what is the advantage resulting from the imitation? First of all, it is necessary that the continuity of the old life be cut. And this is impossible less a man be born again, according to the Lord's word; John 3:3 for the regeneration, as indeed the name shows, is a beginning of a second life. So before beginning the second, it is necessary to put an end to the first. For just as in the case of runners who turn and take the second course, a kind of halt and pause intervenes between the movements in the opposite direction, so also in making a change in lives it seemed necessary for death to come as mediator between the two, ending all that goes before, and beginning all that comes after. How then do we achieve the descent into hell? By imitating, through baptism, the burial of Christ. For the bodies of the baptized are, as it were, buried in the water. Baptism then symbolically signifies the putting off of the works of the flesh; as the apostle says, you were "circumcised with the circumcision made without hands, in putting off the body of the sins of the flesh by the circumcision of Christ; buried with him in baptism." Colossians 2:11-12 And there is, as it were, a cleansing of the soul from the filth that has grown on it from the carnal mind, as it is written, "You shall wash me, and I shall be whiter than snow." On this account we do not, as is the fashion of the Jews, wash ourselves at each defilement, but own the baptism of salvation to be one. For there the death on behalf of the world is one, and one the resurrection of the dead, whereof baptism is a type. For this cause the Lord, who is the Dispenser of our life, gave us the covenant of baptism, containing a type of life and death, for the water fulfils the image of death, and the Spirit gives us the earnest of life. Hence it follows that the answer to our question why the water was associated with the Spirit is clear: the reason is because in baptism two ends were proposed; on the one hand, the destroying of the body of sin, that it may never bear fruit unto death; on the other hand, our living unto the Spirit, and having our fruit in holiness; the water receiving the body as in a tomb figures death, while the Spirit pours in the quickening power, renewing our souls from the deadness of sin unto their original life. This then is what it is to be born again of water and of the Spirit, the being made dead being effected in the water, while our life is wrought in us through the Spirit. In three immersions, then, and with three invocations, the great mystery of baptism is performed, to the end that the type of death may be fully figured, and that by the tradition of the divine knowledge the baptized may have their souls enlightened. It follows that if there is any grace in the water, it is not of the nature of the water, but of the presence of the Spirit. For baptism is "not the putting away of the filth of the flesh, but the answer of a good conscience towards God." 1 Peter 3:21 So in training us for the life that follows on the resurrection the Lord sets out all the manner of life required by the Gospel, laying down for us the law of gentleness, of endurance of wrong, of freedom from the defilement that comes of the love of pleasure, and from covetousness, to the end that we may of set purpose win beforehand and achieve all that the life to come of its inherent nature possesses. If therefore any one in attempting a definition were to describe the gospel as a forecast of the life that follows on the resurrection, he would not seem to me to go beyond what is meet and right. Let us now return to our main topic.

36. Through the Holy Spirit comes our restoration to paradise, our ascension into the kingdom of heaven, our return to the adoption

of sons, our liberty to call God our Father, our being made
partakers of the grace of Christ, our being called children of light,
our sharing in eternal glory, and, in a word, our being brought into
a state of all "fullness of blessing," Romans 15:29 both in this
world and in the world to come, of all the good gifts that are in
store for us, by promise hereof, through faith, beholding the
reflection of their grace as though they were already present, we
await the full enjoyment. If such is the earnest, what the perfection?
If such the first fruits, what the complete fulfilment? Furthermore,
from this too may be apprehended the difference between the
grace that comes from the Spirit and the baptism by water: in that
John indeed baptized with water, but our Lord Jesus Christ by the
Holy Ghost. "I indeed," he says, "baptize you with water unto
repentance; but he that comes after me is mightier than I, whose
shoes I am not worthy to bear: he shall baptize you with the Holy
Ghost and with fire." Matthew 3:11 Here He calls the trial at the
judgment the baptism of fire, as the apostle says, "The fire shall try
every man's work, of what sort it is." 1 Corinthians 3:13 And again,
"The day shall declare it, because it shall be revealed by fire." 1
Corinthians 3:13 And ere now there have been some who in their
championship of true religion have undergone the death for
Christ's sake, not in mere similitude, but in actual fact, and so have
needed none of the outward signs of water for their salvation,
because they were baptized in their own blood. Thus I write not to
disparage the baptism by water, but to overthrow the arguments of
those who exalt themselves against the Spirit; who confound things
that are distinct from one another, and compare those which admit
of no comparison.

## Chapter 16
**That the Holy Spirit is in every conception separable from the
Father and the Son, alike in the creation of perceptible**

**objects, in the dispensation of human affairs, and in the judgment to come.**

37. Let us then revert to the point raised from the outset, that in all things the Holy Spirit is inseparable and wholly incapable of being parted from the Father and the Son. St. Paul, in the passage about the gift of tongues, writes to the Corinthians, "If you all prophesy and there come in one that believes not, or one unlearned, he is convinced of all, he is judged of all; and thus are the secrets of the heart made manifest; and so falling down on his face he will worship God and report that God is in you of a truth." 1 Corinthians 14:24-25 If then God is known to be in the prophets by the prophesying that is acting according to the distribution of the gifts of the Spirit, let our adversaries consider what kind of place they will attribute to the Holy Spirit. Let them say whether it is more proper to rank Him with God or to thrust Him forth to the place of the creature. Peter's words to Sapphira, "How is it that you have agreed together to tempt the Spirit of the Lord? You have not lied unto men, but unto God," show that sins against the Holy Spirit and against God are the same; and thus you might learn that in every operation the Spirit is closely conjoined with, and inseparable from, the Father and the Son. God works the differences of operations, and the Lord the diversities of administrations, but all the while the Holy Spirit is present too of His own will, dispensing distribution of the gifts according to each recipient's worth. For, it is said, "there are diversities of gifts, but the same Spirit; and differences of administrations, but the same Lord; and there are diversities of operations, but it is the same God which works all in all." "But all these," it is said, "works that one and the self-same Spirit, dividing to every man severally as He will." 1 Corinthians 12:11 It must not however be supposed because in this passage the apostle names in the first place the Spirit, in the

second the Son, and in the third God the Father, that therefore
their rank is reversed. The apostle has only started in accordance
with our habits of thought; for when we receive gifts, the first that
occurs to us is the distributer, next we think of the sender, and then
we lift our thoughts to the fountain and cause of the boons.

38. Moreover, from the things created at the beginning may be
learned the fellowship of the Spirit with the Father and the Son.
The pure, intelligent, and supermundane powers are and are styled
holy, because they have their holiness of the grace given by the
Holy Spirit. Accordingly the mode of the creation of the heavenly
powers is passed over in Silence, for the historian of the
cosmogony has revealed to us only the creation of things
perceptible by sense. But do thou, who hast power from the things
that are seen to form an analogy of the unseen, glorify the Maker
by whom all things were made, visible and invisible, principalities
and powers, authorities, thrones, and dominions, and all other
reasonable natures whom we cannot name. And in the creation
bethink you first, I pray you, of the original cause of all things that
are made, the Father; of the creative cause, the Son; of the
perfecting cause, the Spirit; so that the ministering spirits subsist by
the will of the Father, are brought into being by the operation of
the Son, and perfected by the presence of the Spirit. Moreover, the
perfection of angels is sanctification and continuance in it. And let
no one imagine me either to affirm that there are three original
hypostases or to allege the operation of the Son to be imperfect.
For the first principle of existing things is One, creating through
the Son and perfecting through the Spirit. The operation of the
Father who works all in all is not imperfect, neither is the creating
work of the Son incomplete if not perfected by the Spirit. The
Father, who creates by His sole will, could not stand in any need of
the Son, but nevertheless He wills through the Son; nor could the

Son, who works according to the likeness of the Father, need co-operation, but the Son too wills to make perfect through the Spirit. "For by the word of the Lord were the heavens made, and all the host of them by the breath [the Spirit] of His mouth." The Word then is not a mere significant impression on the air, borne by the organs of speech; nor is the Spirit of His mouth a vapour, emitted by the organs of respiration; but the Word is He who "was with God in the beginning" and "was God," John 1:1 and the Spirit of the mouth of God is "the Spirit of truth which proceeds from the Father." John 15:26 You are therefore to perceive three, the Lord who gives the order, the Word who creates, and the Spirit who confirms. And what other thing could confirmation be than the perfecting according to holiness? This perfecting expresses the confirmation's firmness, unchangeableness, and fixity in good. But there is no sanctification without the Spirit. The powers of the heavens are not holy by nature; were it so there would in this respect be no difference between them and the Holy Spirit. It is in proportion to their relative excellence that they have their meed of holiness from the Spirit. The branding-iron is conceived of together with the fire; and yet the material and the fire are distinct. Thus too in the case of the heavenly powers; their substance is, perhaps, an aerial spirit, or an immaterial fire, as it is written, "Who makes his angels spirits and his ministers a flame of fire;" wherefore they exist in space and become visible, and appear in their proper bodily form to them that are worthy. But their sanctification, being external to their substance, superinduces their perfection through the communion of the Spirit. They keep their rank by their abiding in the good and true, and while they retain their freedom of will, never fall away from their patient attendance on Him who is truly good. It results that, if by your argument you do away with the Spirit, the hosts of the angels are disbanded, the dominions of archangels are destroyed, all is thrown into confusion, and their life loses law, order, and distinctness. For how are angels to cry "Glory to God in the highest" Luke 2:14 without being empowered by the Spirit? For "No man can say that Jesus is the Lord but by the Holy Ghost, and no man speaking by the Spirit of God calls Jesus accursed;" 1 Corinthians 12:3 as might be said by wicked and hostile spirits, whose fall establishes our statement of the freedom of the will of the invisible powers; being, as they are, in a condition of equipoise between virtue and vice, and on this account needing the succour of the Spirit. I indeed maintain that even Gabriel Luke 1:11 in no other way foretells events to come than by the foreknowledge of the Spirit, by reason of the fact that one of the boons distributed by the Spirit is prophecy. And whence did he who was ordained to announce the mysteries of the vision to the Man of Desires derive the wisdom whereby he was enabled to teach hidden things, if not from the Holy Spirit? The revelation of mysteries is indeed the peculiar function of the Spirit, as it is written, "God has revealed them unto us by His Spirit." 1 Corinthians 2:10 And how could "thrones, dominions, principalities and powers" Colossians 1:16 live their blessed life, did they not "behold the face of the Father which is in heaven"? Matthew 18:10 But to behold it is impossible without the Spirit! Just as at night, if you withdraw the light from the house, the eyes fall blind and their faculties become inactive, and the worth of objects cannot be discerned, and gold is trodden on in ignorance as though it were iron, so in the order of the intellectual world it is impossible for the high life of Law to abide without the Spirit. For it so to abide were as likely as that an army should maintain its discipline in the absence of its commander, or a chorus its harmony without the guidance of the Coryphæus. How could the Seraphim cry "Holy, Holy, Holy," Isaiah 6:3 were they not taught by the Spirit how often true religion requires them to lift their voice in this ascription of glory? Do "all His angels" and "all His hosts" praise

God? It is through the co-operation of the Spirit. Do "thousand thousand" of angels stand before Him, and "ten thousand times ten thousand" ministering spirits? Daniel 7:10 They are blamelessly doing their proper work by the power of the Spirit. All the glorious and unspeakable harmony of the highest heavens both in the service of God, and in the mutual concord of the celestial powers, can therefore only be preserved by the direction of the Spirit. Thus with those beings who are not gradually perfected by increase and advance, but are perfect from the moment of the creation, there is in creation the presence of the Holy Spirit, who confers on them the grace that flows from Him for the completion and perfection of their essence.

39. But when we speak of the dispensations made for man by our great God and Saviour Jesus Christ, who will gainsay their having been accomplished through the grace of the Spirit? Whether you wish to examine ancient evidence—the blessings of the patriarchs, the succour given through the legislation, the types, the prophecies, the valorous feats in war, the signs wrought through just men;— or on the other hand the things done in the dispensation of the coming of our Lord in the flesh—all is through the Spirit. In the first place He was made an unction, and being inseparably present was with the very flesh of the Lord, according to that which is written, "Upon whom you shall see the Spirit descending and remaining on Him, the same is" John 1:33 "my beloved Son;" Matthew 3:17 and "Jesus of Nazareth" whom "God anointed with the Holy Ghost." Acts 10:38 After this every operation was wrought with the co-operation of the Spirit. He was present when the Lord was being tempted by the devil; for, it is said, "Jesus was led up of the Spirit into the wilderness to be tempted." Matthew 4:1 He was inseparably with Him while working His wonderful works; for, it is said, "If I by the Spirit of God cast out devils."

Matthew 12:28 And He did not leave Him when He had risen from
the dead; for when renewing man, and, by breathing on the face of
the disciples, restoring the grace, that came of the inbreathing of
God, which man had lost, what did the Lord say? "Receive the
Holy Ghost: whose soever sins ye remit, they are remitted unto
them; and whose soever ye retain, they are retained." John 20:22-23
And is it not plain and incontestable that the ordering of the
Church is effected through the Spirit? For He gave, it is said, "in
the church, first Apostles, secondarily prophets, thirdly teachers,
after that miracles, then gifts of healing, helps, governments,
diversities of tongues," 1 Corinthians 12:28 for this order is
ordained in accordance with the division of the gifts that are of the
Spirit.

40. Moreover by any one who carefully uses his reason it will be
found that even at the moment of the expected appearance of the
Lord from heaven the Holy Spirit will not, as some suppose, have
no functions to discharge: on the contrary, even in the day of His
revelation, in which the blessed and only potentate 1 Timothy 6:15
will judge the world in righteousness, Acts 17:31 the Holy Spirit
will be present with Him. For who is so ignorant of the good
things prepared by God for them that are worthy, as not to know
that the crown of the righteous is the grace of the Spirit, bestowed
in more abundant and perfect measure in that day, when spiritual
glory shall be distributed to each in proportion as he shall have
nobly played the man? For among the glories of the saints are
"many mansions" in the Father's house, that is differences of
dignities: for as "star differs from star in glory, so also is the
resurrection of the dead." 1 Corinthians 15:41-42 They, then, that
were sealed by the Spirit unto the day of redemption, and preserve
pure and undiminished the first fruits which they received of the
Spirit, are they that shall hear the words "well done thou good and

faithful servant; you have been faithful over a few things, I will make you ruler over many things." Matthew 25:21 In like manner they which have grieved the Holy Spirit by the wickedness of their ways, or have not wrought for Him that gave to them, shall be deprived of what they have received, their grace being transferred to others; or, according to one of the evangelists, they shall even be wholly cut asunder, Matthew 24:51 — the cutting asunder meaning complete separation from the Spirit. The body is not divided, part being delivered to chastisement, and part let off; for when a whole has sinned it were like the old fables, and unworthy of a righteous judge, for only the half to suffer chastisement. Nor is the soul cut in two—that soul the whole of which possesses the sinful affection throughout, and works the wickedness in co-operation with the body. The cutting asunder, as I have observed, is the separation for aye of the soul from the Spirit. For now, although the Spirit does not suffer admixture with the unworthy, He nevertheless does seem in a manner to be present with them that have once been sealed, awaiting the salvation which follows on their conversion; but then He will be wholly cut off from the soul that has defiled His grace. For this reason "In Hell there is none that makes confession; in death none that remembers God," because the succour of the Spirit is no longer present. How then is it possible to conceive that the judgment is accomplished without the Holy Spirit, wherein the word points out that He is Himself the prize Philippians 3:14 of the righteous, when instead of the earnest is given that which is perfect, and the first condemnation of sinners, when they are deprived of that which they seem to have? But the greatest proof of the conjunction of the Spirit with the Father and the Son is that He is said to have the same relation to God which the spirit in us has to each of us. "For what man" it is said, "knows the things of a man, save the spirit of man which is in him? Even

so the things of God knows no man but the Spirit of God." 1
Corinthians 2:11

On this point I have said enough.

## Chapter 17
**Against those who say that the Holy Ghost is not to be
numbered with, but numbered under, the Father and the Son.
Wherein moreover there is a summary notice of the faith
concerning right sub-numeration.**

41. What, however, they call sub-numeration, and in what sense
they use this word, cannot even be imagined without difficulty. It is
well known that it was imported into our language from the
"wisdom of the world;" but a point for our present consideration
will be whether it has any immediate relation to the subject under
discussion. Those who are adepts in vain investigations tell us that,
while some nouns are common and of widely extended denotation,
others are more specific, and that the force of some is more limited
than that of others. Essence, for instance, is a common noun,
predicable of all things both animate and inanimate; while animal is
more specific, being predicated of fewer subjects than the former,
though of more than those which are considered under it, as it
embraces both rational and irrational nature. Again, human is more
specific than animal, and man than human, and than man the
individual Peter, Paul, or John. Do they then mean by sub-
numeration the division of the common into its subordinate parts?
But I should hesitate to believe they have reached such a pitch of
infatuation as to assert that the God of the universe, like some
common quality conceivable only by reason and without actual
existence in any hypostasis, is divided into subordinate divisions,
and that then this subdivision is called sub-numeration. This would
hardly be said even by men melancholy mad, for, besides its

impiety, they are establishing the very opposite argument to their own contention. For the subdivisions are of the same essence as that from which they have been divided. The very obviousness of the absurdity makes it difficult for us to find arguments to confute their unreasonableness; so that really their folly looks like an advantage to them; just as soft and yielding bodies offer no resistance, and therefore cannot be struck a stout blow. It is impossible to bring a vigorous confutation to bear on a palpable absurdity. The only course open to us is to pass by their abominable impiety in silence. Yet our love for the brethren and the importunity of our opponents makes silence impossible.

42. What is it that they maintain? Look at the terms of their imposture. "We assert that connumeration is appropriate to subjects of equal dignity, and sub-numeration to those which vary in the direction of inferiority." "Why," I rejoined, do you say this? I fail to understand your extraordinary wisdom. Do you mean that gold is numbered with gold, and that lead is unworthy of the connumeration, but, because of the cheapness of the material, is subnumerated to gold? And do you attribute so much importance to number as that it can either exalt the value of what is cheap, or destroy the dignity of what is valuable? Therefore, again, you will number gold under precious stones, and such precious stones as are smaller and without lustre under those which are larger and brighter in colour. But what will not be said by men who spend their time in nothing else but either 'to tell or to hear some new thing'? Acts 17:21 Let these supporters of impiety be classed for the future with Stoics and Epicureans. What sub-numeration is even possible of things less valuable in relation to things very valuable? How is a brass obol to be numbered under a golden stater? "Because," they reply, "we do not speak of possessing two coins, but one and one." But which of these is subnumerated to the

other? Each is similarly mentioned. If then you number each by itself, you cause an equality value by numbering them in the same way but, if you join them, you make their value one by numbering them one with the other. But if the sub-numeration belongs to the one which is numbered second, then it is in the power of the counter to begin by counting the brass coin. Let us, however, pass over the confutation of their ignorance, and turn our argument to the main topic.

43. Do you maintain that the Son is numbered under the Father, and the Spirit under the Son, or do you confine your sub-numeration to the Spirit alone? If, on the other hand, you apply this sub-numeration also to the Son, you revive what is the same impious doctrine, the unlikeness of the substance, the lowliness of rank, the coming into being in later time, and once for all, by this one term, you will plainly again set circling all the blasphemies against the Only-begotten. To controvert these blasphemies would be a longer task than my present purpose admits of; and I am the less bound to undertake it because the impiety has been refuted elsewhere to the best of my ability. If on the other hand they suppose the sub-numeration to benefit the Spirit alone, they must be taught that the Spirit is spoken of together with the Lord in precisely the same manner in which the Son is spoken of with the Father. "The name of the Father and of the Son and of the Holy Ghost" Matthew 28:19 is delivered in like manner, and, according to the co-ordination of words delivered in baptism, the relation of the Spirit to the Son is the same as that of the Son to the Father. And if the Spirit is co-ordinate with the Son, and the Son with the Father, it is obvious that the Spirit is also co-ordinate with the Father. When then the names are ranked in one and the same co-ordinate series, what room is there for speaking on the one hand of connumeration, and on the other of sub-numeration? Nay, without

exception, what thing ever lost its own nature by being numbered? Is it not the fact that things when numbered remain what they naturally and originally were, while number is adopted among us as a sign indicative of the plurality of subjects? For some bodies we count, some we measure, and some we weigh; those which are by nature continuous we apprehend by measure; to those which are divided we apply number (with the exception of those which on account of their fineness are measured); while heavy objects are distinguished by the inclination of the balance. It does not however follow that, because we have invented for our convenience symbols to help us to arrive at the knowledge of quantity, we have therefore changed the nature of the things signified. We do not speak of "weighing under" one another things which are weighed, even though one be gold and the other tin; nor yet do we "measure under" things that are measured; and so in the same way we will not "number under" things which are numbered. And if none of the rest of things admits of sub-numeration how can they allege that the Spirit ought to be subnumerated? Labouring as they do under heathen unsoundness, they imagine that things which are inferior, either by grade of rank or subjection of substance, ought to be subnumerated.

## Chapter 18
**In what manner in the confession of the three hypostases we preserve the pious dogma of the Monarchia. Wherein also is the refutation of them that allege that the Spirit is subnumerated.**

44. In delivering the formula of the Father, the Son, and the Holy Ghost, Matthew 28:19 our Lord did not connect the gift with number. He did not say "into First, Second, and Third," nor yet into one, two, and three, but He gave us the boon of the knowledge of the faith which leads to salvation, by means of holy

names. So that what saves us is our faith. Number has been devised as a symbol indicative of the quantity of objects. But these men, who bring ruin on themselves from every possible source, have turned even the capacity for counting against the faith. Nothing else undergoes any change in consequence of the addition of number, and yet these men in the case of the divine nature pay reverence to number, lest they should exceed the limits of the honour due to the Paraclete. But, O wisest sirs, let the unapproachable be altogether above and beyond number, as the ancient reverence of the Hebrews wrote the unutterable name of God in peculiar characters, thus endeavouring to set forth its infinite excellence. Count, if you must; but you must not by counting do damage to the faith. Either let the ineffable be honoured by silence; or let holy things be counted consistently with true religion. There is one God and Father, one Only-begotten, and one Holy Ghost. We proclaim each of the hypostases singly; and, when count we must, we do not let an ignorant arithmetic carry us away to the idea of a plurality of Gods.

45. For we do not count by way of addition, gradually making increase from unity to multitude, and saying one, two, and three— nor yet first, second, and third. For "I," God, "am the first, and I am the last." Isaiah 44:6 And hitherto we have never, even at the present time, heard of a second God. Worshipping as we do God of God, we both confess the distinction of the Persons, and at the same time abide by the Monarchy. We do not fritter away the theology in a divided plurality, because one Form, so to say, united in the invariableness of the Godhead, is beheld in God the Father, and in God the Only begotten. For the Son is in the Father and the Father in the Son; since such as is the latter, such is the former, and such as is the former, such is the latter; and herein is the Unity. So that according to the distinction of Persons, both are one and one,

and according to the community of Nature, one. How, then, if one and one, are there not two Gods? Because we speak of a king, and of the king's image, and not of two kings. The majesty is not cloven in two, nor the glory divided. The sovereignty and authority over us is one, and so the doxology ascribed by us is not plural but one; because the honour paid to the image passes on to the prototype. Now what in the one case the image is by reason of imitation, that in the other case the Son is by nature; and as in works of art the likeness is dependent on the form, so in the case of the divine and uncompounded nature the union consists in the communion of the Godhead. One, moreover, is the Holy Spirit, and we speak of Him singly, conjoined as He is to the one Father through the one Son, and through Himself completing the adorable and blessed Trinity. Of Him the intimate relationship to the Father and the Son is sufficiently declared by the fact of His not being ranked in the plurality of the creation, but being spoken of singly; for he is not one of many, but One. For as there is one Father and one Son, so is there one Holy Ghost. He is consequently as far removed from created Nature as reason requires the singular to be removed from compound and plural bodies; and He is in such wise united to the Father and to the Son as unit has affinity with unit.

46. And it is not from this source alone that our proofs of the natural communion are derived, but from the fact that He is moreover said to be "of God;" 2 Corinthians 1:12 not indeed in the sense in which "all things are of God," but in the sense of proceeding out of God, not by generation, like the Son, but as Breath of His mouth. But in no way is the "mouth" a member, nor the Spirit breath that is dissolved; but the word "mouth" is used so far as it can be appropriate to God, and the Spirit is a Substance having life, gifted with supreme power of sanctification. Thus the close relation is made plain, while the mode of the ineffable

existence is safeguarded. He is moreover styled 'Spirit of Christ,' as being by nature closely related to Him. Wherefore "If any man have not the Spirit of Christ, he is none of His." Romans 8:9 Hence He alone worthily glorifies the Lord, for, it is said, "He shall glorify me," John 16:14 not as the creature, but as "Spirit of truth," John 14:17 clearly showing forth the truth in Himself, and, as Spirit of wisdom, in His own greatness revealing "Christ the Power of God and the wisdom of God." 1 Corinthians 1:24 And as Paraclete He expresses in Himself the goodness of the Paraclete who sent Him, and in His own dignity manifests the majesty of Him from whom He proceeded. There is then on the one hand a natural glory, as light is the glory of the sun; and on the other a glory bestowed judicially and of free will ' ab extra' on them that are worthy. The latter is twofold. "A son," it is said, "honours his father, and a servant his master." Malachi 1:6 Of these two the one, the servile, is given by the creature; the other, which may be called the intimate, is fulfilled by the Spirit. For, as our Lord said of Himself, "I have glorified You on the earth: I have finished the work which you gave me to do;" John 17:4 so of the Paraclete He says "He shall glorify me: for He shall receive of mine, and shall show it unto you." John 16:14 And as the Son is glorified of the Father when He says "I have both glorified it and will glorify it again," John 12:28 so is the Spirit glorified through His communion with both Father and Son, and through the testimony of the Only-begotten when He says "All manner of sin and blasphemy shall be forgiven unto men: but the blasphemy against the Holy Ghost shall not be forgiven unto men." Matthew 12:31

47. And when, by means of the power that enlightens us, we fix our eyes on the beauty of the image of the invisible God, and through the image are led up to the supreme beauty of the spectacle of the archetype, then, I ween, is with us inseparably the

Spirit of knowledge, in Himself bestowing on them that love the vision of the truth the power of beholding the Image, not making the exhibition from without, but in Himself leading on to the full knowledge. "No man knows the Father save the Son." And so "no man can say that Jesus is the Lord but by the Holy Ghost." 1 Corinthians 12:3 For it is not said through the Spirit, but by the Spirit, and "God is a spirit, and they that worship Him must worship Him in spirit and in truth," John 4:24 as it is written "in your light shall we see light," namely by the illumination of the Spirit, "the true light which lights every man that comes into the world." John 1:9 It results that in Himself He shows the glory of the Only begotten, and on true worshippers He in Himself bestows the knowledge of God. Thus the way of the knowledge of God lies from One Spirit through the One Son to the One Father, and conversely the natural Goodness and the inherent Holiness and the royal Dignity extend from the Father through the Only-begotten to the Spirit. Thus there is both acknowledgment of the hypostases and the true dogma of the Monarchy is not lost. They on the other hand who support their sub-numeration by talking of first and second and third ought to be informed that into the undefiled theology of Christians they are importing the polytheism of heathen error. No other result can be achieved by the fell device of sub-numeration than the confession of a first, a second, and a third God. For us is sufficient the order prescribed by the Lord. He who confuses this order will be no less guilty of transgressing the law than are the impious heathen.

Enough has been now said to prove, in contravention of their error, that the communion of Nature is in no wise dissolved by the manner of sub-numeration. Let us, however, make a concession to our contentious and feeble minded adversary, and grant that what is second to anything is spoken of in sub-numeration to it. Now let us see what follows. "The first man" it is said "is of the earth earthy, the second man is the Lord from heaven." 1 Corinthians 15:47 Again "that was not first which is spiritual but that which is natural and afterward that which is spiritual." 1 Corinthians 15:46 If then the second is subnumerated to the first, and the subnumerated is inferior in dignity to that to which it was subnumerated, according to you the spiritual is inferior in honour to the natural, and the heavenly man to the earthy.

## Chapter 19
## Against those who assert that the Spirit ought not to be glorified.

48. "Be it so," it is rejoined, "but glory is by no means so absolutely due to the Spirit as to require His exaltation by us in doxologies." Whence then could we get demonstrations of the dignity of the Spirit, "passing all understanding," Philippians 4:7 if His communion with the Father and the Son were not reckoned by our opponents as good for testimony of His rank? It is, at all events, possible for us to arrive to a certain extent at intelligent apprehension of the sublimity of His nature and of His unapproachable power, by looking at the meaning of His title, and at the magnitude of His operations, and by His good gifts bestowed on us or rather on all creation. He is called Spirit, as "God is a Spirit," John 4:24 and "the breath of our nostrils, the anointed of the Lord." He is called holy, 1 John 1:20 as the Father is holy, and the Son is holy, for to the creature holiness was brought in from without, but to the Spirit holiness is the fulfilment of nature, and it is for this reason that He is described not as being sanctified, but as sanctifying. He is called good, as the Father is good, and He who was begotten of the Good is good, and to the Spirit His goodness is essence. He is called upright, as "the Lord is upright," in that He is Himself truth, and is Himself Righteousness, 2 Corinthians 3:8-9

having no divergence nor leaning to one side or to the other, on account of the immutability of His substance. He is called Paraclete, like the Only begotten, as He Himself says, "I will ask the Father, and He will give you another comforter." Thus names are borne by the Spirit in common with the Father and the Son, and He gets these titles from His natural and close relationship. From what other source could they be derived? Again He is called royal, Spirit of truth, and Spirit of wisdom. Isaiah 11:2 "The Spirit of God," it is said "has made me," Job 33:4 and God filled Bezaleel with "the divine Spirit of wisdom and understanding and knowledge." Such names as these are super-eminent and mighty, but they do not transcend His glory.

49. And His operations, what are they? For majesty ineffable, and for numbers innumerable. How shall we form a conception of what extends beyond the ages? What were His operations before that creation whereof we can conceive? How great the grace which He conferred on creation? What the power exercised by Him over the ages to come? He existed; He pre-existed; He co-existed with the Father and the Son before the ages. It follows that, even if you can conceive of anything beyond the ages, you will find the Spirit yet further above and beyond. And if you think of the creation, the powers of the heavens were established by the Spirit, the establishment being understood to refer to disability to fall away from good. For it is from the Spirit that the powers derive their close relationship to God, their inability to change to evil, and their continuance in blessedness. Is it Christ's advent? The Spirit is forerunner. Is there the incarnate presence? The Spirit is inseparable. Working of miracles, and gifts of healing are through the Holy Spirit. Demons were driven out by the Spirit of God. The devil was brought to naught by the presence of the Spirit. Remission of sins was by the gift of the Spirit, for "you were

washed, you were sanctified,...in the name of the Lord Jesus Christ, and in the holy Spirit of our God." There is close relationship with God through the Spirit, for "God has sent forth the Spirit of His Son into your hearts, crying Abba, Father." Galatians 4:6 The resurrection from the dead is effected by the operation of the Spirit, for "You send forth your spirit, they are created; and You renew the face of the earth." If here creation may be taken to mean the bringing of the departed to life again, how mighty is not the operation of the Spirit, Who is to us the dispenser of the life that follows on the resurrection, and attunes our souls to the spiritual life beyond? Or if here by creation is meant the change to a better condition of those who in this life have fallen into sin, (for it is so understood according to the usage of Scripture, as in the words of Paul "if any man be in Christ he is a new creature" 2 Corinthians 5:17), the renewal which takes place in this life, and the transmutation from our earthly and sensuous life to the heavenly conversation which takes place in us through the Spirit, then our souls are exalted to the highest pitch of admiration. With these thoughts before us are we to be afraid of going beyond due bounds in the extravagance of the honour we pay? Shall we not rather fear lest, even though we seem to give Him the highest names which the thoughts of man can conceive or man's tongue utter, we let our thoughts about Him fall too low?

It is the Spirit which says, as the Lord says, "Get you down, and go with them, doubting nothing: for I have sent them." Acts 10:20 Are these the words of an inferior, or of one in dread? "Separate me Barnabas and Saul for the work whereunto I have called them." Acts 13:2 Does a slave speak thus? And Isaiah, "The Lord God and His Spirit has sent me," and "the Spirit came down from the Lord and guided them." And pray do not again understand by this guidance some humble service, for the Word witnesses that it was the work of God—"Thou leddest your people," it is said "like a flock," and "Thou that leadest Joseph like a flock," and "He led them on safely, so that they feared not." Thus when you hear that when the Comforter has come, He will put you in remembrance, and "guide you into all truth," do not misrepresent the meaning.

50. But, it is said that "He makes intercession for us." Romans 8:26-27 It follows then that, as the suppliant is inferior to the benefactor, so far is the Spirit inferior in dignity to God. But have you never heard concerning the Only-begotten that He "is at the right hand of God, who also makes intercession for us"? Romans 8:34 Do not, then, because the Spirit is in you—if indeed He is at all in you—nor yet because He teaches us who were blinded, and guides us to the choice of what profits us—do not for this reason allow yourself to be deprived of the right and holy opinion concerning Him. For to make the loving kindness of your benefactor a ground of ingratitude were indeed a very extravagance of unfairness. "Grieve not the Holy Spirit;" Ephesians 4:30 hear the words of Stephen, the first fruits of the martyrs, when he reproaches the people for their rebellion and disobedience; "you do always," he says, "resist the Holy Ghost;" Acts 7:51 and again Isaiah,— "They vexed His Holy Spirit, therefore He was turned to be their enemy;" Isaiah 63:10 and in another passage, "the house of Jacob angered the Spirit of the Lord." Are not these passages indicative of authoritative power? I leave it to the judgment of my readers to determine what opinions we ought to hold when we hear these passages; whether we are to regard the Spirit as an instrument, a subject, of equal rank with the creature, and a fellow servant of ourselves, or whether, on the contrary, to the ears of the pious the mere whisper of this blasphemy is not most grievous. Do you call the Spirit a servant? But, it is said, "the servant knows not what his Lord does," John 15:15 and yet the Spirit knows the

things of God, as "the spirit of man that is in him." 1 Corinthians 2:11

## Chapter 20
**Against those who maintain that the Spirit is in the rank neither of a servant nor of a master, but in that of the free.**

51. He is not a slave, it is said; not a master, but free. Oh the terrible insensibility, the pitiable audacity, of them that maintain this! Shall I rather lament in them their ignorance or their blasphemy? They try to insult the doctrines that concern the divine nature by comparing them with the human, and endeavour to apply to the ineffable nature of God that common custom of human life whereby the difference of degrees is variable, not perceiving that among men no one is a slave by nature. For men are either brought under a yoke of slavery by conquest, as when prisoners are taken in war; or they are enslaved on account of poverty, as the Egyptians were oppressed by Pharaoh; or, by a wise and mysterious dispensation, the worst children are by their fathers' order condemned to serve the wiser and the better; and this any righteous enquirer into the circumstances would declare to be not a sentence of condemnation but a benefit. For it is more profitable that the man who, through lack of intelligence, has no natural principle of rule within himself, should become the chattel of another, to the end that, being guided by the reason of his master, he may be like a chariot with a charioteer, or a boat with a steersman seated at the tiller. For this reason Jacob by his father's blessing became lord of Esau, Genesis 27:29 in order that the foolish son, who had not intelligence, his proper guardian, might, even though he wished it not, be benefited by his prudent brother. So Canaan shall be "a servant unto his brethren" Genesis 9:25 because, since his father Ham was unwise, he was uninstructed in virtue. In this world, then, it is thus that men are made slaves, but they who have escaped

poverty or war, or do not require the tutelage of others, are free. It follows that even though one man be called master and another servant, nevertheless, both in view of our mutual equality of rank and as chattels of our Creator, we are all fellow slaves. But in that other world what can you bring out of bondage? For no sooner were they created than bondage was commenced. The heavenly bodies exercise no rule over one another, for they are unmoved by ambition, but all bow down to God, and render to Him alike the awe which is due to Him as Master and the glory which falls to Him as Creator. For "a son honours his father and a servant his master," Malachi 1:6 and from all God asks one of these two things; for "if I then be a Father where is my honour? And if I be a Master where is my fear?" Malachi 1:6 Otherwise the life of all men, if it were not under the oversight of a master, would be most pitiable; as is the condition of the apostate powers who, because they stiffen their neck against God Almighty, fling off the reins of their bondage,— not that their natural constitution is different; but the cause is in their disobedient disposition to their Creator. Whom then do you call free? Him who has no King? Him who has neither power to rule another nor willingness to be ruled? Among all existent beings no such nature is to be found. To entertain such a conception of the Spirit is obvious blasphemy. If He is a creature of course He serves with all the rest, for "all things," it is said "are your servants," but if He is above Creation, then He shares in royalty.

## Chapter 21
### Proof from Scripture that the Spirit is called Lord.

52. But why get an unfair victory for our argument by fighting over these undignified questions, when it is within our power to prove that the excellence of the glory is beyond dispute by adducing more lofty considerations? If, indeed, we repeat what we have been

taught by Scripture, every one of the Pneumatomachi will perhaps raise a loud and vehement outcry, stop their ears, pick up stones or anything else that comes to hand for a weapon, and charge against us. But our own security must not be regarded by us before the truth. We have learned from the Apostle, "the Lord direct your hearts into the love of God and into the patient waiting for Christ" for our tribulations. Who is the Lord that directs into the love of God and into the patient waiting for Christ for tribulations? Let those men answer us who are for making a slave of the Holy Spirit. For if the argument had been about God the Father, it would certainly have said, 'the Lord direct you into His own love,' or if about the Son, it would have added 'into His own patience.' Let them then seek what other Person there is who is worthy to be honoured with the title of Lord. And parallel with this is that other passage, "and the Lord make you to increase and abound in love one toward another, and toward all men, even as we do towards you; to the end He may establish your hearts unblamable in holiness before God, even our Father, at the coming of our Lord Jesus Christ with all His saints." 1 Thessalonians 3:12-13 Now what Lord does he entreat to establish the hearts of the faithful at Thessalonica, unblamable in holiness before God even our Father, at the coming of our Lord? Let those answer who place the Holy Ghost among the ministering spirits that are sent forth on service. They cannot. Wherefore let them hear yet another testimony which distinctly calls the Spirit Lord. "The Lord," it is said, "is that Spirit;" and again "even as from the Lord the Spirit." But to leave no ground for objection, I will quote the actual words of the Apostle;— "For even unto this day remains the same veil untaken away in the reading of the Old Testament, which veil is done away in Christ....Nevertheless, when it shall turn to the Lord, the veil shall be taken away. Now the Lord is that Spirit." Why does he speak thus? Because he who abides in the bare sense of the letter, and in it busies himself with the observances of the Law, has, as it were, got his own heart enveloped in the Jewish acceptance of the letter, like a veil; and this befalls him because of his ignorance that the bodily observance of the Law is done away by the presence of Christ, in that for the future the types are transferred to the reality. Lamps are made needless by the advent of the sun; and, on the appearance of the truth, the occupation of the Law is gone, and prophecy is hushed into silence. He, on the contrary, who has been empowered to look down into the depth of the meaning of the Law, and, after passing through the obscurity of the letter, as through a veil, to arrive within things unspeakable, is like Moses taking off the veil when he spoke with God. He, too, turns from the letter to the Spirit. So with the veil on the face of Moses corresponds the obscurity of the teaching of the Law, and spiritual contemplation with the turning to the Lord. He, then, who in the reading of the Law takes away the letter and turns to the Lord,— and the Lord is now called the Spirit—becomes moreover like Moses, who had his face glorified by the manifestation of God. For just as objects which lie near brilliant colours are themselves tinted by the brightness which is shed around, so is he who fixes his gaze firmly on the Spirit by the Spirit's glory somehow transfigured into greater splendour, having his heart lighted up, as it were, by some light streaming from the truth of the Spirit. And, this is "being changed from the glory" of the Spirit "into" His own "glory," not in niggard degree, nor dimly and indistinctly, but as we might expect any one to be who is enlightened by the Spirit. Do you not, O man, fear the Apostle when he says "You are the temple of God, and the Spirit of God dwells in you"? 1 Corinthians 3:16 Could he ever have brooked to honour with the title of "temple" the quarters of a slave? How can he who calls Scripture "God-inspired," 2 Timothy 3:16 because it was written through the inspiration of the Spirit, use the language of one who insults and belittles Him?

91

## Chapter 22
## Establishment of the natural communion of the Spirit from His being, equally with the Father and the Son, unapproachable in thought.

53. Moreover the surpassing excellence of the nature of the Spirit is to be learned not only from His having the same title as the Father and the Son, and sharing in their operations, but also from His being, like the Father and the Son, unapproachable in thought. For what our Lord says of the Father as being above and beyond human conception, and what He says of the Son, this same language He uses also of the Holy Ghost. "O righteous Father," He says, "the world has not known You," John 17:25 meaning here by the world not the complex whole compounded of heaven and earth, but this life of ours subject to death, and exposed to innumerable vicissitudes. And when discoursing of Himself He says, "Yet a little while and the world sees me no more, but you see me;" John 14:19 again in this passage, applying the word world to those who being bound down by this material and carnal life, and beholding the truth by material sight alone, were ordained, through their unbelief in the resurrection, to see our Lord no more with the eyes of the heart. And He said the same concerning the Spirit. "The Spirit of truth," He says, "whom the world cannot receive, because it sees Him not, neither knows Him: but you know Him, for He dwells with you." John 14:17 For the carnal man, who has never trained his mind to contemplation, but rather keeps it buried deep in lust of the flesh, as in mud, is powerless to look up to the spiritual light of the truth. And so the world, that is life enslaved by the affections of the flesh, can no more receive the grace of the Spirit than a weak eye the light of a sunbeam. But the Lord, who by His teaching bore witness to purity of life, gives to His disciples the power of now both beholding and contemplating the Spirit. For

"now," He says, "You are clean through the word which I have spoken unto you," John 15:3 wherefore "the world cannot receive Him, because it sees Him not,...but you know Him; for he dwells with you." John 14:17 And so says Isaiah;— "He that spread forth the earth and that which comes out of it; he that gives breath unto the people upon it, and Spirit to them that trample on it" ; for they that trample down earthly things and rise above them are borne witness to as worthy of the gift of the Holy Ghost. What then ought to be thought of Him whom the world cannot receive, and Whom saints alone can contemplate through pureness of heart? What kind of honours can be deemed adequate to Him?

## Chapter 23
### The glorifying of the enumeration of His attributes.

54. Now of the rest of the Powers each is believed to be in a circumscribed place. The angel who stood by Cornelius Acts 10:3 was not at one and the same moment with Philip; Acts 8:26 nor yet did the angel who spoke with Zacharias from the altar at the same time occupy his own post in heaven. But the Spirit is believed to have been operating at the same time in Habakkuk and in Daniel at Babylon, and to have been at the prison with Jeremiah, and with Ezekiel at the Chebar. Ezekiel 1:1 For the Spirit of the Lord fills the world, Wisdom 1:7 and "whither shall I go from your spirit? Or whither shall I flee from your presence?" And, in the words of the Prophet, "For I am with you, says the Lord...and my spirit remains among you." Haggai 2:4-5 But what nature is it becoming to assign to Him who is omnipresent, and exists together with God? The nature which is all-embracing, or one which is confined to particular places, like that which our argument shows the nature of angels to be? No one would so say. Shall we not then highly exalt Him who is in His nature divine, in His greatness infinite, in His operations powerful, in the blessings He confers, good? Shall we

93

not give Him glory? And I understand glory to mean nothing else than the enumeration of the wonders which are His own. It follows then that either we are forbidden by our antagonists even to mention the good things which flow to us from Him. or on the other hand that the mere recapitulation of His attributes is the fullest possible attribution of glory. For not even in the case of the God and Father of our Lord Jesus Christ and of the Only begotten Son, are we capable of giving Them glory otherwise than by recounting, to the extent of our powers, all the wonders that belong to Them.

## Chapter 24
## Proof of the absurdity of the refusal to glorify the Spirit, from the comparison of things glorified in creation.

55. Furthermore man is "crowned with glory and honour," and "glory, honour and peace" are laid up by promise "to every man that works good." Romans 2:10 There is moreover a special and peculiar glory for Israelites "to whom," it is said "pertains the adoption and the glory...and the service," Romans 9:4 and the Psalmist speaks of a certain glory of his own, "that my glory may sing praise to You ;" and again "Awake up my glory" and according to the Apostle there is a certain glory of sun and moon and stars, and "the ministration of condemnation is glorious." 2 Corinthians 3:9 While then so many things are glorified, do you wish the Spirit alone of all things to be unglorified? Yet the Apostle says "the ministration of the Spirit is glorious." 2 Corinthians 3:8 How then can He Himself be unworthy of glory? How according to the Psalmist can the glory of the just man be great and according to you the glory of the Spirit none? How is there not a plain peril from such arguments of our bringing on ourselves the sin from which there is no escape? If the man who is being saved by works

94

of righteousness glorifies even them that fear the Lord much less would he deprive the Spirit of the glory which is His due.

Grant, they say, that He is to be glorified, but not with the Father and the Son. But what reason is there in giving up the place appointed by the Lord for the Spirit, and inventing some other? What reason is there for robbing of His share of glory Him Who is everywhere associated with the Godhead; in the confession of the Faith, in the baptism of redemption, in the working of miracles, in the indwelling of the saints, in the graces bestowed on obedience? For there is not even one single gift which reaches creation without the Holy Ghost; when not even a single word can be spoken in defence of Christ except by them that are aided by the Spirit, as we have learned in the Gospels from our Lord and Saviour. Matthew 10:19-20 And I know not whether any one who has been partaker of the Holy Spirit will consent that we should overlook all this, forget His fellowship in all things, and tear the Spirit asunder from the Father and the Son. Where then are we to take Him and rank Him? With the creature? Yet all the creature is in bondage, but the Spirit makes free. "And where the Spirit of the Lord is, there is liberty." 2 Corinthians 3:17 Many arguments might be adduced to them that it is unseemly to coordinate the Holy Spirit with created nature, but for the present I will pass them by. Were I indeed to bring forward, in a manner befitting the dignity of the discussion, all the proofs always available on our side, and so overthrow the objections of our opponents, a lengthy dissertation would be required, and my readers might be worn out by my prolixity. I therefore propose to reserve this matter for a special treatise, and to apply myself to the points now more immediately before us.

56. Let us then examine the points one by one. He is good by nature, in the same way as the Father is good, and the Son is good; the creature on the other hand shares in goodness by choosing the

good. He knows "The deep things of God;" 1 Corinthians 2:10-11 the creature receives the manifestation of ineffable things through the Spirit. He quickens together with God, who produces and preserves all things alive, and together with the Son, who gives life. "He that raised up Christ from the dead," it is said, "shall also quicken your mortal bodies by the spirit that dwells in you;" Romans 8:11 and again "my sheep hear my voice,...and I give unto them eternal life;" John 10:27-28 but "the Spirit" also, it is said, "gives life," 2 Corinthians 3:6 and again "the Spirit," it is said, "is life, because of righteousness." Romans 8:10 And the Lord bears witness that "it is the Spirit that quickens; the flesh profits nothing." John 6:63 How then shall we alienate the Spirit from His quickening power, and make Him belong to lifeless nature? Who is so contentious, who is so utterly without the heavenly gift, and unfed by God's good words, who is so devoid of part and lot in eternal hopes, as to sever the Spirit from the Godhead and rank Him with the creature?

57. Now it is urged that the Spirit is in us as a gift from God, and that the gift is not reverenced with the same honour as that which is attributed to the giver. The Spirit is a gift of God, but a gift of life, for the law of "the Spirit of life," it is said, "has made" us "free;" Romans 8:2 and a gift of power, for "you shall receive power after that the Holy Ghost has come upon you." Acts 1:8 Is He on this account to be lightly esteemed? Did not God also bestow His Son as a free gift to mankind? "He that spared not His own Son," it is said, "but delivered Him up for us all, how shall He not with Him also freely give us all things?" Romans 8:32 And in another place, "that we might truly know the things that are freely given us of God," 1 Corinthians 2:12 in reference to the mystery of the Incarnation. It follows then that the maintainers of such arguments, in making the greatness of God's loving kindness an

occasion of blasphemy, have really surpassed the ingratitude of the Jews. They find fault with the Spirit because He gives us freedom to call God our Father. "For God has sent forth the Spirit of His Son into" our "hearts crying Abba, Father," Galatians 4:6 that the voice of the Spirit may become the very voice of them that have received him.

**Chapter 25**

**That Scripture uses the words "in" or "by," ἐν in place of "with." Wherein also it is proved that the word "and" has the same force as "with."**

58. It is, however, asked by our opponents, how it is that Scripture nowhere describes the Spirit as glorified together with the Father and the Son, but carefully avoids the use of the expression "with the Spirit," while it everywhere prefers to ascribe glory "in Him" as being the fitter phrase. I should, for my own part, deny that the word in [or by] implies lower dignity than the word "with;" I should maintain on the contrary that, rightly understood, it leads us up to the highest possible meaning. This is the case where, as we have observed, it often stands instead of with; as for instance, "I will go into your house in burnt offerings," instead of with burnt offerings and "he brought them forth also by silver and gold," that is to say with silver and gold and "you go not forth in our armies" instead of with our armies, and innumerable similar passages. In short I should very much like to learn from this newfangled philosophy what kind of glory the Apostle ascribed by the word in, according to the interpretation which our opponents proffer as derived from Scripture, for I have nowhere found the formula "To You, O Father, be honour and glory, through Your only begotten Son, by [or in] the Holy Ghost,"— a form which to our opponents comes, so to say, as naturally as the air they breathe. You may indeed find each of these clauses separately, but they will nowhere

be able to show them to us arranged in this conjunction. If, then, they want exact conformity to what is written, let them give us exact references. If, on the other hand, they make concession to custom, they must not make us an exception to such a privilege.

59. As we find both expressions in use among the faithful, we use both; in the belief that full glory is equally given to the Spirit by both. The mouths, however, of revilers of the truth may best be stopped by the preposition which, while it has the same meaning as that of the Scriptures, is not so wieldy a weapon for our opponents, (indeed it is now an object of their attack) and is used instead of the conjunction and. For to say "Paul and Silvanus and Timothy" 1 Thessalonians 1:1 is precisely the same thing as to say Paul with Timothy and Silvanus; for the connection of the names is preserved by either mode of expression. The Lord says "The Father, the Son and the Holy Ghost." Matthew 28:19 If I say the Father and the Son with the Holy Ghost shall I make, any difference in the sense? Of the connection of names by means of the conjunction and the instances are many. We read "The grace of our Lord Jesus Christ and the love of God and the fellowship of the Holy Ghost," 2 Corinthians 13:13 and again "I beseech you for the Lord Jesus Christ's sake, and for the love of the Spirit." Romans 15:30 Now if we wish to use with instead of and, what difference shall we have made? I do not see; unless any one according to hard and fast grammatical rules might prefer the conjunction as copulative and making the union stronger, and reject the preposition as of inferior force. But if we had to defend ourselves on these points I do not suppose we should require a defence of many words. As it is, their argument is not about syllables nor yet about this or that sound of a word, but about things differing most widely in power and in truth. It is for this reason that, while the use of the syllables is really a matter of no

importance whatever, our opponents are making the endeavour to authorise some syllables, and hunt out others from the Church. For my own part, although the usefulness of the word is obvious as soon as it is heard, I will nevertheless set forth the arguments which led our fathers to adopt the reasonable course of employing the preposition "with." It does indeed equally well with the preposition "and," confute the mischief of Sabellius; and it sets forth quite as well as "and" the distinction of the hypostases, as in the words "I and my Father will come," and "I and my Father are one." John 10:30 In addition to this the proof it contains of the eternal fellowship and uninterrupted conjunction is excellent. For to say that the Son is with the Father is to exhibit at once the distinction of the hypostases, and the inseparability of the fellowship. The same thing is observable even in mere human matters, for the conjunction "and" intimates that there is a common element in an action, while the preposition "with" declares in some sense as well the communion in action. As, for instance—Paul and Timothy sailed to Macedonia, but both Tychicus and Onesimus were sent to the Colossians. Hence we learn that they did the same thing. But suppose we are told that they sailed with, and were sent with? Then we are informed in addition that they carried out the action in company with one another. Thus while the word "with" upsets the error of Sabellius as no other word can, it routs also sinners who err in the very opposite direction; those, I mean, who separate the Son from the Father and the Spirit from the Son, by intervals of time.

60. As compared with "in," there is this difference, that while "with" sets forth the mutual conjunction of the parties associated—as, for example, of those who sail with, or dwell with, or do anything else in common, "in" shows their relation to that matter in which they happen to be acting. For we no sooner hear

the words "sail in" or "dwell in" than we form the idea of the boat or the house. Such is the distinction between these words in ordinary usage; and laborious investigation might discover further illustrations. I have no time to examine into the nature of the syllables. Since then it has been shown that "with" most clearly gives the sense of conjunction, let it be declared, if you will, to be under safe-conduct, and cease to wage your savage and truceless war against it. Nevertheless, though the word is naturally thus auspicious, yet if any one likes, in the ascription of praise, to couple the names by the syllable "and," and to give glory, as we have taught in the Gospel, in the formula of baptism, Father and Son and Holy Ghost, Matthew 28:19 be it so: no one will make any objection. On these conditions, if you will, let us come to terms. But our foes would rather surrender their tongues than accept this word. It is this that rouses against us their implacable and truceless war. We must offer the ascription of glory to God, it is contended, in the Holy Ghost, and not and to the Holy Ghost, and they passionately cling to this word in, as though it lowered the Spirit. It will therefore be not unprofitable to speak at greater length about it; and I shall be astonished if they do not, when they have heard what we have to urge, reject the in as itself a traitor to their cause, and a deserter to the side of the glory of the Spirit.

## Chapter 26
## That the word "in," in as many senses as it bears, is understood of the Spirit.

61. Now, short and simple as this utterance is, it appears to me, as I consider it, that its meanings are many and various. For of the senses in which "in" is used, we find that all help our conceptions of the Spirit. Form is said to be in Matter; Power to be in what is capable of it; Habit to be in him who is affected by it; and so on. Therefore, inasmuch as the Holy Spirit perfects rational beings,

completing their excellence, He is analogous to Form. For he, who no longer "lives after the flesh," Romans 8:12 but, being "led by the Spirit of God," Romans 8:14 is called a Son of God, being "conformed to the image of the Son of God," Romans 8:29 is described as spiritual. And as is the power of seeing in the healthy eye, so is the operation of the Spirit in the purified soul. Wherefore also Paul prays for the Ephesians that they may have their "eyes enlightened" by "the Spirit of wisdom." Ephesians 1:17-18 And as the art in him who has acquired it, so is the grace of the Spirit in the recipient ever present, though not continuously in operation. For as the art is potentially in the artist, but only in operation when he is working in accordance with it, so also the Spirit is ever present with those that are worthy, but works, as need requires, in prophecies, or in healings, or in some other actual carrying into effect of His potential action. Furthermore as in our bodies is health, or heat, or, generally, their variable conditions, so, very frequently is the Spirit in the soul; since He does not abide with those who, on account of the instability of their will, easily reject the grace which they have received. An instance of this is seen in Saul, 1 Samuel 16:14 and the seventy elders of the children of Israel, except Eldad and Medad, with whom alone the Spirit appears to have remained, and, generally, any one similar to these in character. And like reason in the soul, which is at one time the thought in the heart, and at another speech uttered by the tongue, so is the Holy Spirit, as when He "bears witness with our spirit," Romans 8:16 and when He "cries in our hearts, Abba, Father," Galatians 6:4 or when He speaks on our behalf, as it is said, "It is not ye that speak, but the Spirit of our Father which speaks in you." Matthew 10:20 Again, the Spirit is conceived of, in relation to the distribution of gifts, as a whole in parts. For we all are "members one of another, having gifts differing according to the grace that is given us." Romans 12:5-6 Wherefore "the eye cannot say to the hand, I have no need of you; nor again the head to the feet, I have no need of you," 1 Corinthians 12:21 but all together complete the Body of Christ in the Unity of the Spirit, and render to one another the needful aid that comes of the gifts. "But God has set the members in the body, every one of them, as it has pleased Him." But "the members have the same care for one another," 1 Corinthians 12:25 according to the inborn spiritual communion of their sympathy. Wherefore, "whether one member suffer, all the members suffer with it; or one member be honoured, all the members rejoice with it." 1 Corinthians 12:26 And as parts in the whole so are we individually in the Spirit, because we all "were baptized in one body into one spirit."

62. It is an extraordinary statement, but it is none the less true, that the Spirit is frequently spoken of as the place of them that are being sanctified, and it will become evident that even by this figure the Spirit, so far from being degraded, is rather glorified. For words applicable to the body are, for the sake of clearness, frequently transferred in scripture to spiritual conceptions. Accordingly we find the Psalmist, even in reference to God, saying "Be Thou to me a champion God and a strong place to save me" and concerning the Spirit "behold there is place by me, and stand upon a rock." Plainly meaning the place or contemplation in the Spirit wherein, after Moses had entered there, he was able to see God intelligibly manifested to him. This is the special and peculiar place of true worship; for it is said "Take heed to yourself that thou offer not your burnt offerings in every place...but in the place the Lord your God shall choose." Deuteronomy 12:13-14 Now what is a spiritual burnt offering? "The sacrifice of praise." And in what place do we offer it? In the Holy Spirit. Where have we learned this? From the Lord himself in the words "The true worshippers shall worship the Father in spirit and in truth." This place Jacob saw and said "The

Lord is in this place." Genesis 28:16 It follows that the Spirit is verily the place of the saints and the saint is the proper place for the Spirit, offering himself as he does for the indwelling of God, and called God's Temple. 1 Corinthians 6:19 So Paul speaks in Christ, saying "In the sight of God we speak in Christ," 2 Corinthians 2:17 and Christ in Paul, as he himself says "Since ye seek a proof of Christ speaking in me." 2 Corinthians 13:3 So also in the Spirit he speaks mysteries, 1 Corinthians 14:2 and again the Spirit speaks in him. 1 Peter 1:11

63. In relation to the originate, then, the Spirit is said to be in them "in various portions and in various manners," Hebrews 1:1 while in relation to the Father and the Son it is more consistent with true religion to assert Him not to be in but to be with. For the grace flowing from Him when He dwells in those that are worthy, and carries out His own operations, is well described as existing in those that are able to receive Him. On the other hand His essential existence before the ages, and His ceaseless abiding with Son and Father, cannot be contemplated without requiring titles expressive of eternal conjunction. For absolute and real co-existence is predicated in the case of things which are mutually inseparable. We say, for instance, that heat exists in the hot iron, but in the case of the actual fire it co-exists; and, similarly, that health exists in the body, but that life co-exists with the soul. It follows that wherever the fellowship is intimate, congenital, and inseparable, the word with is more expressive, suggesting, as it does, the idea of inseparable fellowship. Where on the other hand the grace flowing from the Spirit naturally comes and goes, it is properly and truly said to exist in, even if on account of the firmness of the recipients' disposition to good the grace abides with them continually. Thus whenever we have in mind the Spirit's proper rank, we contemplate Him as being with the Father and the Son, but when we think of

the grace that flows from Him operating on those who participate in it, we say that the Spirit is in us. And the doxology which we offer "in the Spirit" is not an acknowledgment of His rank; it is rather a confession of our own weakness, while we show that we are not sufficient to glorify Him of ourselves, but our sufficiency is in the Holy Spirit. Enabled in, [or by,] Him we render thanks to our God for the benefits we have received, according to the measure of our purification from evil, as we receive one a larger and another a smaller share of the aid of the Spirit, that we may offer "the sacrifice of praise to God." Hebrews 13:15 According to one use, then, it is thus that we offer our thanksgiving, as the true religion requires, in the Spirit; although it is not quite unobjectionable that any one should testify of himself "the Spirit of God is in me, and I offer glory after being made wise through the grace that flows from Him." For to a Paul it is becoming to say "I think also that I have the Spirit of God," 1 Corinthians 7:40 and again, "that good thing which was committed to you keep by the Holy Ghost which dwells in us." 2 Timothy 1:14 And of Daniel it is fitting to say that "the Holy Spirit of God is in him," and similarly of men who are like these in virtue.

64. Another sense may however be given to the phrase, that just as the Father is seen in the Son, so is the Son in the Spirit. The "worship in the Spirit" suggests the idea of the operation of our intelligence being carried on in the light, as may be learned from the words spoken to the woman of Samaria. Deceived as she was by the customs of her country into the belief that worship was local, our Lord, with the object of giving her better instruction, said that worship ought to be offered "in Spirit and in Truth," John 4:24 plainly meaning by the Truth, Himself. As then we speak of the worship offered in the Image of God the Father as worship in the Son, so too do we speak of worship in the Spirit as showing in

Himself the Godhead of the Lord. Wherefore even in our worship the Holy Spirit is inseparable from the Father and the Son. If you remain outside the Spirit you will not be able even to worship at all; and on your becoming in Him you will in no way be able to dissever Him from God—any more than you will divorce light from visible objects. For it is impossible to behold the Image of the invisible God except by the enlightenment of the Spirit, and impracticable for him to fix his gaze on the Image to dissever the light from the Image, because the cause of vision is of necessity seen at the same time as the visible objects. Thus fitly and consistently do we behold the "Brightness of the glory" of God by means of the illumination of the Spirit, and by means of the "Express Image" we are led up to Him of whom He is the Express Image and Seal, graven to the like.

## Chapter 27
### Of the origin of the word "with," and what force it has. Also concerning the unwritten laws of the church.

65. The word "in," say our opponents, is exactly appropriate to the Spirit, and sufficient for every thought concerning Him. Why then, they ask, have we introduced this new phrase, saying, "with the Spirit" instead of "in the Holy Spirit," thus employing an expression which is quite unnecessary, and sanctioned by no usage in the churches? Now it has been asserted in the previous portion of this treatise that the word "in" has not been specially allotted to the Holy Spirit, but is common to the Father and the Son. It has also been, in my opinion, sufficiently demonstrated that, so far from detracting anything from the dignity of the Spirit, it leads all, but those whose thoughts are wholly perverted, to the sublimest height. It remains for me to trace the origin of the word "with;" to explain what force it has, and to show that it is in harmony with Scripture.

66. Of the beliefs and practices whether generally accepted or publicly enjoined which are preserved in the Church some we possess derived from written teaching; others we have received delivered to us "in a mystery" by the tradition of the apostles; and both of these in relation to true religion have the same force. And these no one will gainsay—no one, at all events, who is even moderately versed in the institutions of the Church. For were we to attempt to reject such customs as have no written authority, on the ground that the importance they possess is small, we should unintentionally injure the Gospel in its very vitals; or, rather, should make our public definition a mere phrase and nothing more. For instance, to take the first and most general example, who is thence who has taught us in writing to sign with the sign of the cross those who have trusted in the name of our Lord Jesus Christ? What writing has taught us to turn to the East at the prayer? Which of the saints has left us in writing the words of the invocation at the displaying of the bread of the Eucharist and the cup of blessing? For we are not, as is well known, content with what the apostle or the Gospel has recorded, but both in preface and conclusion we add other words as being of great importance to the validity of the ministry, and these we derive from unwritten teaching. Moreover we bless the water of baptism and the oil of the chrism, and besides this the catechumen who is being baptized. On what written authority do we do this? Is not our authority silent and mystical tradition? Nay, by what written word is the anointing of oil itself taught? And whence comes the custom of baptizing thrice? And as to the other customs of baptism from what Scripture do we derive the renunciation of Satan and his angels? Does not this come from that unpublished and secret teaching which our fathers guarded in a silence out of the reach of curious meddling and inquisitive investigation? Well had they learned the lesson that the awful dignity of the mysteries is best preserved by silence. What the

uninitiated are not even allowed to look at was hardly likely to be
publicly paraded about in written documents. What was the
meaning of the mighty Moses in not making all the parts of the
tabernacle open to every one? The profane he stationed without
the sacred barriers; the first courts he conceded to the purer; the
Levites alone he judged worthy of being servants of the Deity;
sacrifices and burnt offerings and the rest of the priestly functions
he allotted to the priests; one chosen out of all he admitted to the
shrine, and even this one not always but on only one day in the
year, and of this one day a time was fixed for his entry so that he
might gaze on the Holy of Holies amazed at the strangeness and
novelty of the sight. Moses was wise enough to know that
contempt stretches to the trite and to the obvious, while a keen
interest is naturally associated with the unusual and the unfamiliar.
In the same manner the Apostles and Fathers who laid down laws
for the Church from the beginning thus guarded the awful dignity
of the mysteries in secrecy and silence, for what is bruited abroad
random among the common folk is no mystery at all. This is the
reason for our tradition of unwritten precepts and practices, that
the knowledge of our dogmas may not become neglected and
contemned by the multitude through familiarity. "Dogma" and
"Kerugma" are two distinct things; the former is observed in
silence; the latter is proclaimed to all the world. One form of this
silence is the obscurity employed in Scripture, which makes the
meaning of "dogmas" difficult to be understood for the very
advantage of the reader: Thus we all look to the East at our prayers,
but few of us know that we are seeking our own old country,
Paradise, which God planted in Eden in the East. Genesis 2:8 We
pray standing, on the first day of the week, but we do not all know
the reason. On the day of the resurrection (or "standing again"
Grk. ἀ νάστασις) we remind ourselves of the grace given to us by
standing at prayer, not only because we rose with Christ, and are

bound to "seek those things which are above," Colossians 3:1 but because the day seems to us to be in some sense an image of the age which we expect, wherefore, though it is the beginning of days, it is not called by Moses first, but one. For he says "There was evening, and there was morning, one day," as though the same day often recurred. Now "one" and "eighth" are the same, in itself distinctly indicating that really "one" and "eighth" of which the Psalmist makes mention in certain titles of the Psalms, the state which follows after this present time, the day which knows no waning or eventide, and no successor, that age which ends not or grows old. Of necessity, then, the church teaches her own foster children to offer their prayers on that day standing, to the end that through continual reminder of the endless life we may not neglect to make provision for our removal there. Moreover all Pentecost is a reminder of the resurrection expected in the age to come. For that one and first day, if seven times multiplied by seven, completes the seven weeks of the holy Pentecost; for, beginning at the first, Pentecost ends with the same, making fifty revolutions through the like intervening days. And so it is a likeness of eternity, beginning as it does and ending, as in a circling course, at the same point. On this day the rules of the church have educated us to prefer the upright attitude of prayer, for by their plain reminder they, as it were, make our mind to dwell no longer in the present but in the future. Moreover every time we fall upon our knees and rise from off them we show by the very deed that by our sin we fell down to earth, and by the loving kindness of our Creator were called back to heaven.

67. Time will fail me if I attempt to recount the unwritten mysteries of the Church. Of the rest I say nothing; but of the very confession of our faith in Father, Son, and Holy Ghost, what is the written source? If it be granted that, as we are baptized, so also under the

obligation to believe, we make our confession in like terms as our baptism, in accordance with the tradition of our baptism and in conformity with the principles of true religion, let our opponents grant us too the right to be as consistent in our ascription of glory as in our confession of faith. If they deprecate our doxology on the ground that it lacks written authority, let them give us the written evidence for the confession of our faith and the other matters which we have enumerated. While the unwritten traditions are so many, and their bearing on "the mystery of godliness" 1 Timothy 3:16 is so important, can they refuse to allow us a single word which has come down to us from the Fathers;— which we found, derived from untutored custom, abiding in unperverted churches;— a word for which the arguments are strong, and which contributes in no small degree to the completeness of the force of the mystery?

68. The force of both expressions has now been explained. I will proceed to state once more wherein they agree and wherein they differ from one another—not that they are opposed in mutual antagonism, but that each contributes its own meaning to true religion. The preposition "in" states the truth rather relatively to ourselves; while "with" proclaims the fellowship of the Spirit with God. Wherefore we use both words, by the one expressing the dignity of the Spirit; by the other announcing the grace that is with us. Thus we ascribe glory to God both "in" the Spirit, and "with" the Spirit; and herein it is not our word that we use, but we follow the teaching of the Lord as we might a fixed rule, and transfer His word to things connected and closely related, and of which the conjunction in the mysteries is necessary. We have deemed ourselves under a necessary obligation to combine in our confession of the faith Him who is numbered with Them at Baptism, and we have treated the confession of the faith as the

origin and parent of the doxology. What, then, is to be done? They must now instruct us either not to baptize as we have received, or not to believe as we were baptized, or not to ascribe glory as we have believed. Let any man prove if he can that the relation of sequence in these acts is not necessary and unbroken; or let any man deny if he can that innovation here must mean ruin everywhere. Yet they never stop dinning in our ears that the ascription of glory "with" the Holy Spirit is unauthorized and unscriptural and the like. We have stated that so far as the sense goes it is the same to say "glory be to the Father and to the Son and to the Holy Ghost," and "glory be to the Father and to the Son with the Holy Ghost." It is impossible for any one to reject or cancel the syllable "and," which is derived from the very words of our Lord, and there is nothing to hinder the acceptance of its equivalent. What amount of difference and similarity there is between the two we have already shown. And our argument is confirmed by the fact that the Apostle uses either word indifferently,— saying at one time "in the name of the Lord Jesus and by the Spirit of our God;" 1 Corinthians 6:11 at another "when you are gathered together, and my Spirit, with the power of our Lord Jesus," 1 Corinthians 5:4 with no idea that it makes any difference to the connection of the names whether he use the conjunction or the preposition.

## Chapter 28
**That our opponents refuse to concede in the case of the Spirit the terms which Scripture uses in the case of men, as reigning together with Christ.**

69. But let us see if we can bethink us of any defence of this usage of our fathers; for they who first originated the expression are more open to blame than we ourselves. Paul in his Letter to the Colossians says, "And you, being dead in your sins and the

uncircumcision...has He quickened together with" Colossians 2:13
Christ. Did then God give to a whole people and to the Church the
boon of the life with Christ, and yet the life with Christ does not
belong to the Holy Spirit? But if this is impious even to think of, is
it not rightly reverent so to make our confession, as They are by
nature in close conjunction? Furthermore what boundless lack of
sensibility does it not show in these men to confess that the Saints
are with Christ, (if, as we know is the case, Paul, on becoming
absent from the body, is present with the Lord, and, after
departing, is with Christ ) and, so far as lies in their power, to refuse
to allow to the Spirit to be with Christ even to the same extent as
men? And Paul calls himself a "labourer together with God" 1
Corinthians 3:9 in the dispensation of the Gospel; will they bring
an indictment for impiety against us, if we apply the term "fellow-
labourer" to the Holy Spirit, through whom in every creature under
heaven the Gospel brings forth fruit? The life of them that have
trusted in the Lord "is hidden," it would seem, "with Christ in
God, and when Christ, who is our life, shall appear, then shall"
they themselves also "appear with Him in glory;" Colossians 3:3-4
and is the Spirit of life Himself, "Who made us free from the law
of sin," Romans 8:2 not with Christ, both in the secret and hidden
life with Him, and in the manifestation of the glory which we
expect to be manifested in the saints? We are "heirs of God and
joint heirs with Christ," Romans 8:17 and is the Spirit without part
or lot in the fellowship of God and of His Christ? "The Spirit itself
bears witness with our spirit that we are the children of God;" and
are we not to allow to the Spirit even that testimony of His
fellowship with God which we have learned from the Lord? For
the height of folly is reached if we through the faith in Christ which
is in the Spirit hope that we shall be raised together with Him and
sit together in heavenly places, whenever He shall change our vile
body from the natural to the spiritual, and yet refuse to assign to

the Spirit any share in the sitting together, or in the glory, or anything else which we have received from Him. Of all the boons of which, in accordance with the indefeasible grant of Him who has promised them, we have believed ourselves worthy, are we to allow none to the Holy Spirit, as though they were all above His dignity? It is yours according to your merit to be "ever with the Lord," and you expect to be caught up "in the clouds to meet the Lord in the air and to be ever with the Lord." 1 Thessalonians 4:17 You declare the man who numbers and ranks the Spirit with the Father and the Son to be guilty of intolerable impiety. Can you really now deny that the Spirit is with Christ?

70. I am ashamed to add the rest. You expect to be glorified together with Christ; ("if so be that we suffer with him that we may be also glorified together;" Romans 8:17) but you do not glorify the "Spirit of holiness" Romans 1:4 together with Christ, as though He were not worthy to receive equal honour even with you. You hope to "reign with" 2 Timothy 2:12 Christ; but you "do despite unto the Spirit of grace" Hebrews 10:29 by assigning Him the rank of a slave and a subordinate. And I say this not to demonstrate that so much is due to the Spirit in the ascription of glory, but to prove the unfairness of those who will not ever give so much as this, and shrink from the fellowship of the Spirit with Son and Father as from impiety. Who could touch on these things without a sigh? Is it not so plain as to be within the perception even of a child that this present state of things preludes the threatened eclipse of the faith? The undeniable has become the uncertain. We profess belief in the Spirit, and then we quarrel with our own confessions. We are baptized, and begin to fight again. We call upon Him as the Prince of Life, and then despise Him as a slave like ourselves. We received Him with the Father and the Son, and we dishonour Him as a part of creation. Those who "know not what they ought to pray for,"

Romans 8:26 even though they be induced to utter a word of the Spirit with awe, as though coming near His dignity, yet prune down all that exceeds the exact proportion of their speech. They ought rather to bewail their weakness, in that we are powerless to express in words our gratitude for the benefits which we are actually receiving; for He "passes all understanding," Philippians 4:7 and convicts speech of its natural inability even to approach His dignity in the least degree; as it is written in the Book of Wisdom, "Exalt Him as much as you can, for even yet will He far exceed; and when you exalt Him put forth all your strength, and be not weary, for you can never go far enough." Verily terrible is the account to be given for words of this kind by you who have heard from God who cannot lie that for blasphemy against the Holy Ghost there is no forgiveness. Luke 12:10

## Chapter 29
## Enumeration of the illustrious men in the Church who in their writings have used the word "with."

71. In answer to the objection that the doxology in the form "with the Spirit" has no written authority, we maintain that if there is no other instance of that which is unwritten, then this must not be received. But if the greater number of our mysteries are admitted into our constitution without written authority, then, in company with the many others, let us receive this one. For I hold it apostolic to abide also by the unwritten traditions. "I praise you," it is said, "that you remember me in all things, and keep the ordinances as I delivered them to you;" 1 Corinthians 11:2 and "Hold fast the traditions which you have been taught whether by word, or our Epistle." 2 Thessalonians 2:15 One of these traditions is the practice which is now before us, which they who ordained from the beginning, rooted firmly in the churches, delivering it to their successors, and its use through long custom advances pace by pace

with time. If, as in a Court of Law, we were at a loss for documentary evidence, but were able to bring before you a large number of witnesses, would you not give your vote for our acquittal? I think so; for "at the mouth of two or three witnesses shall the matter be established." Deuteronomy 19:15 And if we could prove clearly to you that a long period of time was in our favour, should we not have seemed to you to urge with reason that this suit ought not to be brought into court against us? For ancient dogmas inspire a certain sense of awe, venerable as they are with a hoary antiquity. I will therefore give you a list of the supporters of the word (and the time too must be taken into account in relation to what passes unquestioned). For it did not originate with us. How could it? We, in comparison with the time during which this word has been in vogue, are, to use the words of Job, "but of yesterday." Job 8:9 I myself, if I must speak of what concerns me individually, cherish this phrase as a legacy left me by my fathers. It was delivered to me by one who spent a long life in the service of God, and by him I was both baptized, and admitted to the ministry of the church. While examining, so far as I could, if any of the blessed men of old used the words to which objection is now made, I found many worthy of credit both on account of their early date, and also a characteristic in which they are unlike the men of today— because of the exactness of their knowledge. Of these some coupled the word in the doxology by the preposition, others by the conjunction, but were in no case supposed to be acting divergently,— at least so far as the right sense of true religion is concerned.

72. There is the famous Irenæus, and Clement of Rome; Dionysius of Rome, and, strange to say, Dionysius of Alexandria, in his second Letter to his namesake, on "Conviction and Defence," so concludes. I will give you his very words. "Following all these, we,

too, since we have received from the presbyters who were before us a form and rule, offering thanksgiving in the same terms with them, thus conclude our Letter to you. To God the Father and the Son our Lord Jesus Christ, with the Holy Ghost, glory and might for ever and ever; amen." And no one can say that this passage has been altered. He would not have so persistently stated that he had received a form and rule if he had said "in the Spirit." For of this phrase the use is abundant: it was the use of "with" which required defence. Dionysius moreover in the middle of his treatise thus writes in opposition to the Sabellians, "If by the hypostases being three they say that they are divided, there are three, though they like it not. Else let them destroy the divine Trinity altogether." And again: "most divine on this account after the Unity is the Trinity." Clement, in more primitive fashion, writes, "God lives, and the Lord Jesus Christ, and the Holy Ghost." And now let us hear how Irenæus, who lived near the times of the Apostles, mentions the Spirit in his work "Against the Heresies." "The Apostle rightly calls carnal them that are unbridled and carried away to their own desires, having no desire for the Holy Spirit," and in another passage Irenæus says, "The Apostle exclaimed that flesh and blood cannot inherit the kingdom of the heavens lest we, being without share in the divine Spirit, fall short of the kingdom of the heavens." If any one thinks Eusebius of Palestine worthy of credit on account of his wide experience, I point further to the very words he uses in discussing questions concerning the polygamy of the ancients. Stirring up himself to his work, he writes "invoking the holy God of the Prophets, the Author of light, through our Saviour Jesus Christ, with the Holy Spirit."

73. Origen, too, in many of his expositions of the Psalms, we find using the form of doxology "with the Holy Ghost." The opinions which he held concerning the Spirit were not always and

everywhere sound; nevertheless in many passages even he himself reverently recognises the force of established usage, and expresses himself concerning the Spirit in terms consistent with true religion. It is, if I am not mistaken, in the Sixth Book of his Commentary on the Gospel of St. John that he distinctly makes the Spirit an object of worship. His words are:— "The washing or water is a symbol of the cleaning of the soul which is washed clean of all filth that comes of wickedness; but none the less is it also by itself, to him who yields himself to the God-head of the adorable Trinity, through the power of the invocations, the origin and source of blessings." And again, in his Exposition of the Epistle to the Romans "the holy powers," he says "are able to receive the Only-begotten, and the Godhead of the Holy Spirit." Thus I apprehend, the powerful influence of tradition frequently impels men to express themselves in terms contradictory to their own opinions. Moreover this form of the doxology was not unknown even to Africanus the historian. In the Fifth Book of his Epitome of the Times he says "we who know the weight of those terms, and are not ignorant of the grace of faith, render thanks to the Father, who bestowed on us His own creatures, Jesus Christ, the Saviour of the world and our Lord, to whom be glory and majesty with the Holy Ghost, for ever." The rest of the passages may perhaps be viewed with suspicion; or may really have been altered, and the fact of their having been tampered with will be difficult to detect because the difference consists in a single syllable. Those however which I have quoted at length are out of the reach of any dishonest manipulation, and can easily be verified from the actual works.

I will now adduce another piece of evidence which might perhaps seem insignificant, but because of its antiquity must in nowise be omitted by a defendant who is indicted on a charge of innovation. It seemed fitting to our fathers not to receive the gift of the light at

eventide in silence, but, on its appearing, immediately to give
thanks. Who was the author of these words of thanksgiving at the
lighting of the lamps, we are not able to say. The people, however,
utter the ancient form, and no one has ever reckoned guilty of
impiety those who say "We praise Father, Son, and God's Holy
Spirit." And if any one knows the Hymn of Athenogenes, which, as
he was hurrying on to his perfecting by fire, he left as a kind of
farewell gift to his friends, he knows the mind of the martyrs as to
the Spirit. On this head I shall say no more.

74. But where shall I rank the great Gregory, and the words uttered
by him? Shall we not place among Apostles and Prophets a man
who walked by the same Spirit as they; 2 Corinthians 12:18 who
never through all his days diverged from the footprints of the
saints; who maintained, as long as he lived, the exact principles of
evangelical citizenship? I am sure that we shall do the truth a wrong
if we refuse to number that soul with the people of God, shining as
it did like a beacon in the Church of God; for by the fellow-
working of the Spirit the power which he had over demons was
tremendous, and so gifted was he with the grace of the word "for
obedience to the faith among...the nations," Romans 1:5 that,
although only seventeen Christians were handed over to him, he
brought the whole people alike in town and country through
knowledge to God. He too by Christ's mighty name commanded
even rivers to change their course, and caused a lake, which
afforded a ground of quarrel to some covetous brethren, to dry up.
Moreover his predictions of things to come were such as in no wise
to fall short of those of the great prophets. To recount all his
wonderful works in detail would be too long a task. By the
superabundance of gifts, wrought in him by the Spirit in all power
and in signs and in marvels, he was styled a second Moses by the
very enemies of the Church. Thus in all that he through grace

accomplished, alike by word and deed, a light seemed ever to be shining, token of the heavenly power from the unseen which followed him. To this day he is a great object of admiration to the people of his own neighbourhood, and his memory, established in the churches ever fresh and green, is not dulled by length of time. Thus not a practice, not a word, not a mystic rite has been added to the Church besides what he bequeathed to it. Hence truly on account of the antiquity of their institution many of their ceremonies appear to be defective. For his successors in the administration of the Churches could not endure to accept any subsequent discovery in addition to what had had his sanction. Now one of the institutions of Gregory is the very form of the doxology to which objection is now made, preserved by the Church on the authority of his tradition; a statement which may be verified without much trouble by any one who likes to make a short journey. That our Firmilian held this belief is testified by the writings which he has left. The contemporaries also of the illustrious Meletius say that he was of this opinion. But why quote ancient authorities? Now in the East are not the maintainers of true religion known chiefly by this one term, and separated from their adversaries as by a watchword? I have heard from a certain Mesopotamian, a man at once well skilled in the language and of unperverted opinions, that by the usage of his country it is impossible for any one, even though he may wish to do so, to express himself in any other way, and that they are compelled by the idiom of their mother tongue to offer the doxology by the syllable "and," or, I should more accurately say, by their equivalent expressions. We Cappadocians, too, so speak in the dialect of our country, the Spirit having so early as the division of tongues foreseen the utility of the phrase. And what of the whole West, almost from Illyricum to the boundaries of our world? Does it not support this word?

75. How then can I be an innovator and creator of new terms, when I adduce as originators and champions of the word whole nations, cities, custom going back beyond the memory of man, men who were pillars of the church and conspicuous for all knowledge and spiritual power? For this cause this banded array of foes is set in motion against me, and town and village and remotest regions are full of my calumniators. Sad and painful are these things to them that seek for peace, but great is the reward of patience for sufferings endured for the Faith's sake. So besides these let sword flash, let axe be whetted, let fire burn fiercer than that of Babylon, let every instrument of torture be set in motion against me. To me nothing is more fearful than failure to fear the threats which the Lord has directed against them that blaspheme the Spirit. Kindly readers will find a satisfactory defence in what I have said, that I accept a phrase so dear and so familiar to the saints, and confirmed by usage so long, inasmuch as, from the day when the Gospel was first preached up to our own time, it is shown to have been admitted to all full rights within the churches, and, what is of greatest moment, to have been accepted as bearing a sense in accordance with holiness and true religion. But before the great tribunal what have I prepared to say in my defence? This; that I was in the first place led to the glory of the Spirit by the honour conferred by the Lord in associating Him with Himself and with His Father at baptism; Matthew 28:19 and secondly by the introduction of each of us to the knowledge of God by such an initiation; and above all by the fear of the threatened punishment shutting out the thought of all indignity and unworthy conception. But our opponents, what will they say? After showing neither reverence for the Lord's honour nor fear of His threats, what kind of defence will they have for their blasphemy? It is for them to make up their mind about their own action or even now to change it. For my own part I would pray most earnestly that the good God

will make His peace rule in the hearts of all, so that these men who are swollen with pride and set in battle array against us may be calmed by the Spirit of meekness and of love; and that if they have become utterly savage, and are in an untamable state, He will grant to us at least to bear with long suffering all that we have to bear at their hands. In short "to them that have in themselves the sentence of death," 2 Corinthians 1:9 it is not suffering for the sake of the Faith which is painful; what is hard to bear is to fail to fight its battle. The athlete does not so much complain of being wounded in the struggle as of not being able even to secure admission into the stadium. Or perhaps this was the time for silence spoken of by Solomon the wise. Ecclesiastes 3:7 For, when life is buffeted by so fierce a storm that all the intelligence of those who are instructed in the word is filled with the deceit of false reasoning and confounded, like an eye filled with dust, when men are stunned by strange and awful noises, when all the world is shaken and everything tottering to its fall, what profits it to cry, as I am really crying, to the wind?

## Chapter 30
## Exposition of the present state of the Churches.

76. To what then shall I liken our present condition? It may be compared, I think, to some naval battle which has arisen out of time old quarrels, and is fought by men who cherish a deadly hate against one another, of long experience in naval warfare, and eager for the fight. Look, I beg you, at the picture thus raised before your eyes. See the rival fleets rushing in dread array to the attack. With a burst of uncontrollable fury they engage and fight it out. Fancy, if you like, the ships driven to and fro by a raging tempest, while thick darkness falls from the clouds and blackens all the scenes so that watchwords are indistinguishable in the confusion, and all distinction between friend and foe is lost. To fill up the details of

the imaginary picture, suppose the sea swollen with billows and whirled up from the deep, while a vehement torrent of rain pours down from the clouds and the terrible waves rise high. From every quarter of heaven the winds beat upon one point, where both the fleets are dashed one against the other. Of the combatants some are turning traitors; some are deserting in the very thick of the fight; some have at one and the same moment to urge on their boats, all beaten by the gale, and to advance against their assailants. Jealousy of authority and the lust of individual mastery splits the sailors into parties which deal mutual death to one another. Think, besides all this, of the confused and unmeaning roar sounding over all the sea, from howling winds, from crashing vessels, from boiling surf, from the yells of the combatants as they express their varying emotions in every kind of noise, so that not a word from admiral or pilot can be heard. The disorder and confusion is tremendous, for the extremity of misfortune, when life is despaired of, gives men license for every kind of wickedness. Suppose, too, that the men are all smitten with the incurable plague of mad love of glory, so that they do not cease from their struggle each to get the better of the other, while their ship is actually settling down into the deep.

77. Turn now I beg you from this figurative description to the unhappy reality. Did it not at one time appear that the Arian schism, after its separation into a sect opposed to the Church of God, stood itself alone in hostile array? But when the attitude of our foes against us was changed from one of long standing and bitter strife to one of open warfare, then, as is well known, the war was split up in more ways than I can tell into many subdivisions, so that all men were stirred to a state of inveterate hatred alike by common party spirit and individual suspicion. But what storm at sea was ever so fierce and wild as this tempest of the Churches? In it every landmark of the Fathers has been moved; every foundation,

every bulwark of opinion has been shaken: everything buoyed up on the unsound is dashed about and shaken down. We attack one another. We are overthrown by one another. If our enemy is not the first to strike us, we are wounded by the comrade at our side. If a foeman is stricken and falls, his fellow soldier tramples him down. There is at least this bond of union between us that we hate our common foes, but no sooner have the enemy gone by than we find enemies in one another. And who could make a complete list of all the wrecks? Some have gone to the bottom on the attack of the enemy, some through the unsuspected treachery of their allies, some from the blundering of their own officers. We see, as it were, whole churches, crews and all, dashed and shattered upon the sunken reefs of disingenuous heresy, while others of the enemies of the Spirit of Salvation have seized the helm and made shipwreck of the faith. 1 Timothy 1:19 And then the disturbances wrought by the princes of the world 1 Corinthians 2:6 have caused the downfall of the people with a violence unmatched by that of hurricane or whirlwind. The luminaries of the world, which God set to give light to the souls of the people, have been driven from their homes, and a darkness verily gloomy and disheartening has settled on the Churches. The terror of universal ruin is already imminent, and yet their mutual rivalry is so unbounded as to blunt all sense of danger. Individual hatred is of more importance than the general and common warfare, for men by whom the immediate gratification of ambition is esteemed more highly than the rewards that await us in a time to come, prefer the glory of getting the better of their opponents to securing the common welfare of mankind. So all men alike, each as best he can, lift the hand of murder against one another. Harsh rises the cry of the combatants encountering one another in dispute; already all the Church is almost full of the inarticulate screams, the unintelligible noises, rising from the ceaseless agitations that divert the right rule of the doctrine of true religion, now in the direction of excess, now in that of defect. On the one hand are they who confound the Persons and are carried away into Judaism; on the other hand are they that, through the opposition of the natures, pass into heathenism. Between these opposite parties inspired Scripture is powerless to mediate; the traditions of the apostles cannot suggest terms of arbitration. Plain speaking is fatal to friendship, and disagreement in opinion all the ground that is wanted for a quarrel. No oaths of confederacy are so efficacious in keeping men true to sedition as their likeness in error. Every one is a theologue though he have his soul branded with more spots than can be counted. The result is that innovators find a plentiful supply of men ripe for faction, while self-appointed scions of the house of place-hunters reject the government of the Holy Spirit and divide the chief dignities of the Churches. The institutions of the Gospel have now everywhere been thrown into confusion by want of discipline; there is an indescribable pushing for the chief places while every self-advertiser tries to force himself into high office. The result of this lust for ordering is that our people are in a state of wild confusion for lack of being ordered; the exhortations of those in authority are rendered wholly purposeless and void, because there is not a man but, out of his ignorant impudence, thinks that it is just as much his duty to give orders to other people, as it is to obey any one else.

78. So, since no human voice is strong enough to be heard in such a disturbance, I reckon silence more profitable than speech, for if there is any truth in the words of the Preacher, "The words of wise men are heard in quiet," Ecclesiastes 9:17 in the present condition of things any discussion of them must be anything but becoming. I am moreover restrained by the Prophet's saying, "Therefore the prudent shall keep silence in that time, for it is an evil time," Amos 5:13 a time when some trip up their neighbours' heels, some stamp

on a man when he is down, and others clap their hands with joy, but there is not one to feel for the fallen and hold out a helping hand, although according to the ancient law he is not uncondemned, who passes by even his enemy's beast of burden fallen under his load. Ezekiel 23:5 This is not the state of things now. Why not? The love of many has waxed cold; Matthew 24:12 brotherly concord is destroyed, the very name of unity is ignored, brotherly admonitions are heard no more, nowhere is there Christian pity, nowhere falls the tear of sympathy. Now there is no one to receive "the weak in faith," Romans 14:1 but mutual hatred has blazed so high among fellow clansmen that they are more delighted at a neighbour's fall than at their own success. Just as in a plague, men of the most regular lives suffer from the same sickness as the rest, because they catch the disease by communication with the infected, so nowadays by the evil rivalry which possesses our souls we are carried away to an emulation in wickedness, and are all of us each as bad as the others. Hence merciless and sour sit the judges of the erring; unfeeling and hostile are the critics of the well disposed. And to such a depth is this evil rooted among us that we have become more brutish than the brutes; they do at least herd with their fellows, but our most savage warfare is with our own people.

79. For all these reasons I ought to have kept silence, but I was drawn in the other direction by love, which "seeks not her own," 1 Corinthians 13:5 and desires to overcome every difficulty put in her way by time and circumstance. I was taught too by the children at Babylon, that, when there is no one to support the cause of true religion, we ought alone and all unaided to do our duty. They from out of the midst of the flame lifted up their voices in hymns and praise to God, reeking not of the host that set the truth at naught, but sufficient, three only that they were, with one another.

Wherefore we too are undismayed at the cloud of our enemies, and, resting our hope on the aid of the Spirit, have, with all boldness, proclaimed the truth. Had I not so done, it would truly have been terrible that the blasphemers of the Spirit should so easily be emboldened in their attack upon true religion, and that we, with so mighty an ally and supporter at our side, should shrink from the service of that doctrine, which by the tradition of the Fathers has been preserved by an unbroken sequence of memory to our own day. A further powerful incentive to my undertaking was the warm fervour of your "love unfeigned," and the seriousness and taciturnity of your disposition; a guarantee that you would not publish what I was about to say to all the world—not because it would not be worth making known, but to avoid casting pearls before swine. Matthew 7:6 My task is now done. If you find what I have said satisfactory, let this make an end to our discussion of these matters. If you think any point requires further elucidation, pray do not hesitate to pursue the investigation with all diligence, and to add to your information by putting any uncontroversial question. Either through me or through others the Lord will grant full explanation on matters which have yet to be made clear, according to the knowledge supplied to the worthy by the Holy Spirit. Amen

.

# Hexaemeron

**Homily 1**
**In the Beginning God made the Heaven and the Earth.**

1. It is right that any one beginning to narrate the formation of the world should begin with the good order which reigns in visible things. I am about to speak of the creation of heaven and earth, which was not spontaneous, as some have imagined, but drew its origin from God. What ear is worthy to hear such a tale? How earnestly the soul should prepare itself to receive such high lessons! How pure it should be from carnal affections, how unclouded by worldly disquietudes, how active and ardent in its researches, how eager to find in its surroundings an idea of God which may be worthy of Him!

But before weighing the justice of these remarks, before examining all the sense contained in these few words, let us see who addresses them to us. Because, if the weakness of our intelligence does not allow us to penetrate the depth of the thoughts of the writer, yet we shall be involuntarily drawn to give faith to his words by the force of his authority. Now it is Moses who has composed this history; Moses, who, when still at the breast, is described as exceeding fair; Moses, whom the daughter of Pharaoh adopted; who received from her a royal education, and who had for his teachers the wise men of Egypt; Moses, who disdained the pomp of royalty, and, to share the humble condition of his compatriots, preferred to be persecuted with the people of God rather than to enjoy the fleeting delights of sin; Moses, who received from nature such a love of justice that, even before the leadership of the people of God was committed to him, he was impelled, by a natural horror of evil, to

127

pursue malefactors even to the point of punishing them by death; Moses, who, banished by those whose benefactor he had been, hastened to escape from the tumults of Egypt and took refuge in Ethiopia, living there far from former pursuits, and passing forty years in the contemplation of nature; Moses, finally, who, at the age of eighty, saw God, as far as it is possible for man to see Him; or rather as it had not previously been granted to man to see Him, according to the testimony of God Himself, "If there be a prophet among you, I the Lord will make myself known unto him in a vision, and will speak unto him in a dream. My servant Moses is not so, who is faithful in all mine house, with him will I speak mouth to mouth, even apparently and not in dark speeches." It is this man, whom God judged worthy to behold Him, face to face, like the angels, who imparts to us what he has learned from God. Let us listen then to these words of truth written without the help of the "enticing words of man's wisdom" 1 Corinthians 2:4 by the dictation of the Holy Spirit; words destined to produce not the applause of those who hear them, but the salvation of those who are instructed by them.

2. "In the beginning God created the heaven and the earth." Genesis 1:1 I stop struck with admiration at this thought. What shall I first say? Where shall I begin my story? Shall I show forth the vanity of the Gentiles? Shall I exalt the truth of our faith? The philosophers of Greece have made much ado to explain nature, and not one of their systems has remained firm and unshaken, each being overturned by its successor. It is vain to refute them; they are sufficient in themselves to destroy one another. Those who were too ignorant to rise to a knowledge of a God, could not allow that an intelligent cause presided at the birth of the Universe; a primary error that involved them in sad consequences. Some had recourse to material principles and attributed the origin of the Universe to

the elements of the world. Others imagined that atoms, and indivisible bodies, molecules and ducts, form, by their union, the nature of the visible world. Atoms reuniting or separating, produce births and deaths and the most durable bodies only owe their consistency to the strength of their mutual adhesion: a true spider's web woven by these writers who give to heaven, to earth, and to sea so weak an origin and so little consistency! It is because they knew not how to say "In the beginning God created the heaven and the earth." Deceived by their inherent atheism it appeared to them that nothing governed or ruled the universe, and that was all was given up to chance. To guard us against this error the writer on the creation, from the very first words, enlightens our understanding with the name of God; "In the beginning God created." What a glorious order! He first establishes a beginning, so that it might not be supposed that the world never had a beginning. Then he adds "Created" to show that which was made was a very small part of the power of the Creator. In the same way that the potter, after having made with equal pains a great number of vessels, has not exhausted either his art or his talent; thus the Maker of the Universe, whose creative power, far from being bounded by one world, could extend to the infinite, needed only the impulse of His will to bring the immensities of the visible world into being. If then the world has a beginning, and if it has been created, enquire who gave it this beginning, and who was the Creator: or rather, in the fear that human reasonings may make you wander from the truth, Moses has anticipated enquiry by engraving in our hearts, as a seal and a safeguard, the awful name of God: "In the beginning God created"— It is He, beneficent Nature, Goodness without measure, a worthy object of love for all beings endowed with reason, the beauty the most to be desired, the origin of all that exists, the source of life, intellectual light, impenetrable wisdom, it is He who "in the beginning created heaven and earth."

3. Do not then imagine, O man! That the visible world is without a beginning; and because the celestial bodies move in a circular course, and it is difficult for our senses to define the point where the circle begins, do not believe that bodies impelled by a circular movement are, from their nature, without a beginning. Without doubt the circle (I mean the plane figure described by a single line) is beyond our perception, and it is impossible for us to find out where it begins or where it ends; but we ought not on this account to believe it to be without a beginning. Although we are not sensible of it, it really begins at some point where the draughtsman has begun to draw it at a certain radius from the centre. Thus seeing that figures which move in a circle always return upon themselves, without for a single instant interrupting the regularity of their course, do not vainly imagine to yourselves that the world has neither beginning nor end. "For the fashion of this world passes away" 1 Corinthians 7:31 and "Heaven and earth shall pass away." Matthew 24:35 The dogmas of the end, and of the renewing of the world, are announced beforehand in these short words put at the head of the inspired history. "In the beginning God made." That which was begun in time is condemned to come to an end in time. If there has been a beginning do not doubt of the end. Of what use then are geometry— the calculations of arithmetic— the study of solids and far-famed astronomy, this laborious vanity, if those who pursue them imagine that this visible world is co-eternal with the Creator of all things, with God Himself; if they attribute to this limited world, which has a material body, the same glory as to the incomprehensible and invisible nature; if they cannot conceive that a whole, of which the parts are subject to corruption and change, must of necessity end by itself submitting to the fate of its parts? But they have become "vain in their imaginations and their foolish heart was darkened. Professing themselves to be wise, they became fools." Romans 1:21-22 Some have affirmed that heaven

co-exists with God from all eternity; others that it is God Himself without beginning or end, and the cause of the particular arrangement of all things.

4. One day, doubtless, their terrible condemnation will be the greater for all this worldly wisdom, since, seeing so clearly into vain sciences, they have wilfully shut their eyes to the knowledge of the truth. These men who measure the distances of the stars and describe them, both those of the North, always shining brilliantly in our view, and those of the southern pole visible to the inhabitants of the South, but unknown to us; who divide the Northern zone and the circle of the Zodiac into an infinity of parts, who observe with exactitude the course of the stars, their fixed places, their declensions, their return and the time that each takes to make its revolution; these men, I say, have discovered all except one thing: the fact that God is the Creator of the universe, and the just Judge who rewards all the actions of life according to their merit. They have not known how to raise themselves to the idea of the consummation of all things, the consequence of the doctrine of judgment, and to see that the world must change if souls pass from this life to a new life. In reality, as the nature of the present life presents an affinity to this world, so in the future life our souls will enjoy a lot conformable to their new condition. But they are so far from applying these truths, that they do but laugh when we announce to them the end of all things and the regeneration of the age. Since the beginning naturally precedes that which is derived from it, the writer, of necessity, when speaking to us of things which had their origin in time, puts at the head of his narrative these words— "In the beginning God created."

5. It appears, indeed, that even before this world an order of things existed of which our mind can form an idea, but of which we can say nothing, because it is too lofty a subject for men who are but

beginners and are still babes in knowledge. The birth of the world was preceded by a condition of things suitable for the exercise of supernatural powers, outstripping the limits of time, eternal and infinite. The Creator and Demiurge of the universe perfected His works in it, spiritual light for the happiness of all who love the Lord, intellectual and invisible natures, all the orderly arrangement of pure intelligences who are beyond the reach of our mind and of whom we cannot even discover the names. They fill the essence of this invisible world, as Paul teaches us. "For by him were all things created that are in heaven, and that are in earth, visible and invisible whether they be thrones or dominions or principalities or powers" Colossians 1:16 or virtues or hosts of angels or the dignities of archangels. To this world at last it was necessary to add a new world, both a school and training place where the souls of men should be taught and a home for beings destined to be born and to die. Thus was created, of a nature analogous to that of this world and the animals and plants which live thereon, the succession of time, for ever pressing on and passing away and never stopping in its course. Is not this the nature of time, where the past is no more, the future does not exist, and the present escapes before being recognised? And such also is the nature of the creature which lives in time,— condemned to grow or to perish without rest and without certain stability. It is therefore fit that the bodies of animals and plants, obliged to follow a sort of current, and carried away by the motion which leads them to birth or to death, should live in the midst of surroundings whose nature is in accord with beings subject to change. Thus the writer who wisely tells us of the birth of the Universe does not fail to put these words at the head of the narrative. "In the beginning God created;" that is to say, in the beginning of time. Therefore, if he makes the world appear in the beginning, it is not a proof that its birth has preceded that of all other things that were made. He only wishes to tell us that, after the invisible and intellectual world, the visible world, the world of the senses, began to exist.

The first movement is called beginning. "To do right is the beginning of the good way." Just actions are truly the first steps towards a happy life. Again, we call "beginning" the essential and first part from which a thing proceeds, such as the foundation of a house, the keel of a vessel; it is in this sense that it is said, "The fear of the Lord is the beginning of wisdom," Proverbs 9:10 that is to say that piety is, as it were, the groundwork and foundation of perfection. Art is also the beginning of the works of artists, the skill of Bezaleel began the adornment of the tabernacle. Often even the good which is the final cause is the beginning of actions. Thus the approbation of God is the beginning of almsgiving, and the end laid up for us in the promises the beginning of all virtuous efforts.

6. Such being the different senses of the word beginning, see if we have not all the meanings here. You may know the epoch when the formation of this world began, it, ascending into the past, you endeavour to discover the first day. You will thus find what was the first movement of time; then that the creation of the heavens and of the earth were like the foundation and the groundwork, and afterwards that an intelligent reason, as the word beginning indicates, presided in the order of visible things. You will finally discover that the world was not conceived by chance and without reason, but for an useful end and for the great advantage of all beings, since it is really the school where reasonable souls exercise themselves, the training ground where they learn to know God; since by the sight of visible and sensible things the mind is led, as by a hand, to the contemplation of invisible things. "For," as the Apostle says, "the invisible things of him from the creation of the world are clearly seen, being understood by the things that are made." Romans 1:20 Perhaps these words "In the beginning God

created" signify the rapid and imperceptible moment of creation. The beginning, in effect, is indivisible and instantaneous. The beginning of the road is not yet the road, and that of the house is not yet the house; so the beginning of time is not yet time and not even the least particle of it. If some objector tell us that the beginning is a time, he ought then, as he knows well, to submit it to the division of time— a beginning, a middle and an end. Now it is ridiculous to imagine a beginning of a beginning. Further, if we divide the beginning into two, we make two instead of one, or rather make several, we really make an infinity, for all that which is divided is divisible to the infinite. Thus then, if it is said, "In the beginning God created," it is to teach us that at the will of God the world arose in less than an instant, and it is to convey this meaning more clearly that other interpreters have said: "God made summarily" that is to say all at once and in a moment. But enough concerning the beginning, if only to put a few points out of many.

7. Among arts, some have in view production, some practice, others theory. The object of the last is the exercise of thought, that of the second, the motion of the body. Should it cease, all stops; nothing more is to be seen. Thus dancing and music have nothing behind; they have no object but themselves. In creative arts on the contrary the work lasts after the operation. Such is architecture— such are the arts which work in wood and brass and weaving, all those indeed which, even when the artisan has disappeared, serve to show an industrious intelligence and to cause the architect, the worker in brass or the weaver, to be admired on account of his work. Thus, then, to show that the world is a work of art displayed for the beholding of all people; to make them know Him who created it, Moses does not use another word. "In the beginning," he says "God created." He does not say "God worked," "God formed," but "God created." Among those who have imagined

that the world co-existed with God from all eternity, many have denied that it was created by God, but say that it exists spontaneously, as the shadow of this power. God, they say, is the cause of it, but an involuntary cause, as the body is the cause of the shadow and the flame is the cause of the brightness. It is to correct this error that the prophet states, with so much precision, "In the beginning God created." He did not make the thing itself the cause of its existence. Being good, He made it an useful work. Being wise, He made it everything that was most beautiful. Being powerful He made it very great. Moses almost shows us the finger of the supreme artisan taking possession of the substance of the universe, forming the different parts in one perfect accord, and making a harmonious symphony result from the whole.

"In the beginning God made heaven and earth." By naming the two extremes, he suggests the substance of the whole world, according to heaven the privilege of seniority, and putting earth in the second rank. All intermediate beings were created at the same time as the extremities. Thus, although there is no mention of the elements, fire, water and air, imagine that they were all compounded together, and you will find water, air and fire, in the earth. For fire leaps out from stones; iron which is dug from the earth produces under friction fire in plentiful measure. A marvellous fact! Fire shut up in bodies lurks there hidden without harming them, but no sooner is it released than it consumes that which has hitherto preserved it. The earth contains water, as diggers of wells teach us. It contains air too, as is shown by the vapours that it exhales under the sun's warmth when it is damp. Now, as according to their nature, heaven occupies the higher and earth the lower position in space, (one sees, in fact, that all which is light ascends towards heaven, and heavy substances fall to the ground); as therefore height and depth are the points the most

135

opposed to each other it is enough to mention the most distant parts to signify the inclusion of all which fills up intervening Space. Do not ask, then, for an enumeration of all the elements; guess, from what Holy Scripture indicates, all that is passed over in silence.

8. "In the beginning God created the heaven and the earth." If we were to wish to discover the essence of each of the beings which are offered for our contemplation, or come under our senses, we should be drawn away into long digressions, and the solution of the problem would require more words than I possess, to examine fully the matter. To spend time on such points would not prove to be to the edification of the Church. Upon the essence of the heavens we are contented with what Isaiah says, for, in simple language, he gives us sufficient idea of their nature, "The heaven was made like smoke," that is to say, He created a subtle substance, without solidity or density, from which to form the heavens. As to the form of them we also content ourselves with the language of the same prophet, when praising God "that stretches out the heavens as a curtain and spreads them out as a tent to dwell in." In the same way, as concerns the earth, let us resolve not to torment ourselves by trying to find out its essence, not to tire our reason by seeking for the substance which it conceals. Do not let us seek for any nature devoid of qualities by the conditions of its existence, but let us know that all the phenomena with which we see it clothed regard the conditions of its existence and complete its essence. Try to take away by reason each of the qualities it possesses, and you will arrive at nothing. Take away black, cold, weight, density, the qualities which concern taste, in one word all these which we see in it, and the substance vanishes.

If I ask you to leave these vain questions, I will not expect you to try and find out the earth's point of support. The mind would reel on beholding its reasonings losing themselves without end. Do you say that the earth reposes on a bed of air? How, then, can this soft substance, without consistency, resist the enormous weight which presses upon it? How is it that it does not slip away in all directions, to avoid the sinking weight, and to spread itself over the mass which overwhelms it? Do you suppose that water is the foundation of the earth? You will then always have to ask yourself how it is that so heavy and opaque a body does not pass through the water; how a mass of such a weight is held up by a nature weaker than itself. Then you must seek a base for the waters, and you will be in much difficulty to say upon what the water itself rests.

9. Do you suppose that a heavier body prevents the earth from falling into the abyss? Then you must consider that this support needs itself a support to prevent it from falling. Can we imagine one? Our reason again demands yet another support, and thus we shall fall into the infinite, always imagining a base for the base which we have already found. And the further we advance in this reasoning the greater force we are obliged to give to this base, so that it may be able to support all the mass weighing upon it. Put then a limit to your thought, so that your curiosity in investigating the incomprehensible may not incur the reproaches of Job, and you be not asked by him, "Whereupon are the foundations thereof fastened?" Job 38:6 If ever you hear in the Psalms, "I bear up the pillars of it;" see in these pillars the power which sustains it. Because what means this other passage, "He has founded it upon the sea," if not that the water is spread all around the earth? How then can water, the fluid element which flows down every declivity, remain suspended without ever flowing? You do not reflect that the idea of the earth suspended by itself throws your reason into a like but even greater difficulty, since from its nature it is heavier. But let us admit that the earth rests upon itself, or let us say that it

rides the waters, we must still remain faithful to thought of true religion and recognise that all is sustained by the Creator's power. Let us then reply to ourselves, and let us reply to those who ask us upon what support this enormous mass rests, "In His hands are the ends of the earth." It is a doctrine as infallible for our own information as profitable for our hearers.

10. There are inquirers into nature who with a great display of words give reasons for the immobility of the earth. Placed, they say, in the middle of the universe and not being able to incline more to one side than the other because its centre is everywhere the same distance from the surface, it necessarily rests upon itself; since a weight which is everywhere equal cannot lean to either side. It is not, they go on, without reason or by chance that the earth occupies the centre of the universe. It is its natural and necessary position. As the celestial body occupies the higher extremity of space all heavy bodies, they argue, that we may suppose to have fallen from these high regions, will be carried from all directions to the centre, and the point towards which the parts are tending will evidently be the one to which the whole mass will be thrust together. If stones, wood, all terrestrial bodies, fall from above downwards, this must be the proper and natural place of the whole earth. If, on the contrary, a light body is separated from the centre, it is evident that it will ascend towards the higher regions. Thus heavy bodies move from the top to the bottom, and following this reasoning, the bottom is none other than the centre of the world. Do not then be surprised that the world never falls: it occupies the centre of the universe, its natural place. By necessity it is obliged to remain in its place, unless a movement contrary to nature should displace it. If there is anything in this system which might appear probable to you, keep your admiration for the source of such perfect order, for the wisdom of God. Grand phenomena do not

strike us the less when we have discovered something of their wonderful mechanism. Is it otherwise here? At all events let us prefer the simplicity of faith to the demonstrations of reason.

11. We might say the same thing of the heavens. With what a noise of words the sages of this world have discussed their nature! Some have said that heaven is composed of four elements as being tangible and visible, and is made up of earth on account of its power of resistance, with fire because it is striking to the eye, with air and water on account of the mixture. Others have rejected this system as improbable, and introduced into the world, to form the heavens, a fifth element after their own fashioning. There exists, they say, an æthereal body which is neither fire, air, earth, nor water, nor in one word any simple body. These simple bodies have their own natural motion in a straight line, light bodies upwards and heavy bodies downwards; now this motion upwards and downwards is not the same as circular motion; there is the greatest possible difference between straight and circular motion. It therefore follows that bodies whose motion is so various must vary also in their essence. But, it is not even possible to suppose that the heavens should be formed of primitive bodies which we call elements, because the reunion of contrary forces could not produce an even and spontaneous motion, when each of the simple bodies is receiving a different impulse from nature. Thus it is a labour to maintain composite bodies in continual movement, because it is impossible to put even a single one of their movements in accord and harmony with all those that are in discord; since what is proper to the light particle, is in warfare with that of a heavier one. If we attempt to rise we are stopped by the weight of the terrestrial element; if we throw ourselves down we violate the igneous part of our being in dragging it down contrary to its nature. Now this struggle of the elements effects their dissolution. A body to which

violence is done and which is placed in opposition to nature, after a short but energetic resistance, is soon dissolved into as many parts as it had elements, each of the constituent parts returning to its natural place. It is the force of these reasons, say the inventors of the fifth kind of body for the genesis of heaven and the stars, which constrained them to reject the system of their predecessors and to have recourse to their own hypothesis. But yet another fine speaker arises and disperses and destroys this theory to give predominance to an idea of his own invention.

Do not let us undertake to follow them for fear of falling into like frivolities; let them refute each other, and, without disquieting ourselves about essence, let us say with Moses "God created the heavens and the earth." Let us glorify the supreme Artificer for all that was wisely and skillfully made; by the beauty of visible things let us raise ourselves to Him who is above all beauty; by the grandeur of bodies, sensible and limited in their nature, let us conceive of the infinite Being whose immensity and omnipotence surpass all the efforts of the imagination. Because, although we ignore the nature of created things, the objects which on all sides attract our notice are so marvellous, that the most penetrating mind cannot attain to the knowledge of the least of the phenomena of the world, either to give a suitable explanation of it or to render due praise to the Creator, to Whom belong all glory, all honour and all power world without end. Amen.

## Homily 2
### "The Earth was Invisible and Unfinished."

1. In the few words which have occupied us this morning we have found such a depth of thought that we despair of penetrating further. If such is the fore court of the sanctuary, if the portico of the temple is so grand and magnificent, if the splendour of its

beauty thus dazzles the eyes of the soul, what will be the holy of
holies? Who will dare to try to gain access to the innermost shrine?
Who will look into its secrets? To gaze into it is indeed forbidden
us, and language is powerless to express what the mind conceives.
However, since there are rewards, and most desirable ones,
reserved by the just Judge for the intention alone of doing good, do
not let us hesitate to continue our researches. Although we may not
attain to the truth, if, with the help of the Spirit, we do not fall
away from the meaning of Holy Scripture we shall not deserve to
be rejected, and, with the help of grace, we shall contribute to the
edification of the Church of God.

"The earth," says Holy Scripture, "was invisible and unfinished."
The heavens and the earth were created without distinction. How
then is it that the heavens are perfect while the earth is still
unformed and incomplete? In one word, what was the unfinished
condition of the earth? And for what reason was it invisible? The
fertility of the earth is its perfect finishing; growth of all kinds of
plants, the upspringing of tall trees, both productive and sterile,
flowers' sweet scents and fair colours, and all that which, a little
later, at the voice of God came forth from the earth to beautify her,
their universal Mother. As nothing of all this yet existed, Scripture
is right in calling the earth "without form." We could also say of
the heavens that they were still imperfect and had not received their
natural adornment, since at that time they did not shine with the
glory of the sun and of the moon and were not crowned by the
choirs of the stars. These bodies were not yet created. Thus you
will not diverge from the truth in saying that the heavens also were
"without form." The earth was invisible for two reasons: it may be
because man, the spectator, did not yet exist, or because being
submerged under the waters which over-flowed the surface, it
could not be seen, since the waters had not yet been gathered

together into their own places, where God afterwards collected them, and gave them the name of seas. What is invisible? First of all that which our fleshly eye cannot perceive; our mind, for example; then that which, visible in its nature, is hidden by some body which conceals it, like iron in the depths of the earth. It is in this sense, because it was hidden under the waters, that the earth was still invisible. However, as light did not yet exist, and as the earth lay in darkness, because of the obscurity of the air above it, it should not astonish us that for this reason Scripture calls it "invisible."

2. But the corrupters of the truth, who, incapable of submitting their reason to Holy Scripture, distort at will the meaning of the Holy Scriptures, pretend that these words mean matter. For it is matter, they say, which from its nature is without form and invisible—being by the conditions of its existence without quality and without form and figure. The Artificer submitting it to the working of His wisdom clothed it with a form, organized it, and thus gave being to the visible world.

If matter is uncreated, it has a claim to the same honours as God, since it must be of equal rank with Him. Is this not the summit of wickedness, that an extreme deformity, without quality, without form, shape, ugliness without configuration, to use their own expression, should enjoy the same prerogatives with Him, Who is wisdom, power and beauty itself, the Creator and the Demiurge of the universe? This is not all. If matter is so great as to be capable of being acted on by the whole wisdom of God, it would in a way raise its hypostasis to an equality with the inaccessible power of God, since it would be able to measure by itself all the extent of the divine intelligence. If it is insufficient for the operations of God, then we fall into a more absurd blasphemy, since we condemn God for not being able, on account of the want of matter, to finish His own works. The poverty of human nature has deceived these reasoners. Each of our crafts is exercised upon some special matter— the art of the smith upon iron, that of the carpenter on wood. In all, there is the subject, the form and the work which results from the form. Matter is taken from without— art gives the form— and the work is composed at the same time of form and of matter.

Such is the idea that they make for themselves of the divine work. The form of the world is due to the wisdom of the supreme Artificer; matter came to the Creator from without; and thus the world results from a double origin. It has received from outside its matter and its essence, and from God its form and figure. They thus come to deny that the mighty God has presided at the formation of the universe, and pretend that He has only brought a crowning contribution to a common work, that He has only contributed some small portion to the genesis of beings: they are incapable from the debasement of their reasonings of raising their glances to the height of truth. Here below arts are subsequent to matter— introduced into life by the indispensable need of them. Wool existed before weaving made it supply one of nature's imperfections. Wood existed before carpentering took possession of it, and transformed it each day to supply new wants, and made us see all the advantages derived from it, giving the oar to the sailor, the winnowing fan to the labourer, the lance to the soldier. But God, before all those things which now attract our notice existed, after casting about in His mind and determining to bring into being time which had no being, imagined the world such as it ought to be, and created matter in harmony with the form which He wished to give it. He assigned to the heavens the nature adapted for the heavens, and gave to the earth an essence in accordance with its form. He formed, as He wished, fire, air and water, and gave to each the essence which the object of its existence required. Finally, He welded all the diverse parts of the universe by links of indissoluble attachment and established between them so perfect a fellowship and harmony that the most distant, in spite of their distance, appeared united in one universal sympathy. Let those men therefore renounce their fabulous imaginations, who, in spite of the weakness of their argument, pretend to measure a power as incomprehensible to man's reason as it is unutterable by man's voice.

3. God created the heavens and the earth, but not only half—He created all the heavens and all the earth, creating the essence with the form. For He is not an inventor of figures, but the Creator even of the essence of beings. Further let them tell us how the efficient power of God could deal with the passive nature of matter, the latter furnishing the matter without form, the former possessing the science of the form without matter, both being in need of each other; the Creator in order to display His art, matter in order to cease to be without form and to receive a form. But let us stop here and return to our subject.

"The earth was invisible and unfinished." In saying "In the beginning God created the heavens and the earth," the sacred writer passed over many things in silence, water, air, fire and the results from them, which, all forming in reality the true complement of the world, were, without doubt, made at the same time as the universe. By this silence, history wishes to train the activity or our intelligence, giving it a weak point for starting, to impel it to the discovery of the truth. Thus, we are not told of the creation of water; but, as we are told that the earth was invisible, ask yourself what could have covered it, and prevented it from being seen? Fire could not conceal it. Fire brightens all about it, and spreads light rather than darkness around. No more was it air that enveloped the earth. Air by nature is of little density and transparent. It receives all kinds of visible object, and transmits them to the spectators. Only one supposition remains; that which floated on the surface of the earth was water— the fluid essence which had not yet been confined to its own place. Thus the earth was not only invisible; it was still incomplete. Even today excessive damp is a hindrance to the productiveness of the earth. The same cause at the same time prevents it from being seen, and from being complete, for the proper and natural adornment of the earth is its completion: grain waving in the valleys— meadows green with grass and rich with many coloured flowers— fertile glades and hill-tops shaded by forests. Of all this nothing was yet produced; the earth was in travail with it in virtue of the power that she had received from the Creator. But she was waiting for the appointed time and the divine order to bring forth.

4. "Darkness was upon the face of the deep." Genesis 1:2 A new source for fables and most impious imaginations if one distorts the sense of these words at the will of one's fancies. By "darkness" these wicked men do not understand what is meant in reality— air not illumined, the shadow produced by the interposition of a body, or finally a place for some reason deprived of light. For them "darkness" is an evil power, or rather the personification of evil, having his origin in himself in opposition to, and in perpetual struggle with, the goodness of God. If God is light, they say, without any doubt the power which struggles against Him must be darkness, "Darkness" not owing its existence to a foreign origin, but an evil existing by itself. "Darkness" is the enemy of souls, the primary cause of death, the adversary of virtue. The words of the Prophet, they say in their error, show that it exists and that it does not proceed from God. From this what perverse and impious dogmas have been imagined! What grievous wolves, Acts 20:29

tearing the flock of the Lord, have sprung from these words to cast themselves upon souls! Is it not from hence that have come forth Marcions and Valentini, and the detestable heresy of the Manicheans, which you may without going far wrong call the putrid humour of the churches.

O man, why wander thus from the truth, and imagine for yourself that which will cause your perdition? The word is simple and within the comprehension of all. "The earth was invisible." Why? Because the "deep" was spread over its surface. What is "the deep"? A mass of water of extreme depth. But we know that we can see many bodies through clear and transparent water. How then was it that no part of the earth appeared through the water? Because the air which surrounded it was still without light and in darkness. The rays of the sun, penetrating the water, often allow us to see the pebbles which form the bed of the river, but in a dark night it is impossible for our glance to penetrate under the water. Thus, these words "the earth was invisible" are explained by those that follow; "the deep" covered it and itself was in darkness. Thus, the deep is not a multitude of hostile powers, as has been imagined; nor "darkness" an evil sovereign force in enmity with good. In reality two rival principles of equal power, if engaged without ceasing in a war of mutual attacks, will end in self destruction. But if one should gain the mastery it would completely annihilate the conquered. Thus, to maintain the balance in the struggle between good and evil is to represent them as engaged in a war without end and in perpetual destruction, where the opponents are at the same time conquerors and conquered. If good is the stronger, what is there to prevent evil being completely annihilated? But if that be the case, the very utterance of which is impious, I ask myself how it is that they themselves are not filled with horror to think that they have imagined such abominable blasphemies.

It is equally impious to say that evil has its origin from God; because the contrary cannot proceed from its contrary. Life does not engender death; darkness is not the origin of light; sickness is not the maker of health. In the changes of conditions there are transitions from one condition to the contrary; but in genesis each being proceeds from its like, and not from its contrary. If then evil is neither uncreate nor created by God, from whence comes its nature? Certainly that evil exists, no one living in the world will deny. What shall we say then? Evil is not a living animated essence; it is the condition of the soul opposed to virtue, developed in the careless on account of their falling away from good.

5. Do not then go beyond yourself to seek for evil, and imagine that there is an original nature of wickedness. Each of us, let us acknowledge it, is the first author of his own vice. Among the ordinary events of life, some come naturally, like old age and sickness, others by chance like unforeseen occurrences, of which the origin is beyond ourselves, often sad, sometimes fortunate, as for instance the discovery of a treasure when digging a well, or the meeting of a mad dog when going to the market place. Others depend upon ourselves, such as ruling one's passions, or not putting a bridle on one's pleasures, to be master of our anger, or to raise the hand against him who irritates us, to tell the truth, or to lie, to have a sweet and well-regulated disposition, or to be fierce and swollen and exalted with pride. Here you are the master of your actions. Do not look for the guiding cause beyond yourself, but recognise that evil, rightly so called, has no other origin than our voluntary falls. If it were involuntary, and did not depend upon ourselves, the laws would not have so much terror for the guilty, and the tribunals would not be so without pity when they condemn wretches according to the measure of their crimes. But enough concerning evil rightly so called. Sickness, poverty, obscurity, death,

finally all human afflictions, ought not to be ranked as evils; since we do not count among the greatest boons things which are their opposites. Among these afflictions, some are the effect of nature, others have obviously been for many a source of advantage. Let us then be silent for the moment about these metaphors and allegories, and, simply following without vain curiosity the words of Holy Scripture, let us take from darkness the idea which it gives us.

But reason asks, was darkness created with the world? Is it older than light? Why in spite of its inferiority has it preceded it? Darkness, we reply, did not exist in essence; it is a condition produced in the air by the withdrawal of light. What then is that light which disappeared suddenly from the world, so that darkness should cover the face of the deep? If anything had existed before the formation of this sensible and perishable world, no doubt we conclude it would have been in light. The orders of angels, the heavenly hosts, all intellectual natures named or unnamed, all the ministering spirits, did not live in darkness, but enjoyed a condition fitted for them in light and spiritual joy.

No one will contradict this; least of all he who looks for celestial light as one of the rewards promised to virtue, the light which, as Solomon says, is always a light to the righteous, the light which made the Apostle say "Giving thanks unto the Father, which has made us meet to be partakers of the inheritance of the saints in light." Colossians 1:12 Finally, if the condemned are sent into outer darkness evidently those who are made worthy of God's approval, are at rest in heavenly light. When then, according to the order of God, the heaven appeared, enveloping all that its circumference included, a vast and unbroken body separating outer things from those which it enclosed, it necessarily kept the space inside in darkness for want of communication with the outer light. Three things are, indeed, needed to form a shadow, light, a body, a dark place. The shadow of heaven forms the darkness of the world. Understand, I pray you, what I mean, by a simple example; by raising for yourself at mid-day a tent of some compact and impenetrable material, and shutting yourself up in it in sudden darkness. Suppose that original darkness was like this, not subsisting directly by itself, but resulting from some external causes. If it is said that it rested upon the deep, it is because the extremity of air naturally touches the surface of bodies; and as at that time the water covered everything, we are obliged to say that darkness was upon the face of the deep.

6. And the Spirit of God was borne upon the face of the waters. Does this spirit mean the diffusion of air? The sacred writer wishes to enumerate to you the elements of the world, to tell you that God created the heavens, the earth, water, and air and that the last was now diffused and in motion; or rather, that which is truer and confirmed by the authority of the ancients, by the Spirit of God, he means the Holy Spirit. It is, as has been remarked, the special name, the name above all others that Scripture delights to give to the Holy Spirit, and always by the spirit of God the Holy Spirit is meant, the Spirit which completes the divine and blessed Trinity. You will find it better therefore to take it in this sense. How then did the Spirit of God move upon the waters? The explanation that I am about to give you is not an original one, but that of a Syrian, who was as ignorant in the wisdom of this world as he was versed in the knowledge of the Truth. He said, then, that the Syriac word was more expressive, and that being more analogous to the Hebrew term it was a nearer approach to the scriptural sense. This is the meaning of the word; by "was borne" the Syrians, he says, understand: it cherished the nature of the waters as one sees a bird cover the eggs with her body and impart to them vital force from her own warmth. Such is, as nearly as possible, the meaning of

these words— the Spirit was borne: let us understand, that is, prepared the nature of water to produce living beings: a sufficient proof for those who ask if the Holy Spirit took an active part in the creation of the world.

7. And God said, Let there be light. Genesis 1:3 The first word of God created the nature of light; it made darkness vanish, dispelled gloom, illuminated the world, and gave to all beings at the same time a sweet and gracious aspect. The heavens, until then enveloped in darkness, appeared with that beauty which they still present to our eyes. The air was lighted up, or rather made the light circulate mixed with its substance, and, distributing its splendour rapidly in every direction, so dispersed itself to its extreme limits. Up it sprang to the very æther and heaven. In an instant it lighted up the whole extent of the world, the North and the South, the East and the West. For the æther also is such a subtle substance and so transparent that it needs not the space of a moment for light to pass through it. Just as it carries our sight instantaneously to the object of vision, so without the least interval, with a rapidity that thought cannot conceive, it receives these rays of light in its uttermost limits. With light the æther becomes more pleasing and the waters more limpid. These last, not content with receiving its splendour, return it by the reflection of light and in all directions send forth quivering flashes. The divine word gives every object a more cheerful and a more attractive appearance, just as when men in deep sea pour in oil they make the place about them clear. So, with a single word and in one instant, the Creator of all things gave the boon of light to the world.

Let there be light. The order was itself an operation, and a state of things was brought into being, than which man's mind cannot even imagine a pleasanter one for our enjoyment. It must be well understood that when we speak of the voice, of the word, of the command of God, this divine language does not mean to us a sound which escapes from the organs of speech, a collision of air struck by the tongue; it is a simple sign of the will of God, and, if we give it the form of an order, it is only the better to impress the souls whom we instruct.

And God saw the light, that it was good. Genesis 1:4 How can we worthily praise light after the testimony given by the Creator to its goodness? The word, even among us, refers the judgment to the eyes, incapable of raising itself to the idea that the senses have already received. But, if beauty in bodies results from symmetry of parts, and the harmonious appearance of colours, how in a simple and homogeneous essence like light, can this idea of beauty be preserved? Would not the symmetry in light be less shown in its parts than in the pleasure and delight at the sight of it? Such is also the beauty of gold, which it owes not to the happy mingling of its parts, but only to its beautiful colour which has a charm attractive to the eyes.

Thus again, the evening star is the most beautiful of the stars: not that the parts of which it is composed form a harmonious whole; but thanks to the unalloyed and beautiful brightness which meets our eyes. And further, when God proclaimed the goodness of light, it was not in regard to the charm of the eye but as a provision for future advantage, because at that time there were as yet no eyes to judge of its beauty. "And God divided the light from the darkness;" Genesis 1:4 that is to say, God gave them natures incapable of mixing, perpetually in opposition to each other, and put between them the widest space and distance.

8. "And God called the light Day and the darkness he called Night." Genesis 1:5 Since the birth of the sun, the light that it diffuses in the air, when shining on our hemisphere, is day; and the

shadow produced by its disappearance is night. But at that time it was not after the movement of the sun, but following this primitive light spread abroad in the air or withdrawn in a measure determined by God, that day came and was followed by night.

"And the evening and the morning were the first day." Genesis 1:5 Evening is then the boundary common to day and night; and in the same way morning constitutes the approach of night to day. It was to give day the privileges of seniority that Scripture put the end of the first day before that of the first night, because night follows day: for, before the creation of light, the world was not in night, but in darkness. It is the opposite of day which was called night, and it did not receive its name until after day. Thus were created the evening and the morning. Scripture means the space of a day and a night, and afterwards no more says day and night, but calls them both under the name of the more important: a custom which you will find throughout Scripture. Everywhere the measure of time is counted by days, without mention of nights. "The days of our years," says the Psalmist. "Few and evil have the days of the years of my life been," Genesis 47:9 said Jacob, and elsewhere "all the days of my life." Thus under the form of history the law is laid down for what is to follow. And the evening and the morning were one day. Why does Scripture say "one day the first day"? Before speaking to us of the second, the third, and the fourth days, would it not have been more natural to call that one the first which began the series? If it therefore says "one day," it is from a wish to determine the measure of day and night, and to combine the time that they contain. Now twenty-four hours fill up the space of one day— we mean of a day and of a night; and if, at the time of the solstices, they have not both an equal length, the time marked by Scripture does not the less circumscribe their duration. It is as though it said: twenty-four hours measure the space of a day, or that, in reality a day is the time that the heavens starting from one point take to return there. Thus, every time that, in the revolution of the sun, evening and morning occupy the world, their periodical succession never exceeds the space of one day. But must we believe in a mysterious reason for this? God who made the nature of time measured it out and determined it by intervals of days; and, wishing to give it a week as a measure, he ordered the week to revolve from period to period upon itself, to count the movement of time, forming the week of one day revolving seven times upon itself: a proper circle begins and ends with itself. Such is also the character of eternity, to revolve upon itself and to end nowhere. If then the beginning of time is called "one day" rather than "the first day," it is because Scripture wishes to establish its relationship with eternity. It was, in reality, fit and natural to call "one" the day whose character is to be one wholly separated and isolated from all the others. If Scripture speaks to us of many ages, saying everywhere, "age of age, and ages of ages," we do not see it enumerate them as first, second, and third. It follows that we are hereby shown not so much limits, ends and succession of ages, as distinctions between various states and modes of action. "The day of the Lord," Scripture says, "is great and very terrible," Joel 2:11 and elsewhere "Woe unto you that desire the day of the Lord: to what end is it for you? The day of the Lord is darkness and not light." Amos 5:18 A day of darkness for those who are worthy of darkness. No; this day without evening, without succession and without end is not unknown to Scripture, and it is the day that the Psalmist calls the eighth day, because it is outside this time of weeks. Thus whether you call it day, or whether you call it eternity, you express the same idea. Give this state the name of day; there are not several, but only one. If you call it eternity still it is unique and not manifold. Thus it is in order that you may carry your thoughts forward towards a future life, that Scripture marks by the word "one" the day which is the type of eternity, the first fruits of days, the contemporary of light, the holy Lord's day honoured by the Resurrection of our Lord. And the evening and the morning were one day.

But, while I am conversing with you about the first evening of the world, evening takes me by surprise, and puts an end to my discourse. May the Father of the true light, Who has adorned day with celestial light, Who has made the fire to shine which illuminates us during the night, Who reserves for us in the peace of a future age a spiritual and everlasting light, enlighten your hearts in the knowledge of truth, keep you from stumbling, and grant that "you may walk honestly as in the day." Romans 13:13 Thus shall you shine as the sun in the midst of the glory of the saints, and I shall glory in you in the day of Christ, to Whom belong all glory and power for ever and ever. Amen.

## Homily 3
## On the Firmament.

1. We have now recounted the works of the first day, or rather of one day. Far be it from me indeed, to take from it the privilege it enjoys of having been for the Creator a day apart, a day which is not counted in the same order as the others. Our discussion yesterday treated of the works of this day, and divided the narrative so as to give you food for your souls in the morning, and joy in the evening. Today we pass on to the wonders of the second day. And here I do not wish to speak of the narrator's talent, but of the grace of Scripture, for the narrative is so naturally told that it pleases and delights all the friends of truth. It is this charm of truth which the Psalmist expresses so emphatically when he says, "How sweet are your words unto my taste, yea, sweeter than honey to my mouth." Yesterday then, as far as we were able, we delighted our souls by

conversing about the oracles of God, and now today we are met together again on the second day to contemplate the wonders of the second day.

I know that many artisans, belonging to mechanical trades, are crowding around me. A day's labour hardly suffices to maintain them; therefore I am compelled to abridge my discourse, so as not to keep them too long from their work. What shall I say to them? The time which you lend to God is not lost: he will return it to you with large interest. Whatever difficulties may trouble you the Lord will disperse them. To those who have preferred spiritual welfare, He will give health of body, keenness of mind, success in business, and unbroken prosperity. And, even if in this life our efforts should not realise our hopes, the teachings of the Holy Spirit are none the less a rich treasure for the ages to come. Deliver your heart, then, from the cares of this life and give close heed to my words. Of what avail will it be to you if you are here in the body, and your heart is anxious about your earthly treasure?

2. And God said "Let there be a firmament in the midst of the waters, and let it divide the waters from the waters." Genesis 1:6 Yesterday we heard God's decree, "Let there be light." Today it is, "Let there be a firmament." There appears to be something more in this. The word is not limited to a simple command. It lays down the reason necessitating the structure of the firmament: it is, it is said, to separate the waters from the waters. And first let us ask how God speaks? Is it in our manner? Does His intelligence receive an impression from objects, and, after having conceived them, make them known by particular signs appropriate to each of them? Has He consequently recourse to the organs of voice to convey His thoughts? Is He obliged to strike the air by the articulate movements of the voice, to unveil the thought hidden in His heart? Would it not seem like an idle fable to say that God should need

such a circuitous method to manifest His thoughts? And is it not more conformable with true religion to say, that the divine will and the first impetus of divine intelligence are the Word of God? It is He whom Scripture vaguely represents, to show us that God has not only wished to create the world, but to create it with the help of a co-operator. Scripture might continue the history as it is begun: In the beginning God created the heaven and the earth; afterwards He created light, then He created the firmament. But, by making God command and speak, the Scripture tacitly shows us Him to Whom this order and these words are addressed. It is not that it grudges us the knowledge of the truth, but that it may kindle our desire by showing us some trace and indication of the mystery. We seize with delight, and carefully keep, the fruit of laborious efforts, while a possession easily attained is despised. Such is the road and the course which Scripture follows to lead us to the idea of the Only begotten. And certainly, God's immaterial nature had no need of the material language of voice, since His very thoughts could be transmitted to His fellow-worker. What need then of speech, for those Who by thought alone could communicate their counsels to each other? Voice was made for hearing, and hearing for voice. Where there is neither air, nor tongue, nor ear, nor that winding canal which carries sounds to the seat of sensation in the head, there is no need for words: thoughts of the soul are sufficient to transmit the will. As I said then, this language is only a wise and ingenious contrivance to set our minds seeking the Person to whom the words are addressed.

3. In the second place, does the firmament that is called heaven differ from the firmament that God made in the beginning? Are there two heavens? The philosophers, who discuss heaven, would rather lose their tongues than grant this. There is only one heaven, they pretend; and it is of a nature neither to admit of a second, nor

of a third, nor of several others. The essence of the celestial body quite complete constitutes its vast unity. Because, they say, every body which has a circular motion is one and finite. And if this body is used in the construction of the first heaven, there will be nothing left for the creation of a second or a third. Here we see what those imagine who put under the Creator's hand uncreated matter; a lie that follows from the first fable. But we ask the Greek sages not to mock us before they are agreed among themselves. Because there are among them some who say there are infinite heavens and worlds. When grave demonstrations shall have upset their foolish system, when the laws of geometry shall have established that, according to the nature of heaven, it is impossible that there should be two, we shall only laugh the more at this elaborate scientific trifling. These learned men see not merely one bubble but several bubbles formed by the same cause, and they doubt the power of creative wisdom to bring several heavens into being! We find, however, if we raise our eyes towards the omnipotence of God, that the strength and grandeur of the heavens differ from the drops of water bubbling on the surface of a fountain. How ridiculous, then, is their argument of impossibility! As for myself, far from not believing in a second, I seek for the third whereon the blessed Paul was found worthy to gaze. And does not the Psalmist in saying "heaven of heavens" give us an idea of their plurality? Is the plurality of heaven stranger than the seven circles through which nearly all the philosophers agree that the seven planets pass—circles which they represent to us as placed in connection with each other like casks fitting the one into the other? These circles, they say, carried away in a direction contrary to that of the world, and striking the æther, make sweet and harmonious sounds, unequalled by the sweetest melody. And if we ask them for the witness of the senses, what do they say? That we, accustomed to this noise from our birth, on account of hearing it always, have lost the sense of it;

like men in smithies with their ears incessantly dinned. If I refuted this ingenious frivolity, the untruth of which is evident from the first word, it would seem as though I did not know the value of time, and mistrusted the intelligence of such an audience.

But let me leave the vanity of outsiders to those who are without, and return to the theme proper to the Church. If we believe some of those who have preceded us, we have not here the creation of a new heaven, but a new account of the first. The reason they give is, that the earlier narrative briefly described the creation of heaven and earth; while here scripture relates in greater detail the manner in which each was created. I, however, since Scripture gives to this second heaven another name and its own function, maintain that it is different from the heaven which was made at the beginning; that it is of a stronger nature and of a special use to the universe.

4. "And God said, let there be a firmament in the midst of the waters, and let it divide the waters from the waters. And God made the firmament, and divided the waters which were under the firmament from the waters which were above the firmament." Genesis 1:6-7 Before laying hold of the meaning of Scripture let us try to meet objections from other quarters. We are asked how, if the firmament is a spherical body, as it appears to the eye, its convex circumference can contain the water which flows and circulates in higher regions? What shall we answer? One thing only: because the interior of a body presents a perfect concavity it does not necessarily follow that its exterior surface is spherical and smoothly rounded. Look at the stone vaults of baths, and the structure of buildings of cave form; the dome, which forms the interior, does not prevent the roof from having ordinarily a flat surface. Let these unfortunate men cease, then, from tormenting us and themselves about the impossibility of our retaining water in the higher regions.

Now we must say something about the nature of the firmament, and why it received the order to hold the middle place between the waters. Scripture constantly makes use of the word firmament to express extraordinary strength. "The Lord my firmament and refuge." "I have strengthened the pillars of it." "Praise him in the firmament of his power." The heathen writers thus call a strong body one which is compact and full, to distinguish it from the mathematical body. A mathematical body is a body which exists only in the three dimensions, breadth, depth, and height. A firm body, on the contrary, adds resistance to the dimensions. It is the custom of Scripture to call firmament all that is strong and unyielding. It even uses the word to denote the condensation of the air: He, it says, who strengthens the thunder. Scripture means by the strengthening of the thunder, the strength and resistance of the wind, which, enclosed in the hollows of the clouds, produces the noise of thunder when it breaks through with violence. Here then, according to me, is a firm substance, capable of retaining the fluid and unstable element water; and as, according to the common acceptation, it appears that the firmament owes its origin to water, we must not believe that it resembles frozen water or any other matter produced by the filtration of water; as, for example, rock crystal, which is said to owe its metamorphosis to excessive congelation, or the transparent stone which forms in mines. This pellucid stone, if one finds it in its natural perfection, without cracks inside, or the least spot of corruption, almost rivals the air in clearness. We cannot compare the firmament to one of these substances. To hold such an opinion about celestial bodies would be childish and foolish; and although everything may be in everything, fire in earth, air in water, and of the other elements the one in the other; although none of those which come under our senses are pure and without mixture, either with the element which serves as a medium for it, or with that which is contrary to it; I,

nevertheless, dare not affirm that the firmament was formed of one
of these simple substances, or of a mixture of them, for I am taught
by Scripture not to allow my imagination to wander too far afield.
But do not let us forget to remark that, after these divine words "let
there be a firmament," it is not said "and the firmament was made"
but, "and God made the firmament, and divided the waters."
Genesis 1:7 Hear, O you deaf! See, O you blind!— who, then, is
deaf? He who does not hear this startling voice of the Holy Spirit.
Who is blind? He who does not see such clear proofs of the Only
begotten. "Let there be a firmament." It is the voice of the primary
and principal Cause. "And God made the firmament." Here is a
witness to the active and creative power of God.

5. But let us continue our explanation: "Let it divide the waters
from the waters." Genesis 1:6 The mass of waters, which from all
directions flowed over the earth, and was suspended in the air, was
infinite, so that there was no proportion between it and the other
elements. Thus, as it has been already said, the abyss covered the
earth. We give the reason for this abundance of water. None of you
assuredly will attack our opinion; not even those who have the
most cultivated minds, and whose piercing eye can penetrate this
perishable and fleeting nature; you will not accuse me of advancing
impossible or imaginary theories, nor will you ask me upon what
foundation the fluid element rests. By the same reason which
makes them attract the earth, heavier than water, from the
extremities of the world to suspend it in the centre, they will grant
us without doubt that it is due both to its natural attraction
downwards and its general equilibrium, that this immense quantity
of water rests motionless upon the earth. Therefore the prodigious
mass of waters was spread around the earth; not in proportion with
it and infinitely larger, thanks to the foresight of the supreme
Artificer, Who, from the beginning, foresaw what was to come, and

at the first provided all for the future needs of the world. But what need was there for this superabundance of water? The essence of fire is necessary for the world, not only in the economy of earthly produce, but for the completion of the universe; for it would be imperfect if the most powerful and the most vital of its elements were lacking. Now fire and water are hostile to and destructive of each other. Fire, if it is the stronger, destroys water, and water, if in greater abundance, destroys fire. As, therefore, it was necessary to avoid an open struggle between these elements, so as not to bring about the dissolution of the universe by the total disappearance of one or the other, the sovereign Disposer created such a quantity of water that in spite of constant diminution from the effects of fire, it could last until the time fixed for the destruction of the world. He who planned all with weight and measure, He who, according to the word of Job, knows the number of the drops of rain, knew how long His work would last, and for how much consumption of fire He ought to allow. This is the reason of the abundance of water at the creation. Further, there is no one so strange to life as to need to learn the reason why fire is essential to the world. Not only all the arts which support life, the art of weaving, that of shoemaking, of architecture, of agriculture, have need of the help of fire, but the vegetation of trees, the ripening of fruits, the breeding of land and water animals, and their nourishment, all existed from heat from the beginning, and have been since maintained by the action of heat. The creation of heat was then indispensable for the formation and the preservation of beings, and the abundance of waters was no less so in the presence of the constant and inevitable consumption by fire.

6. Survey creation; you will see the power of heat reigning over all that is born and perishes. On account of it comes all the water spread over the earth, as well as that which is beyond our sight and

is dispersed in the depths of the earth. On account of it are abundance of fountains, springs or wells, courses of rivers, both mountain torrents and ever flowing streams, for the storing of moisture in many and various reservoirs. From the East, from the winter solstice flows the Indus, the greatest river of the earth, according to geographers. From the middle of the East proceed the Bactrus, the Choaspes, and the Araxes, from which the Tanais detaches itself to fall into the Palus-Mæotis. Add to these the Phasis which descends from Mount Caucasus, and countless other rivers, which, from northern regions, flow into the Euxine Sea. From the warm countries of the West, from the foot of the Pyrenees, arise the Tartessus and the Ister, of which the one discharges itself into the sea beyond the Pillars and the other, after flowing through Europe, falls into Euxine Sea. Is there any need to enumerate those which the Ripæan mountains pour forth in the heart of Scythia, the Rhone, and so many other rivers, all navigable, which after having watered the countries of the western Gauls and of Celts and of the neighbouring barbarians, flow into the Western sea? And others from the higher regions of the South flow through Ethiopia, to discharge themselves some into our sea, others into inaccessible seas, the Ægon the Nyses, the Chremetes, and above all the Nile, which is not of the character of a river when, like a sea, it inundates Egypt. Thus the habitable part of our earth is surrounded by water, linked together by vast seas and irrigated by countless perennial rivers, thanks to the ineffable wisdom of Him Who ordered all to prevent this rival element to fire from being entirely destroyed.

However, a time will come, when all shall be consumed by fire; as Isaiah says of the God of the universe in these words, "That says to the deep, Be dry, and I will dry up your rivers." Isaiah 44:27 Reject then the foolish wisdom of this world, and receive with me the more simple but infallible doctrine of truth.

7. Therefore we read: "Let there be a firmament in the midst of the waters, and let it divide the waters from the waters." I have said what the word firmament in Scripture means. It is not in reality a firm and solid substance which has weight and resistance; this name would otherwise have better suited the earth. But, as the substance of superincumbent bodies is light, without consistency, and cannot be grasped by any one of our senses, it is in comparison with these pure and imperceptible substances that the firmament has received its name. Imagine a place fit to divide the moisture, sending it, if pure and filtered, into higher regions, and making it fall, if it is dense and earthy; to the end that by the gradual withdrawal of the moist particles the same temperature may be preserved from the beginning to the end. You do not believe in this prodigious quantity of water; but you do not take into account the prodigious quantity of heat, less considerable no doubt in bulk, but exceedingly powerful nevertheless, if you consider it as destructive of moisture. It attracts surrounding moisture, as the melon shows us, and consumes it as quickly when attracted, as the flame of the lamp draws to it the fuel supplied by the wick and burns it up. Who doubts that the æther is an ardent fire? If an impassable limit had not been assigned to it by the Creator, what would prevent it from setting on fire and consuming all that is near it, and absorbing all the moisture from existing things? The aerial waters which veil the heavens with vapours that are sent forth by rivers, fountains, marshes, lakes, and seas, prevent the æther from invading and burning up the universe. Thus we see even this sun, in the summer season, dry up in a moment a damp and marshy country, and make it perfectly arid. What has become of all the water? Let these masters of omniscience tell us. Is it not plain to every one that it has risen in vapour, and has been consumed by the heat of the sun? They say, none the less, that even the sun is without heat. What time they lose in words! And see what proof they lean upon to

resist what is perfectly plain. Its colour is white, and neither reddish nor yellow. It is not then fiery by nature, and its heat results, they say, from the velocity of its rotation. What do they gain? That the sun does not seem to absorb moisture? I do not, however, reject this statement, although it is false, because it helps my argument. I said that the consumption of heat required this prodigious quantity of water. That the sun owes its heat to its nature, or that heat results from its action, makes no difference, provided that it produces the same effects upon the same matter. If you kindle fire by rubbing two pieces of wood together, or if you light them by holding them to a flame, you will have absolutely the same effect. Besides, we see that the great wisdom of Him who governs all, makes the sun travel from one region to another, for fear that, if it remained always in the same place, its excessive heat would destroy the order of the universe. Now it passes into southern regions about the time of the winter solstice, now it returns to the sign of the equinox; from thence it betakes itself to northern regions during the summer solstice, and keeps up by this imperceptible passage a pleasant temperature throughout all the world.

Let the learned people see if they do not disagree among themselves. The water which the sun consumes is, they say, what prevents the sea from rising and flooding the rivers; the warmth of the sun leaves behind the salts and the bitterness of the waters, and absorbs from them the pure and drinkable particles, thanks to the singular virtue of this planet in attracting all that is light and in allowing to fall, like mud and sediment, all which is thick and earthy. From thence come the bitterness, the salt taste and the power of withering and drying up which are characteristic of the sea. While as is notorious, they hold these views, they shift their ground and say that moisture cannot be lessened by the sun.

8. "And God called the firmament heaven." Genesis 1:8 The nature of right belongs to another, and the firmament only shares it on account of its resemblance to heaven. We often find the visible region called heaven, on account of the density and continuity of the air within our ken, and deriving its name "heaven" from the word which means to see. It is of it that Scripture says, "The fowl of the air," "Fowl that may fly...in the open firmament of heaven;" Genesis 1:20 and, elsewhere, "They mount up to heaven." Moses, blessing the tribe of Joseph, desires for it the fruits and the dews of heaven, of the suns of summer and the conjunctions of the moon, and blessings from the tops of the mountains and from the everlasting hills, in one word, from all which fertilises the earth. In the curses on Israel it is said, "And your heaven that is over your head shall be brass." Deuteronomy 28:23 What does this mean? It threatens him with a complete drought, with an absence of the aerial waters which cause the fruits of the earth to be brought forth and to grow.

Since, then, Scripture says that the dew or the rain falls from heaven, we understand that it is from those waters which have been ordered to occupy the higher regions. When the exhalations from the earth, gathered together in the heights of the air, are condensed under the pressure of the wind, this aerial moisture diffuses itself in vaporous and light clouds; then mingling again, it forms drops which fall, dragged down by their own weight; and this is the origin of rain. When water beaten by the violence of the wind, changes into foam, and passing through excessive cold quite freezes, it breaks the cloud, and falls as snow. You can thus account for all the moist substances that the air suspends over our heads.

And do not let any one compare with the inquisitive discussions of philosophers upon the heavens, the simple and inartificial character of the utterances of the Spirit; as the beauty of chaste women surpasses that of a harlot, so our arguments are superior to those of our opponents. They only seek to persuade by forced reasoning. With us truth presents itself naked and without artifice. But why torment ourselves to refute the errors of philosophers, when it is sufficient to produce their mutually contradictory books, and, as quiet spectators, to watch the war? For those thinkers are not less numerous, nor less celebrated, nor more sober in speech in fighting their adversaries, who say that the universe is being consumed by fire, and that from the seeds which remain in the ashes of the burnt world all is being brought to life again. Hence in the world there is destruction and palingenesis to infinity. All, equally far from the truth, find each on their side by-ways which lead them to error.

9. But as far as concerns the separation of the waters I am obliged to contest the opinion of certain writers in the Church who, under the shadow of high and sublime conceptions, have launched out into metaphor, and have only seen in the waters a figure to denote spiritual and incorporeal powers. In the higher regions, above the firmament, dwell the better; in the lower regions, earth and matter are the dwelling place of the malignant. So, say they, God is praised by the waters that are above the heaven, that is to say, by the good powers, the purity of whose soul makes them worthy to sing the praises of God. And the waters which are under the heaven represent the wicked spirits, who from their natural height have fallen into the abyss of evil. Turbulent, seditious, agitated by the tumultuous waves of passion, they have received the name of sea, because of the instability and the inconstancy of their movements. Let us reject these theories as dreams and old women's tales. Let us understand that by water water is meant; for the dividing of the waters by the firmament let us accept the reason which has been given us. Although, however, waters above the heaven are invited to give glory to the Lord of the Universe, do not let us think of

them as intelligent beings; the heavens are not alive because they "declare the glory of God," nor the firmament a sensible being because it "shows His handiwork." And if they tell you that the heavens mean contemplative powers, and the firmament active powers which produce good, we admire the theory as ingenious without being able to acknowledge the truth of it. For thus dew, the frost, cold and heat, which in Daniel are ordered to praise the Creator of all things, will be intelligent and invisible natures. But this is only a figure, accepted as such by enlightened minds, to complete the glory of the Creator. Besides, the waters above the heavens, these waters privileged by the virtue which they possess in themselves, are not the only waters to celebrate the praises of God. "Praise the Lord from the earth, you dragons and all deeps." Thus the singer of the Psalms does not reject the deeps which our inventors of allegories rank in the divisions of evil; he admits them to the universal choir of creation, and the deeps sing in their language a harmonious hymn to the glory of the Creator.

10. "And God saw that it was good." God does not judge of the beauty of His work by the charm of the eyes, and He does not form the same idea of beauty that we do. What He esteems beautiful is that which presents in its perfection all the fitness of art, and that which tends to the usefulness of its end. He, then, who proposed to Himself a manifest design in His works, approved each one of them, as fulfilling its end in accordance with His creative purpose. A hand, an eye, or any portion of a statue lying apart from the rest, would look beautiful to no one. But if each be restored to its own place, the beauty of proportion, until now almost unperceived, would strike even the most uncultivated. But the artist, before uniting the parts of his work, distinguishes and recognises the beauty of each of them, thinking of the object that he has in view. It is thus that Scripture depicts to us the Supreme

Artist, praising each one of His works; soon, when His work is complete, He will accord well deserved praise to the whole together. Let me here end my discourse on the second day, to allow my industrious hearers to examine what they have just heard. May their memory retain it for the profit of their soul; may they by careful meditation inwardly digest and benefit by what I say. As for those who live by their work, let me allow them to attend all day to their business, so that they may come, with a soul free from anxiety, to the banquet of my discourse in the evening. May God who, after having made such great things, put such weak words in my mouth, grant you the intelligence of His truth, so that you may raise yourselves from visible things to the invisible Being, and that the grandeur and beauty of creatures may give you a just idea of the Creator. For the visible things of Him from the creation of the world are clearly seen, and His power and divinity are eternal. Thus earth, air, sky, water, day, night, all visible things, remind us of who is our Benefactor. We shall not therefore give occasion to sin, we shall not give place to the enemy within us, if by unbroken recollection we keep God ever dwelling in our hearts, to Whom be all glory and all adoration, now and for ever, world without end. Amen.

## Homily 4
### Upon the gathering together of the waters.

1. There are towns where the inhabitants, from dawn to eve, feast their eyes on the tricks of innumerable conjurors. They are never tired of hearing dissolute songs which cause much impurity to spring up in their souls, and they are often called happy, because they neglect the cares of business and trades useful to life, and pass the time, which is assigned to them on this earth, in idleness and pleasure. They do not know that a theatre full of impure sights is, for those who sit there, a common school of vice; that these

melodious and meretricious songs insinuate themselves into men's souls, and all who hear them, eager to imitate the notes of harpers and pipers, are filled with filthiness. Some others, who are wild after horses, think they are backing their horses in their dreams; they harness their chariots, change their drivers, and even in sleep are not free from the folly of the day. And shall we, whom the Lord, the great worker of marvels, calls to the contemplation of His own works, tire of looking at them, or be slow to hear the words of the Holy Spirit? Shall we not rather stand around the vast and varied workshop of divine creation and, carried back in mind to the times of old, shall we not view all the order of creation? Heaven, poised like a dome, to quote the words of the prophet; earth, this immense mass which rests upon itself; the air around it, of a soft and fluid nature, a true and continual nourishment for all who breathe it, of such tenuity that it yields and opens at the least movement of the body, opposing no resistance to our motions, while, in a moment, it streams back to its place, behind those who cleave it; water, finally, that supplies drink for man, or may be designed for our other needs, and the marvellous gathering together of it into definite places which have been assigned to it: such is the spectacle which the words which I have just read will show you.

2. "And God said, Let the waters under the heaven be gathered together unto one place, and let the dry land appear, and it was so." And the water which was under the heaven gathered together unto one place; "And God called the dry land earth and the gathering together of the waters called He seas." Genesis 1:9-10 What trouble you have given me in my previous discourses by asking me why the earth was invisible, why all bodies are naturally endued with colour, and why all colour comes under the sense of sight. And, perhaps, my reason did not appear sufficient to you, when I said that the

earth, without being naturally invisible, was so to us, because of the mass of water that entirely covered it. Hear then how Scripture explains itself. "Let the waters be gathered together, and let the dry land appear." The veil is lifted and allows the earth, hitherto invisible, to be seen. Perhaps you will ask me new questions. And first, is it not a law of nature that water flows downwards? Why, then, does Scripture refer this to the fiat of the Creator? As long as water is spread over a level surface, it does not flow; it is immovable. But when it finds any slope, immediately the foremost portion falls, then the one that follows takes its place, and that one is itself replaced by a third. Thus incessantly they flow, pressing the one on the other, and the rapidity of their course is in proportion to the mass of water that is being carried, and the declivity down which it is borne. If such is the nature of water, it was supererogatory to command it to gather into one place. It was bound, on account of its natural instability, to fall into the most hollow part of the earth and not to stop until the levelling of its surface. We see how there is nothing so level as the surface of water. Besides, they add, how did the waters receive an order to gather into one place, when we see several seas, separated from each other by the greatest distances? To the first question I reply: Since God's command, you know perfectly well the motion of water; you know that it is unsteady and unstable and falls naturally over declivities and into hollow places. But what was its nature before this command made it take its course? You do not know yourself, and you have heard from no eye-witness. Think, in reality, that a word of God makes the nature, and that this order is for the creature a direction for its future course. There was only one creation of day and night, and since that moment they have incessantly succeeded each other and divided time into equal parts.

3. "Let the waters be gathered together." It was ordered that it should be the natural property of water to flow, and in obedience to this order, the waters are never weary in their course. In speaking thus, I have only in view the flowing property of waters. Some flow of their own accord like springs and rivers, others are collected and stationary. But I speak now of flowing waters. "Let the waters be gathered together unto one place." Have you never thought, when standing near a spring which is sending forth water abundantly, Who makes this water spring from the bowels of the earth? Who forced it up? Where are the store-houses which send it forth? To what place is it hastening? How is it that it is never exhausted here, and never overflows there? All this comes from that first command; it was for the waters a signal for their course.

In all the story of the waters remember this first order, "let the waters be gathered together." To take their assigned places they were obliged to flow, and, once arrived there, to remain in their place and not to go farther. Thus in the language of Ecclesiastes, "All the waters run into the sea; yet the sea is not full." Ecclesiastes 1:6-7 Waters flow in virtue of God's order, and the sea is enclosed in limits according to this first law, "Let the waters be gathered together unto one place." For fear the water should spread beyond its bed, and in its successive invasions cover one by one all countries, and end by flooding the whole earth, it received the order to gather unto one place. Thus we often see the furious sea raising mighty waves to the heaven, and, when once it has touched the shore, break its impetuosity in foam and retire. "Fear ye not me, says the Lord....which have placed the sand for the bound of the sea." Jeremiah 5:22 A grain of sand, the weakest thing possible, curbs the violence of the ocean. For what would prevent the Red Sea from invading the whole of Egypt, which lies lower, and uniting itself to the other sea which bathes its shores, were it not fettered by the fiat of the Creator? And if I say that Egypt is lower than the Red Sea, it is because experience has convinced us of it every time that an attempt has been made to join the sea of Egypt to the Indian Ocean, of which the Red Sea is a part. Thus we have renounced this enterprise, as also have the Egyptian Sesostris, who conceived the idea, and Darius the Mede who afterwards wished to carry it out.

I report this fact to make you understand the full force of the command, "Let the waters be gathered unto one place"; that is to say, let there be no other gathering, and, once gathered, let them not disperse.

4. To say that the waters were gathered in one place indicates that previously they were scattered in many places. The mountains, intersected by deep ravines, accumulated water in their valleys, when from every direction the waters betook themselves to the one gathering place. What vast plains, in their extent resembling wide seas, what valleys, what cavities hollowed in many different ways, at that time full of water, must have been emptied by the command of God! But we must not therefore say, that if the water covered the face of the earth, all the basins which have since received the sea were originally full. Where can the gathering of the waters have come from if the basins were already full? These basins, we reply, were only prepared at the moment when the water had to unite in a single mass. At that time the sea which is beyond Gadeira and the vast ocean, so dreaded by navigators, which surrounds the isle of Britain and western Spain, did not exist. But, all of a sudden, God created this vast space, and the mass of waters flowed in.

Now if our explanation of the creation of the world may appear contrary to experience, (because it is evident that all the waters did not flow together in one place,) many answers may be made, all obvious as soon as they are stated. Perhaps it is even ridiculous to reply to such objections. Ought they to bring forward in opposition ponds and accumulations of rain water, and think that this is enough to upset our reasonings? Evidently the chief and most complete affluence of the waters was what received the name of gathering unto one place. For wells are also gathering places for water, made by the hand of man to receive the moisture diffused in the hollow of the earth. This name of gathering does not mean any chance massing of water, but the greatest and most important one, wherein the element is shown collected together. In the same way that fire, in spite of its being divided into minute particles which are sufficient for our needs here, is spread in a mass in the æther; in the same way that air, in spite of a like minute division, has occupied the region round the earth; so also water, in spite of the small amount spread abroad everywhere, only forms one gathering together, that which separates the whole element from the rest. Without doubt the lakes as well those of the northern regions and those that are to be found in Greece, in Macedonia, in Bithynia and in Palestine, are gatherings together of waters; but here it means the greatest of all, that gathering the extent of which equals that of the earth. The first contain a great quantity of water; no one will deny this. Nevertheless no one could reasonably give them the name of seas, not even if they are like the great sea, charged with salt and sand. They instance for example, the Lacus Asphaltitis in Judæa, and the Serbonian lake which extends between Egypt and Palestine in the Arabian desert. These are lakes, and there is only one sea, as those affirm who have travelled round the earth. Although some authorities think the Hyrcanian and Caspian Seas are enclosed in their own boundaries, if we are to believe the geographers, they communicate with each other and together discharge themselves into the Great Sea. It is thus that, according to their account, the Red Sea and that beyond Gadeira only form one. Then why did

God call the different masses of water seas? This is the reason; the waters flowed into one place, and their different accumulations, that is to say, the gulfs that the earth embraced in her folds, received from the Lord the name of seas: North Sea, South Sea, Eastern Sea, and Western Sea. The seas have even their own names, the Euxine, the Propontis, the Hellespont, the Ægean, the Ionian, the Sardinian, the Sicilian, the Tyrrhene, and many other names of which an exact enumeration would now be too long, and quite out of place. See why God calls the gathering together of waters seas. But let us return to the point from which the course of my argument has diverted me.

5. And God said: "Let the waters be gathered together unto one place and let the dry land appear." He did not say let the earth appear, so as not to show itself again without form, mud-like, and in combination with the water, nor yet endued with proper form and virtue. At the same time, lest we should attribute the drying of the earth to the sun, the Creator shows it to us dried before the creation of the sun. Let us follow the thought Scripture gives us. Not only the water which was covering the earth flowed off from it, but all that which had filtered into its depths withdrew in obedience to the irresistible order of the sovereign Master. And it was so. This is quite enough to show that the Creator's voice had effect: however, in several editions, there is added "And the water which was under the heavens gathered itself unto one place and the dry land was seen;" words that other interpreters have not given, and which do not appear conformable to Hebrew usage. In fact, after the assertion, "and it was so," it is superfluous to repeat exactly the same thing. In accurate copies these words are marked with an obelus, which is the sign of rejection.

"And God called the dry land earth; and the gathering together of the waters called He seas." Genesis 1:10 Why does Scripture say above that the waters were gathered together unto one place, and that the dry earth appeared? Why does it add here the dry land appeared, and God gave it the name of earth? It is that dryness is the property which appears to characterize the nature of the subject, while the word earth is only its simple name. Just as reason is the distinctive faculty of man, and the word man serves to designate the being gifted with this faculty, so dryness is the special and peculiar quality of the earth. The element essentially dry receives therefore the name of earth, as the animal who has a neigh for a characteristic cry is called a horse. The other elements, like the earth, have received some peculiar property which distinguishes them from the rest, and makes them known for what they are. Thus water has cold for its distinguishing property; air, moisture; fire, heat. But this theory really applies only to the primitive elements of the world. The elements which contribute to the formation of bodies, and come under our senses, show us these qualities in combination, and in the whole of nature our eyes and senses can find nothing which is completely singular, simple and pure. Earth is at the same time dry and cold; water, cold and moist; air, moist and warm; fire, warm and dry. It is by the combination of their qualities that the different elements can mingle. Thanks to a common quality each of them mixes with a neighbouring element, and this natural alliance attaches it to the contrary element. For example, earth, which is at the same time dry and cold, finds in cold a relationship which unites it to water, and by the means of water unites itself to air. Water placed between the two, appears to give each a hand, and, on account of its double quality, allies itself to earth by cold and to air by moisture. Air, in its turn, takes the middle place and plays the part of a mediator between the inimical natures of water and fire, united to the first by moisture, and to the second by heat. Finally fire, of a nature at the same time warm and dry, is linked to air by warmth, and by its dryness reunites itself to the earth. And from this accord and from this mutual mixture of elements, results a circle and an harmonious choir whence each of the elements deserves its name. I have said this in order to explain why God has given to the dry land the name of earth, without however calling the earth dry. It is because dryness is not one of those qualities which the earth acquired afterwards, but one of those which constituted its essence from the beginning. Now that which causes a body to exist, is naturally antecedent to its posterior qualities and has a pre-eminence over them. It is then with reason that God chose the most ancient characteristic of the earth whereby to designate it.

6. "And God saw that it was good." Genesis 1:10 Scripture does not merely wish to say that a pleasing aspect of the sea presented itself to God. It is not with eyes that the Creator views the beauty of His works. He contemplates them in His ineffable wisdom. A fair sight is the sea all bright in a settled calm; fair too, when, ruffled by a light breeze of wind, its surface shows tints of purple and azure,— when, instead of lashing with violence the neighbouring shores, it seems to kiss them with peaceful caresses. However, it is not in this that Scripture makes God find the goodness and charm of the sea. Here it is the purpose of the work which makes the goodness.

In the first place sea water is the source of all the moisture of the earth. It filters through imperceptible conduits, as is proved by the subterranean openings and caves whither its waves penetrate; it is received in oblique and sinuous canals; then, driven out by the wind, it rises to the surface of the earth, and breaks it, having become drinkable and free from its bitterness by this long percolation. Often, moved by the same cause, it springs even from mines that it has crossed, deriving warmth from them, and rises boiling, and bursts forth of a burning heat, as may be seen in islands and on the sea coast; even inland in certain places, in the neighbourhood of rivers, to compare little things with great, almost the same phenomena occur. To what do these words tend? To prove that the earth is all undermined with invisible conduits, where the water travels everywhere underground from the sources of the sea.

7. Thus, in the eyes of God, the sea is good, because it makes the under current of moisture in the depths of the earth. It is good again, because from all sides it receives the rivers without exceeding its limits. It is good, because it is the origin and source of the waters in the air. Warmed by the rays of the sun, it escapes in vapour, is attracted into the high regions of the air, and is there cooled on account of its rising high above the refraction of the rays from the ground, and, the shade of the clouds adding to this refrigeration, it is changed into rain and fattens the earth. If people are incredulous, let them look at caldrons on the fire, which, though full of water, are often left empty because all the water is boiled and resolved into vapour. Sailors, too, boil even sea water, collecting the vapour in sponges, to quench their thirst in pressing need.

Finally the sea is good in the eyes of God, because it girdles the isles, of which it forms at the same time the rampart and the beauty, because it brings together the most distant parts of the earth, and facilitates the inter-communication of mariners. By this means it gives us the boon of general information, supplies the merchant with his wealth, and easily provides for the necessities of life, allowing the rich to export their superfluities, and blessing the poor with the supply of what they lack.

But whence do I perceive the goodness of the Ocean, as it appeared in the eyes of the Creator? If the Ocean is good and worthy of praise before God, how much more beautiful is the assembly of a Church like this, where the voices of men, of children, and of women, arise in our prayers to God mingling and resounding like the waves which beat upon the shore. This Church also enjoys a profound calm, and malicious spirits cannot trouble it with the breath of heresy. Deserve, then, the approbation of the Lord by remaining faithful to such good guidance, in our Lord Jesus Christ, to whom be glory and power for ever and ever. Amen.

## Homily 5
## The Germination of the Earth.

1. "And God said Let the earth bring forth grass, the herb yielding seed, and the fruit tree yielding fruit after his kind, whose seed is in itself." Genesis 1:11 It was deep wisdom that commanded the earth, when it rested after discharging the weight of the waters, first to bring forth grass, then wood as we see it doing still at this time. For the voice that was then heard and this command were as a natural and permanent law for it; it gave fertility and the power to produce fruit for all ages to come; "Let the earth bring forth." The production of vegetables shows first germination. When the germs begin to sprout they form grass; this develops and becomes a plant, which insensibly receives its different articulations, and reaches its maturity in the seed. Thus all things which sprout and are green are developed. "Let the earth bring forth green grass." Let the earth bring forth by itself without having any need of help from without. Some consider the sun as the source of all productiveness on the earth. It is, they say, the action of the sun's heat which attracts the vital force from the centre of the earth to the surface. The reason why the adornment of the earth was before the sun is the following; that those who worship the sun, as the source of life, may renounce their error. If they be well persuaded that the earth was adorned before the genesis of the sun, they will retract their

unbounded admiration for it, because they see grass and plants vegetate before it rose. If then the food for the flocks was prepared, did our race appear less worthy of a like solicitude? He, who provided pasture for horses and cattle, thought before all of your riches and pleasures. If he fed your cattle, it was to provide for all the needs of your life. And what object was there in the bringing forth of grain, if not for your subsistence? Moreover, many grasses and vegetables serve for the food of man.

2. "Let the earth bring forth grass yielding seed after his kind." So that although some kind of grass is of service to animals, even their gain is our gain too, and seeds are especially designed for our use. Such is the true meaning of the words that I have quoted. "Let the earth bring forth grass, the herb yielding seed after his kind." In this manner we can re-establish the order of the words, of which the construction seems faulty in the actual version, and the economy of nature will be rigorously observed. In fact, first comes germination, then verdure, then the growth of the plant, which after having attained its full growth arrives at perfection in seed.

How then, they say, can Scripture describe all the plants of the earth as seed-bearing, when the reed, couch-grass, mint, crocus, garlic, and the flowering rush and countless other species, produce no seed? To this we reply that many vegetables have their seminal virtue in the lower part and in the roots. The need, for example, after its annual growth sends forth a protuberance from its roots, which takes the place of seed for future trees. Numbers of other vegetables are the same and all over the earth reproduce by the roots. Nothing then is truer than that each plant produces its seed or contains some seminal virtue; this is what is meant by "after its kind." So that the shoot of a reed does not produce an olive tree, but from a reed grows another reed, and from one sort of seed a plant of the same sort always germinates. Thus, all which sprang from the earth, in its first bringing forth, is kept the same to our time, thanks to the constant reproduction of kind.

"Let the earth bring forth." See how, at this short word, at this brief command, the cold and sterile earth travailed and hastened to bring forth its fruit, as it cast away its sad and dismal covering to clothe itself in a more brilliant robe, proud of its proper adornment and displaying the infinite variety of plants.

I want creation to penetrate you with so much admiration that everywhere, wherever you may be, the least plant may bring to you the clear remembrance of the Creator. If you see the grass of the fields, think of human nature, and remember the comparison of the wise Isaiah. "All flesh is grass, and all the goodliness thereof is as the flower of the field." Truly the rapid flow of life, the short gratification and pleasure that an instant of happiness gives a man, all wonderfully suit the comparison of the prophet. Today he is vigorous in body, fattened by luxury, and in the prime of life, with complexion fair like the flowers, strong and powerful and of irresistible energy; tomorrow and he will be an object of pity, withered by age or exhausted by sickness. Another shines in all the splendour of a brilliant fortune, and around him are a multitude of flatterers, an escort of false friends on the track of his good graces; a crowd of kinsfolk, but of no true kin; a swarm of servants who crowd after him to provide for his food and for all his needs; and in his comings and goings this innumerable suite, which he drags after him, excites the envy of all whom he meets. To fortune may be added power in the State, honours bestowed by the imperial throne, the government of a province, or the command of armies; a herald who precedes him is crying in a loud voice; lictors right and left also fill his subjects with awe, blows, confiscations, banishments, imprisonments, and all the means by which he strikes intolerable terror into all whom he has to rule. And what then?

One night, a fever, a pleurisy, or an inflammation of the lungs, snatches away this man from the midst of men, stripped in a moment of all his stage accessories, and all this, his glory, is proved a mere dream. Therefore the Prophet has compared human glory to the weakest flower.

3. Up to this point, the order in which plants shoot bears witness to their first arrangement. Every herb, every plant proceeds from a germ. If, like the couch-grass and the crocus, it throws out a shoot from its root and from this lower protuberance, it must always germinate and start outwards. If it proceeds from a seed, there is still, by necessity, first a germ, then the sprout, then green foliage, and finally the fruit which ripens upon a stalk hitherto dry and thick. "Let the earth bring forth grass." When the seed falls into the earth, which contains the right combination of heat and moisture, it swells and becomes porous, and, grasping the surrounding earth, attracts to itself all that is suitable for it and that has affinity to it. These particles of earth, however small they may be, as they fall and insinuate themselves into all the pores of the seed, broaden its bulk and make it send forth roots below, and shoot upwards, sending forth stalks no less numerous than the roots. As the germ is always growing warm, the moisture, pumped up through the roots, and helped by the attraction of heat, draws a proper amount of nourishment from the soil, and distributes it to the stem, to the bark, to the husk, to the seed itself and to the beards with which it is armed. It is owing to these successive accretions that each plant attains its natural development, as well grain as vegetables, herbs or brushwood. A single plant, a blade of grass is sufficient to occupy all your intelligence in the contemplation of the skill which produced it. Why is the wheat stalk better with joints? Are they not like fastenings, which help it to bear easily the weight of the ear, when it is swollen with fruit and bends towards the earth? Thus,

while oats, which have no weight to bear at the top, are without these supports, nature has provided them for wheat. It has hidden the grain in a case, so that it may not be exposed to birds' pillage, and has furnished it with a rampart of barbs, which, like darts, protect it against the attacks of tiny creatures.

4. What shall I say? What shall I leave unsaid? In the rich treasures of creation it is difficult to select what is most precious; the loss of what is omitted is too severe. "Let the earth bring forth grass;" and instantly, with useful plants, appear noxious plants; with grain, hemlock; with the other nutritious plants, hellebore, monkshood, mandrake and the juice of the poppy. What then? Shall we show no gratitude for so many beneficial gifts, and reproach the Creator for those which may be harmful to our life? And shall we not reflect that all has not been created in view of the wants of our bellies? The nourishing plants, which are destined for our use, are close at hand, and known by all the world. But in creation nothing exists without a reason. The blood of the bull is a poison: ought this animal then, whose strength is so serviceable to man, not to have been created, or, if created, to have been bloodless? But you have sense enough in yourself to keep you free from deadly things. What! Sheep and goats know how to turn away from what threatens their life, discerning danger by instinct alone: and you, who have reason and the art of medicine to supply what you need, and the experience of your forebears to tell you to avoid all that is dangerous, you tell me that you find it difficult to keep yourself from poisons! But not a single thing has been created without reason, not a single thing is useless. One serves as food to some animal; medicine has found in another a relief for one of our maladies. Thus the starling eats hemlock, its constitution rendering it insusceptible to the action of the poison. Thanks to the tenuity of the pores of its heart, the malignant juice is no sooner swallowed

than it is digested, before its chill can attack the vital parts. The quail, thanks to its peculiar temperament, whereby it escapes the dangerous effects, feeds on hellebore. There are even circumstances where poisons are useful to men; with mandrake doctors give us sleep; with opium they lull violent pain. Hemlock has ere now been used to appease the rage of unruly diseases; and many times hellebore has taken away long standing disease. These plants, then, instead of making you accuse the Creator, give you a new subject for gratitude.

5. "Let the earth bring forth grass." What spontaneous provision is included in these words—that which is present in the root, in the plant itself, and in the fruit, as well as that which our labour and husbandry add! God did not command the earth immediately to give forth seed and fruit, but to produce germs, to grow green, and to arrive at maturity in the seed; so that this first command teaches nature what she has to do in the course of ages. But, they ask, is it true that the earth produces seed after his kind, when often, after having sown wheat, we gather black grain? This is not a change of kind, but an alteration, a disease of the grain. It has not ceased to be wheat; it is on account of having been burnt that it is black, as one can learn from its name. If a severe frost had burnt it, it would have had another colour and a different flavour. They even pretend that, if it could find suitable earth and moderate temperature, it might return to its first form. Thus, you find nothing in nature contrary to the divine command. As to the darnel and all those bastard grains which mix themselves with the harvest, the tares of Scripture, far from being a variety of grain, have their own origin and their own kind; image of those who alter the doctrine of the Lord and, not being rightly instructed in the word, but, corrupted by the teaching of the evil one, mix themselves with the sound body of the Church to spread their pernicious errors secretly

among purer souls. The Lord thus compares the perfection of those who believe in Him to the growth of seed, "as if a man should cast seed into the ground; and should sleep and rise, night and day, and the seed should spring and grow up, he knows not how. For the earth brings forth fruit of herself; first the blade, then the ear, after that the full grain in the ear." Matthew 4:26-28 "Let the earth bring forth grass." In a moment earth began by germination to obey the laws of the Creator, completed every stage of growth, and brought germs to perfection. The meadows were covered with deep grass, the fertile plains quivered with harvests, and the movement of the grain was like the waving of the sea. Every plant, every herb, the smallest shrub, the least vegetable, arose from the earth in all its luxuriance. There was no failure in this first vegetation: no husbandman's inexperience, no inclemency of the weather, nothing could injure it; then the sentence of condemnation was not fettering the earth's fertility. All this was before the sin which condemned us to eat our bread by the sweat of our brow.

6. "Let the earth," the Creator adds, "bring forth the fruit tree yielding fruit after his kind, whose seed is in itself." Genesis 1:11

At this command every copse was thickly planted; all the trees, fir, cedar, cypress, pine, rose to their greatest height, the shrubs were straightway clothed with thick foliage. The plants called crown-plants, roses, myrtles, laurels, did not exist; in one moment they came into being, each one with its distinctive peculiarities. Most marked differences separated them from other plants, and each one was distinguished by a character of its own. But then the rose was without thorns; since then the thorn has been added to its beauty, to make us feel that sorrow is very near to pleasure, and to remind us of our sin, which condemned the earth to produce thorns and caltrops. But, they say, the earth has received the command to produce trees "yielding fruit whose seed was in itself," and we see many trees which have neither fruit, nor seed. What shall we reply? First, that only the more important trees are mentioned; and then, that a careful examination will show us that every tree has seed, or some property which takes the place of it. The black poplar, the willow, the elm, the white poplar, all the trees of this family, do not produce any apparent fruit; however, an attentive observer finds seed in each of them. This grain which is at the base of the leaf, and which those who busy themselves with inventing words call mischos, has the property of seed. And there are trees which reproduce by their branches, throwing out roots from them. Perhaps we ought even to consider as seeds the saplings which spring from the roots of a tree: for cultivators tear them out to multiply the species. But, we have already said, it is chiefly a question of the trees which contribute most to our life; which offer their various fruits to man and provide him with plentiful nourishment. Such is the vine, which produces wine to make glad the heart of man; such is the olive tree, whose fruit brightens his face with oil. How many things in nature are combined in the same plant! In a vine, roots, green and flexible branches, which spread themselves far over the earth, buds, tendrils, bunches of sour grapes and ripe grapes. The sight of a vine, when observed by an intelligent eye, serves to remind you of your nature. Without doubt you remember the parable where the Lord calls Himself a vine and His Father the husbandman, and every one of us who are grafted by faith into the Church the branches. He invites us to produce fruits in abundance, for fear lest our sterility should condemn us to the fire. cf.John 15:1-6 He constantly compares our souls to vines. "My well beloved," says He, "has a vineyard in a very fruitfull hill," Isaiah 5:1 and elsewhere, I have "planted a vineyard and hedged it round about." Matthew 21:33 Evidently He calls human souls His vine, those souls whom He has surrounded with the authority of

His precepts and a guard of angels. "The angel of the Lord encamps round about them that fear him." And further: He has planted for us, so to say, props, in establishing in His Church apostles, prophets, teachers; and raising our thoughts by the example of the blessed in olden times, He has not allowed them to drag on the earth and be crushed under foot. He wishes that the claspings of love, like the tendrils of the vine, should attach us to our neighbours and make us rest on them, so that, in our continual aspirations towards heaven, we may imitate these vines, which raise themselves to the tops of the tallest trees. He also asks us to allow ourselves to be dug about; and that is what the soul does when it disembarrasses itself from the cares of the world, which are a weight on our hearts. He, then, who is freed from carnal affections and from the love of riches, and, far from being dazzled by them, disdains and despises this miserable vain glory, is, so to say, dug about and at length breathes, free from the useless weight of earthly thoughts. Nor must we, in the spirit of the parable, put forth too much wood, that is to say, live with ostentation, and gain the applause of the world; we must bring forth fruits, keeping the proof of our works for the husbandman. Be "like a green olive tree in the house of God," never destitute of hope, but decked through faith with the bloom of salvation. Thus you will resemble the eternal verdure of this plant and will rival it in fruitfulness, if each day sees you giving abundantly in alms.

7. But let us return to the examination of the ingenious contrivances of creation. How many trees then arose, some to give us their fruits, others to roof our houses, others to build our ships, others to feed our fires! What a variety in the disposition of their several parts! And yet, how difficult is it to find the distinctive property of each of them, and to grasp the difference which separates them from other species. Some strike deep roots, others

186

do not; some shoot straight up and have only one stem, others appear to love the earth and, from their root upwards, divide into several shoots. Those whose long branches stretch up afar into the air, have also deep roots which spread within a large circumference, a true foundation placed by nature to support the weight of the tree. What variety there is in bark! Some plants have smooth bark, others rough, some have only one layer, others several. What a marvellous thing! You may find in the youth and age of plants resemblances to those of man. Young and vigorous, their bark is distended; when they grow old, it is rough and wrinkled. Cut one, it sends forth new buds; the other remains henceforward sterile and as if struck with a mortal wound. But further, it has been observed that pines, cut down, or even submitted to the action of fire, are changed into a forest of oaks. We know besides that the industry of agriculturists remedies the natural defects of certain trees. Thus the sharp pomegranate and bitter almonds, if the trunk of the tree is pierced near the root to introduce into the middle of the pith a fat plug of pine, lose the acidity of their juice, and become delicious fruits. Let not the sinner then despair of himself, when he thinks, if agriculture can change the juices of plants, the efforts of the soul to arrive at virtue, can certainly triumph over all infirmities.

Now there is such a variety of fruits in fruit trees that it is beyond all expression; a variety not only in the fruits of trees of different families, but even in those of the same species, if it be true, as gardeners say, that the sex of a tree influences the character of its fruits. They distinguish male from female in palms; sometimes we see those which they call female lower their branches, as though with passionate desire, and invite the embraces of the male. Then, those who take care of these plants shake over these palms the fertilizing dust from the male palm-tree, the psen as they call it: the tree appears to share the pleasures of enjoyment; then it raises its branches, and its foliage resumes its usual form. The same is said of the fig tree. Some plant wild fig trees near cultivated fig trees, and there are others who, to remedy the weakness of the productive fig tree of our gardens, attach to the branches unripe figs and so retain the fruit which had already begun to drop and to be lost. What lesson does nature here give us? That we must often borrow, even from those who are strangers to the faith, a certain vigour to show forth good works. If you see outside the Church, in pagan life, or in the midst of a pernicious heresy, the example of virtue and fidelity to moral laws, redouble your efforts to resemble the productive fig tree, who by the side of the wild fig tree, gains strength, prevents the fruit from being shed, and nourishes it with more care.

8. Plants reproduce themselves in so many different ways, that we can only touch upon the chief among them. As to fruits themselves, who could review their varieties, their forms, their colours, the peculiar flavour, and the use of each of them? Why do some fruits ripen when exposed bare to the rays of the sun, while others fill out while encased in shells? Trees of which the fruit is tender have, like the fig tree, a thick shade of leaves; those, on the contrary, of which the fruits are stouter, like the nut, are only covered by a light shade. The delicacy of the first requires more care; if the latter had a thicker case, the shade of the leaves would be harmful. Why is the vine leaf serrated, if not that the bunches of grapes may at the same time resist the injuries of the air and receive through the openings all the rays of the sun? Nothing has been done without motive, nothing by chance. All shows ineffable wisdom.

What discourse can touch all? Can the human mind make an exact review, remark every distinctive property, exhibit all the differences, unveil with certainty so many mysterious causes? The same water, pumped up through the root, nourishes in a different way the root itself, the bark of the trunk, the wood and the pith. It becomes leaf, it distributes itself among the branches and twigs and makes the fruits swell— it gives to the plant its gum and its sap. Who will explain to us the difference between all these? There is a difference between the gum of the mastich and the juice of the balsam, a difference between that which distils in Egypt and Libya from the fennel. Amber is, they say, the crystallized sap of plants. And for a proof, see the bits of straws and little insects which have been caught in the sap while still liquid and imprisoned there. In one word, no one without long experience could find terms to express the virtue of it. How, again, does this water become wine in the vine, and oil in the olive tree? Yet what is marvellous is, not to see it become sweet in one fruit, fat and unctuous in another, but to see in sweet fruits an inexpressible variety of flavour. There is one sweetness of the grape, another of the apple, another of the fig, another of the date. I shall willingly give you the gratification of continuing this research. How is it that this same water has sometimes a sweet taste, softened by its remaining in certain plants, and at other times stings the palate because it has become acid by passing through others? How is it, again, that it attains extreme bitterness, and makes the mouth rough when it is found in wormwood and in scammony? That it has in acorns and dogwood a sharp and rough flavour? That in the turpentine tree and the walnut tree it is changed into a soft and oily matter?

9. But what need is there to continue, when in the same fig tree we have the most opposite flavours, as bitter in the sap as it is sweet in the fruit? And in the vine, is it not as sweet in the grapes as it is astringent in the branches? And what a variety of colour! Look how in a meadow this same water becomes red in one flower, purple in another, blue in this one, white in that. And this diversity of colours, is it to be compared to that of scents? But I perceive that

an insatiable curiosity is drawing out my discourse beyond its limits. If I do not stop and recall it to the law of creation, day will fail me while making you see great wisdom in small things.

"Let the earth bring forth the fruit tree yielding fruit." Immediately the tops of the mountains were covered with foliage: paradises were artfully laid out, and an infinitude of plants embellished the banks of the rivers. Some were for the adornment of man's table; some to nourish animals with their fruits and their leaves; some to provide medicinal help by giving us their sap, their juice, their chips, their bark or their fruit. In a word, the experience of ages, profiting from every chance, has not been able to discover anything useful, which the penetrating foresight of the Creator did not first perceive and call into existence. Therefore, when you see the trees in our gardens, or those of the forest, those which love the water or the land, those which bear flowers, or those which do not flower, I should like to see you recognising grandeur even in small objects, adding incessantly to your admiration of, and redoubling your love for the Creator. Ask yourself why He has made some trees evergreen and others deciduous; why, among the first, some lose their leaves, and others always keep them. Thus the olive and the pine shed their leaves, although they renew them insensibly and never appear to be despoiled of their verdure. The palm tree, on the contrary, from its birth to its death, is always adorned with the same foliage. Think again of the double life of the tamarisk; it is an aquatic plant, and yet it covers the desert. Thus, Jeremiah compares it to the worst of characters— the double character.

10. "Let the earth bring forth." This short command was in a moment a vast nature, an elaborate system. Swifter than thought it produced the countless qualities of plants. It is this command which, still at this day, is imposed on the earth, and in the course of each year displays all the strength of its power to produce herbs,

seeds and trees. Like tops, which after the first impulse, continue
their evolutions, turning upon themselves when once fixed in their
centre; thus nature, receiving the impulse of this first command,
follows without interruption the course of ages, until the
consummation of all things. Let us all hasten to attain to it, full of
fruit and of good works; and thus, planted in the house of the Lord
we shall flourish in the court of our God, in our Lord Jesus Christ,
to whom be glory and power for ever and ever. Amen.

**Homily 6**
**The creation of luminous bodies.**

1. At the shows in the circus the spectator must join in the efforts
of the athletes. This the laws of the show indicate, for they
prescribe that all should have the head uncovered when present at
the stadium. The object of this, in my opinion, is that each one
there should not only be a spectator of the athletes, but be, in a
certain measure, a true athlete himself. Thus, to investigate the
great and prodigious show of creation, to understand supreme and
ineffable wisdom, you must bring personal light for the
contemplation of the wonders which I spread before your eyes, and
help me, according to your power, in this struggle, where you are
not so much judges as fellow combatants, for fear lest the truth
might escape you, and lest my error might turn to your common
prejudice. Why these words? It is because we propose to study the
world as a whole, and to consider the universe, not by the light of
worldly wisdom, but by that with which God wills to enlighten His
servant, when He speaks to him in person and without enigmas. It
is because it is absolutely necessary that all lovers of great and
grand shows should bring a mind well prepared to study them. If
sometimes, on a bright night, while gazing with watchful eyes on
the inexpressible beauty of the stars, you have thought of the
Creator of all things; if you have asked yourself who it is that has

dotted heaven with such flowers, and why visible things are even
more useful than beautiful; if sometimes, in the day, you have
studied the marvels of light, if you have raised yourself by visible
things to the invisible Being, then you are a well prepared auditor,
and you can take your place in this august and blessed
amphitheatre. Come in the same way that any one not knowing a
town is taken by the hand and led through it; thus I am going to
lead you, like strangers, through the mysterious marvels of this
great city of the universe. Our first country was in this great city,
whence the murderous dæmon whose enticements seduced man to
slavery expelled us. There you will see man's first origin and his
immediate seizure by death, brought forth by sin, the first born of
the evil spirit. You will know that you are formed of earth, but the
work of God's hands; much weaker than the brute, but ordained to
command beings without reason and soul; inferior as regards
natural advantages, but, thanks to the privilege of reason, capable
of raising yourself to heaven. If we are penetrated by these truths,
we shall know ourselves, we shall know God, we shall adore our
Creator, we shall serve our Master, we shall glorify our Father, we
shall love our Sustainer, we shall bless our Benefactor, we shall not
cease to honour the Prince of present and future life, Who, by the
riches that He showers upon us in this world, makes us believe in
His promises and uses present good things to strengthen our
expectation of the future. Truly, if such are the good things of time,
what will be those of eternity? If such is the beauty of visible
things, what shall we think of invisible things? If the grandeur of
heaven exceeds the measure of human intelligence, what mind shall
be able to trace the nature of the everlasting? If the sun, subject to
corruption, is so beautiful, so grand, so rapid in its movement, so
invariable in its course; if its grandeur is in such perfect harmony
with and due proportion to the universe: if, by the beauty of its
nature, it shines like a brilliant eye in the middle of creation; if

finally, one cannot tire of contemplating it, what will be the beauty of the Sun of Righteousness? If the blind man suffers from not seeing the material sun, what a deprivation is it for the sinner not to enjoy the true light!

2. "And God said, Let there be lights in the firmament of the heaven to give light upon the earth, and to divide the day from the night." Heaven and earth were the first; after them was created light; the day had been distinguished from the night, then had appeared the firmament and the dry element. The water had been gathered into the reservoir assigned to it, the earth displayed its productions, it had caused many kinds of herbs to germinate and it was adorned with all kinds of plants. However, the sun and the moon did not yet exist, in order that those who live in ignorance of God may not consider the sun as the origin and the father of light, or as the maker of all that grows out of the earth. That is why there was a fourth day, and then God said: "Let there be lights in the firmament of the heaven."

When once you have learned Who spoke, think immediately of the hearer. God said, "Let there be lights...and God made two great lights." Who spoke? And Who made? Do you not see a double person? Everywhere, in mystic language, history is sown with the dogmas of theology.

The motive follows which caused the lights to be created. It was to illuminate the earth. Already light was created; why therefore say that the sun was created to give light? And, first, do not laugh at the strangeness of this expression. We do not follow your nicety about words, and we trouble ourselves but little to give them a harmonious turn. Our writers do not amuse themselves by polishing their periods, and everywhere we prefer clearness of words to sonorous expressions. See then if by this expression "to light up," the sacred writer sufficiently made his thought understood. He has put "to give light" instead of "illumination." Now there is nothing here contradictory to what has been said of light. Then the actual nature of light was produced: now the sun's body is constructed to be a vehicle for that original light. A lamp is not fire. Fire has the property of illuminating, and we have invented the lamp to light us in darkness. In the same way, the luminous bodies have been fashioned as a vehicle for that pure, clear, and immaterial light. The Apostle speaks to us of certain lights which shine in the world without being confounded with the true light of the world, the possession of which made the saints luminaries of the souls which they instructed and drew from the darkness of ignorance. This is why the Creator of all things, made the sun in addition to that glorious light, and placed it shining in the heavens.

3. And let no one suppose it to be a thing incredible that the brightness of the light is one thing, and the body which is its material vehicle is another. First, in all composite things, we distinguish substance susceptible of quality, and the quality which it receives. The nature of whiteness is one thing, another is that of the body which is whitened; thus the natures differ which we have just seen reunited by the power of the Creator. And do not tell me that it is impossible to separate them. Even I do not pretend to be able to separate light from the body of the sun; but I maintain that that which we separate in thought, may be separated in reality by the Creator of nature. You cannot, moreover, separate the brightness of fire from the virtue of burning which it possesses; but God, who wished to attract His servant by a wonderful sight, set a fire in the burning bush, which displayed all the brilliancy of flame while its devouring property was dormant. It is that which the Psalmist affirms in saying "The voice of the Lord divides the flames of fire." Thus, in the requital which awaits us after this life, a

mysterious voice seems to tell us that the double nature of fire will be divided; the just will enjoy its light, and the torment of its heat will be the torture of the wicked.

In the revolutions of the moon we find anew proof of what we have advanced. When it stops and grows less it does not consume itself in all its body, but in the measure that it deposits or absorbs the light which surrounds it, it presents to us the image of its decrease or of its increase. If we wish an evident proof that the moon does not consume its body when at rest, we have only to open our eyes. If you look at it in a cloudless and clear sky, you observe, when it has taken the complete form of a crescent, that the part, which is dark and not lighted up, describes a circle equal to that which the full moon forms. Thus the eye can take in the whole circle, if it adds to the illuminated part this obscure and dark curve. And do not tell me that the light of the moon is borrowed, diminishing or increasing in proportion as it approaches or recedes from the sun. That is not now the object of our research; we only wish to prove that its body differs from the light which makes it shine. I wish you to have the same idea of the sun; except however that the one, after having once received light and having mixed it with its substance, does not lay it down again, while the other, turn by turn, putting off and reclothing itself again with light, proves by that which takes place in itself what we have said of the sun.

The sun and moon thus received the command to divide the day from the night. God had already separated light from darkness; then He placed their natures in opposition, so that they could not mingle, and that there could never be anything in common between darkness and light. You see what a shadow is during the day; that is precisely the nature of darkness during the night. If, at the appearance of a light, the shadow always falls on the opposite side; if in the morning it extends towards the setting sun; if in the evening it inclines towards the rising sun, and at mid-day turns towards the north; night retires into the regions opposed to the rays of the sun, since it is by nature only the shadow of the earth. Because, in the same way that, during the day, shadow is produced by a body which intercepts the light, night comes naturally when the air which surrounds the earth is in shadow. And this is precisely what Scripture says, "God divided the light from the darkness." Thus darkness fled at the approach of light, the two being at their first creation divided by a natural antipathy. Now God commanded the sun to measure the day, and the moon, whenever she rounds her disc, to rule the night. For then these two luminaries are almost diametrically opposed; when the sun rises, the full moon disappears from the horizon, to re-appear in the east at the moment the sun sets. It matters little to our subject if in other phases the light of the moon does not correspond exactly with night. It is none the less true, that when at its perfection it makes the stars to turn pale and lightens up the earth with the splendour of its light, it reigns over the night, and in concert with the sun divides the duration of it in equal parts.

4. "And let them be for signs, and for seasons, and for days and years." Genesis 1:14 The signs which the luminaries give are necessary to human life. In fact what useful observations will long experience make us discover, if we ask without undue curiosity! What signs of rain, of drought, or of the rising of the wind, partial or general, violent or moderate! Our Lord indicates to us one of the signs given by the sun when He says, "It will be foul weather today; for the sky is red and lowering." Matthew 16:3 In fact, when the sun rises through a fog, its rays are darkened, but the disc appears burning like a coal and of a bloody red colour. It is the thickness of the air which causes this appearance; as the rays of the sun do not disperse such amassed and condensed air, it cannot certainly be

retained by the waves of vapour which exhale from the earth, and it will cause from superabundance of moisture a storm in the countries over which it accumulates. In the same way, when the moon is surrounded with moisture, or when the sun is encircled with what is called a halo, it is the sign of heavy rain or of a violent storm; again, in the same way, if mock suns accompany the sun in its course they foretell certain celestial phenomena. Finally, those straight lines, like the colours of the rainbow, which are seen on the clouds, announce rain, extraordinary tempests, or, in one word, a complete change in the weather.

Those who devote themselves to the observation of these bodies find signs in the different phases of the moon, as if the air, by which the earth is enveloped, were obliged to vary to correspond with its change of form. Towards the third day of the new moon, if it is sharp and clear, it is a sign of fixed fine weather. If its horns appear thick and reddish it threatens us either with heavy rain or with a gale from the South. Who does not know how useful are these signs in life? Thanks to them, the sailor keeps back his vessel in the harbour, foreseeing the perils with which the winds threaten him, and the traveller beforehand takes shelter from harm, waiting until the weather has become fairer. Thanks to them, husbandmen, busy with sowing seed or cultivating plants, are able to know which seasons are favourable to their labours. Further, the Lord has announced to us that at the dissolution of the universe, signs will appear in the sun, in the moon and in the stars. The sun shall be turned into blood and the moon shall not give her light, signs of the consummation of all things.

5. But those who overstep the borders, making the words of Scripture their apology for the art of casting nativities, pretend that our lives depend upon the motion of the heavenly bodies, and that thus the Chaldæans read in the planets that which will happen to

us. By these very simple words "let them be for signs," they understand neither the variations of the weather, nor the change of seasons; they only see in them, at the will of their imagination, the distribution of human destinies. What do they say in reality? When the planets cross in the signs of the Zodiac, certain figures formed by their meeting give birth to certain destinies, and others produce different destinies.

Perhaps for clearness sake it is not useless to enter into more detail about this vain science. I will say nothing of my own to refute them; I will use their words, bringing a remedy for the infected, and for others a preservative from falling. The inventors of astrology seeing that in the extent of time many signs escaped them, divided it and enclosed each part in narrow limits, as if in the least and shortest interval, in a moment, in the twinkling of an eye, 1 Corinthians 15:52 to speak with the Apostle, the greatest difference should be found between one birth and another. Such an one is born in this moment; he will be a prince over cities and will govern the people, in the fullness of riches and power. Another is born the instant after; he will be poor, miserable, and will wander daily from door to door begging his bread. Consequently they divide the Zodiac into twelve parts, and, as the sun takes thirty days to traverse each of the twelve divisions of this unerring circle, they divide them into thirty more. Each of them forms sixty new ones, and these last are again divided into sixty. Let us see then if, in determining the birth of an infant, it will be possible to observe this rigorous division of time. The child is born. The nurse ascertains the sex; then she awaits the wail which is a sign of its life. Until then how many moments have passed do you think? The nurse announces the birth of the child to the Chaldæan: how many minutes would you count before she opens her mouth, especially if he who records the hour is outside the women's apartments? And we know that he who consults the dial, ought, whether by day or by night, to mark the hour with the most precise exactitude. What a swarm of seconds passes during this time! For the planet of nativity ought to be found, not only in one of the twelve divisions of the Zodiac, and even in one of its first subdivisions, but again in one of the sixtieth parts which divide this last, and even, to arrive at the exact truth, in one of the sixtieth subdivisions that this contains in its turn. And to obtain such minute knowledge, so impossible to grasp from this moment, each planet must be questioned to find its position as regards the signs of the Zodiac and the figures that the planets form at the moment of the child's birth. Thus, if it is impossible to find exactly the hour of birth, and if the least change can upset all, then both those who give themselves up to this imaginary science and those who listen to them open-mouthed, as if they could learn from them the future, are supremely ridiculous.

6. But what effects are produced? Such an one will have curly hair and bright eyes, because he is born under the Ram; such is the appearance of a ram. He will have noble feelings; because the Ram is born to command. He will be liberal and fertile in resources, because this animal gets rid of its fleece without trouble, and nature immediately hastens to reclothe it. Another is born under the Bull: he will be enured to hardship and of a slavish character, because the bull bows under the yoke. Another is born under the Scorpion; like to this venomous reptile he will be a striker. He who is born under the Balance will be just, thanks to the justness of our balances. Is not this the height of folly? This Ram, from whence you draw the nativity of man, is the twelfth part of the heaven, and in entering into it the sun reaches the spring. The Balance and the Bull are likewise twelfth parts of the Zodiac. How can you see there the principal causes which influence the life of man? And why do you take animals to characterize the manners of men who enter this

world? He who is born under the Ram will be liberal, not because
this part of heaven gives this characteristic, but because such is the
nature of the beast. Why then should we frighten ourselves by the
names of these stars and undertake to persuade ourselves with
these bleatings? If heaven has different characteristics derived from
these animals, it is then itself subject to external influences since its
causes depend on the brutes who graze in our fields. A ridiculous
assertion; but how much more ridiculous the pretence of arriving at
the influence on each other of things which have not the least
connection! This pretended science is a true spider's web; if a gnat
or a fly, or some insect equally feeble falls into it it is held
entangled; if a stronger animal approaches, it passes through
without trouble, carrying the weak tissue away with it.

7. They do not, however, stop here; even our acts, where each one
feels his will ruling, I mean, the practice of virtue or of vice,
depend, according to them, on the influence of celestial bodies. It
would be ridiculous seriously to refute such an error, but, as it
holds a great many in its nets, perhaps it is better not to pass it over
in silence. I would first ask them if the figures which the stars
describe do not change a thousand times a day. In the perpetual
motion of planets, some meet in a more rapid course, others make
slower revolutions, and often in an hour we see them look at each
other and then hide themselves. Now, at the hour of birth, it is very
important whether one is looked upon by a beneficent star or by an
evil one, to speak their language. Often then the astrologers do not
seize the moment when a good star shows itself, and, on account
of having let this fugitive moment escape, they enrol the newborn
under the influence of a bad genius. I am compelled to use their
own words. What madness! But, above all, what impiety! For the
evil stars throw the blame of their wickedness upon Him Who
made them. If evil is inherent in their nature, the Creator is the

author of evil. If they make it themselves, they are animals endowed with the power of choice, whose acts will be free and voluntary. Is it not the height of folly to tell these lies about beings without souls? Again, what a want of sense does it show to distribute good and evil without regard to personal merit; to say that a star is beneficent because it occupies a certain place; that it becomes evil, because it is viewed by another star; and that if it moves ever so little from this figure it loses its malign influence.

But let us pass on. If, at every instant of duration, the stars vary their figures, then in these thousand changes, many times a day, there ought to be reproduced the configuration of royal births. Why then does not every day see the birth of a king? Why is there a succession on the throne from father to son? Without doubt there has never been a king who has taken measures to have his son born under the star of royalty. For what man possesses such a power? How then did Uzziah beget Jotham, Jotham Ahaz, Ahaz Hezekiah? And by what chance did the birth of none of them happen in an hour of slavery? If the origin of our virtues and of our vices is not in ourselves, but is the fatal consequence of our birth, it is useless for legislators to prescribe for us what we ought to do, and what we ought to avoid; it is useless for judges to honour virtue and to punish vice. The guilt is not in the robber, not in the assassin: it was willed for him; it was impossible for him to hold back his hand, urged to evil by inevitable necessity. Those who laboriously cultivate the arts are the maddest of men. The labourer will make an abundant harvest without sowing seed and without sharpening his sickle. Whether he wishes it or not, the merchant will make his fortune, and will be flooded with riches by fate. As for us Christians, we shall see our great hopes vanish, since from the moment that man does not act with freedom, there is neither reward for justice, nor punishment for sin. Under the reign of necessity and of fatality there is no place for merit, the first condition of all righteous judgment. But let us stop. You who are sound in yourselves have no need to hear more, and time does not allow us to make attacks without limit against these unhappy men.

8. Let us return to the words which follow. "Let them be for signs and for seasons and for days and years." Genesis 1:14 We have spoken about signs. By times, we understand the succession of seasons, winter, spring, summer and autumn, which we see follow each other in so regular a course, thanks to the regularity of the movement of the luminaries. It is winter when the sun sojourns in the south and produces in abundance the shades of night in our region. The air spread over the earth is chilly, and the damp exhalations, which gather over our heads, give rise to rains, to frosts, to innumerable flakes of snow. When, returning from the southern regions, the sun is in the middle of the heavens and divides day and night into equal parts, the more it sojourns above the earth the more it brings back a mild temperature to us. Then comes spring, which makes all the plants germinate, and gives to the greater part of the trees their new life, and, by successive generation, perpetuates all the land and water animals. From thence the sun, returning to the summer solstice, in the direction of the North, gives us the longest days. And, as it travels farther in the air, it burns that which is over our heads, dries up the earth, ripens the grains and hastens the maturity of the fruits of the trees. At the epoch of its greatest heat, the shadows which the sun makes at mid-day are short, because it shines from above, from the air over our heads. Thus the longest days are those when the shadows are shortest, in the same way that the shortest days are those when the shadows are longest. It is this which happens to all of us "Hetero-skii" (shadowed-on-one-side) who inhabit the northern regions of the earth. But there are people who, two days in the year, are

completely without shade at mid-day, because the sun, being perpendicularly over their heads, lights them so equally from all sides, that it could through a narrow opening shine at the bottom of a well. Thus there are some who call them "askii" (shadowless). For those who live beyond the land of spices see their shadow now on one side, now on another, the only inhabitants of this land of which the shade falls at mid-day; thus they are given the name of "amphiskii," (shadowed-on-both-sides). All these phenomena happen while the sun is passing into northern regions: they give us an idea of the heat thrown on the air, by the rays of the sun and of the effects that they produce. Next we pass to autumn, which breaks up the excessive heat, lessening the warmth little by little, and by a moderate temperature brings us back without suffering to winter, to the time when the sun returns from the northern regions to the southern. It is thus that seasons, following the course of the sun, succeed each other to rule our life.

"Let them be for days" Genesis 1:14 says Scripture, not to produce them but to rule them; because day and night are older than the creation of the luminaries and it is this that the psalm declares to us. "The sun to rule by day...the moon and stars to rule by night." How does the sun rule by day? Because carrying everywhere light with it, it is no sooner risen above the horizon than it drives away darkness and brings us day. Thus we might, without self deception, define day as air lighted by the sun, or as the space of time that the sun passes in our hemisphere. The functions of the sun and moon serve further to mark years. The moon, after having twelve times run her course, forms a year which sometimes needs an intercalary month to make it exactly agree with the seasons. Such was formerly the year of the Hebrews and of the early Greeks. As to the solar year, it is the time that the sun, having started from a certain sign, takes to return to it in its normal progress.

9. "And God made two great lights." Genesis 1:16 The word "great," if, for example we say it of the heaven of the earth or of the sea, may have an absolute sense; but ordinarily it has only a relative meaning, as a great horse, or a great ox. It is not that these animals are of an immoderate size, but that in comparison with their like they deserve the title of great. What idea shall we ourselves form here of greatness? Shall it be the idea that we have of it in the ant and in all the little creatures of nature, which we call great in comparison with those like themselves, and to show their superiority over them? Or shall we predicate greatness of the luminaries, as of the natural greatness inherent in them? As for me, I think so. If the sun and moon are great, it is not in comparison with the smaller stars, but because they have such a circumference that the splendour which they diffuse lights up the heavens and the air, embracing at the same time earth and sea. In whatever part of heaven they may be, whether rising, or setting, or in mid heaven, they appear always the same in the eyes of men, a manifest proof of their prodigious size. For the whole extent of heaven cannot make them appear greater in one place and smaller in another. Objects which we see afar off appear dwarfed to our eyes, and in measure as they approach us we can form a juster idea of their size. But there is no one who can be nearer or more distant from the sun. All the inhabitants of the earth see it at the same distance. Indians and Britons see it of the same size. The people of the East do not see it decrease in magnitude when it sets; those of the West do not find it smaller when it rises. If it is in the middle of the heavens it does not vary in either aspect. Do not be deceived by mere appearance, and because it looks a cubit's breadth, imagine it to be no bigger. At a very great distance objects always lose size in our eyes; sight, not being able to clear the intermediary space, is as it were exhausted in the middle of its course, and only a small part of it reaches the visible object. Our power of sight is small and makes

all we see seem small, affecting what it sees by its own condition. Thus, then, if sight is mistaken its testimony is fallible. Recall your own impressions and you will find in yourself the proof of my words. If you have ever from the top of a high mountain looked at a large and level plain, how big did the yokes of oxen appear to you? How big were the ploughmen themselves? Did they not look like ants? If from the top of a commanding rock, looking over the wide sea, you cast your eyes over the vast extent how big did the greatest islands appear to you? How large did one of those barks of great tonnage, which unfurl their white sails to the blue sea, appear to you. Did it not look smaller than a dove? It is because sight, as I have just told you, loses itself in the air, becomes weak and cannot seize with exactness the object which it sees. And further: your sight shows you high mountains intersected by valleys as rounded and smooth, because it reaches only to the salient parts, and is not able, on account of its weakness, to penetrate into the valleys which separate them. It does not even preserve the form of objects, and thinks that all square towers are round. Thus all proves that at a great distance sight only presents to us obscure and confused objects. The luminary is then great, according to the witness of Scripture, and infinitely greater than it appears.

10. See again another evident proof of its greatness. Although the heaven may be full of stars without number, the light contributed by them all could not disperse the gloom of night. The sun alone, from the time that it appeared on the horizon, while it was still expected and had not yet risen completely above the earth, dispersed the darkness, outshone the stars, dissolved and diffused the air, which was hitherto thick and condensed over our heads, and produced thus the morning breeze and the dew which in fine weather streams over the earth. Could the earth with such a wide extent be lighted up entirely in one moment if an immense disc

were not pouring forth its light over it? Recognise here the wisdom of the Artificer. See how He made the heat of the sun proportionate to this distance. Its heat is so regulated that it neither consumes the earth by excess, nor lets it grow cold and sterile by defect.

To all this the properties of the moon are near akin; she, too, has an immense body, whose splendour only yields to that of the sun. Our eyes, however, do not always see her in her full size. Now she presents a perfectly rounded disc, now when diminished and lessened she shows a deficiency on one side. When waxing she is shadowed on one side, and when she is waning another side is hidden. Now it is not without a secret reason of the divine Maker of the universe, that the moon appears from time to time under such different forms. It presents a striking example of our nature. Nothing is stable in man; here from nothingness he raises himself to perfection; there after having hasted to put forth his strength to attain his full greatness he suddenly is subject to gradual deterioration, and is destroyed by diminution. Thus, the sight of the moon, making us think of the rapid vicissitudes of human things, ought to teach us not to pride ourselves on the good things of this life, and not to glory in our power, not to be carried away by uncertain riches, to despise our flesh which is subject to change, and to take care of the soul, for its good is unmoved. If you cannot behold without sadness the moon losing its splendour by gradual and imperceptible decrease, how much more distressed should you be at the sight of a soul, who, after having possessed virtue, loses its beauty by neglect, and does not remain constant to its affections, but is agitated and constantly changes because its purposes are unstable. What Scripture says is very true, "As for a fool he changes as the moon." Sirach 27:11

I believe also that the variations of the moon do not take place without exerting great influence upon the organization of animals and of all living things. This is because bodies are differently disposed at its waxing and waning. When she wanes they lose their density and become void. When she waxes and is approaching her fullness they appear to fill themselves at the same time with her, thanks to an imperceptible moisture that she emits mixed with heat, which penetrates everywhere. For proof, see how those who sleep under the moon feel abundant moisture filling their heads; see how fresh meat is quickly turned under the action of the moon; see the brain of animals, the moistest part of marine animals, the pith of trees. Evidently the moon must be, as Scripture says, of enormous size and power to make all nature thus participate in her changes.

11. On its variations depends also the condition of the air, as is proved by sudden disturbances which often come after the new moon, in the midst of a calm and of a stillness in the winds, to agitate the clouds and to hurl them against each other; as the flux and reflux in straits, and the ebb and flow of the ocean prove, so that those who live on its shores see it regularly following the revolutions of the moon. The waters of straits approach and retreat from one shore to the other during the different phases of the moon; but, when she is new, they have not an instant of rest, and move in perpetual swaying to and fro, until the moon, reappearing, regulates their reflux. As to the Western sea, we see it in its ebb and flow now return into its bed, and now overflow, as the moon draws it back by her respiration and then, by her expiration, urges it to its own boundaries.

I have entered into these details, to show you the grandeur of the luminaries, and to make you see that, in the inspired words, there is not one idle syllable. And yet my sermon has scarcely touched on any important point; there are many other discoveries about the size and distance of the sun and moon to which any one who will make a serious study of their action and of their characteristics may arrive by the aid of reason. Let me then ingenuously make an avowal of my weakness, for fear that you should measure the mighty works of the Creator by my words. The little that I have said ought the rather to make you conjecture the marvels on which I have omitted to dwell. We must not then measure the moon with the eye, but with the reason. Reason, for the discovery of truth, is much surer than the eye.

Everywhere ridiculous old women's tales, imagined in the delirium of drunkenness, have been circulated; such as that enchantments can remove the moon from its place and make it descend to the earth. How could a magician's charm shake that of which the Most High has laid the foundations? And if once torn out what place could hold it?

Do you wish from slight indications to have a proof of the moon's size? All the towns in the world, however distant from each other, equally receive the light from the moon in those streets that are turned towards its rising. If she did not look on all face to face, those only would be entirely lighted up which were exactly opposite; as to those beyond the extremities of her disc, they would only receive diverted and oblique rays. It is this effect which the light of lamps produces in houses; if a lamp is surrounded by several persons, only the shadow of the person who is directly opposite to it is cast in a straight line, the others follow inclined lines on each side. In the same way, if the body of the moon were not of an immense and prodigious size she could not extend herself alike to all. In reality, when the moon rises in the equinoctial regions, all equally enjoy her light, both those who inhabit the icy zone, under the revolutions of the Bear, and those who dwell in the extreme south in the neighbourhood of the torrid zone. She gives us an idea of her size by appearing to be face to face with all people. Who then can deny the immensity of a body which divides itself equally over such a wide extent?

But enough on the greatness of the sun and moon. May He Who has given us intelligence to recognise in the smallest objects of creation the great wisdom of the Contriver make us find in great bodies a still higher idea of their Creator. However, compared with their Author, the sun and moon are but a fly and an ant. The whole universe cannot give us a right idea of the greatness of God; and it is only by signs, weak and slight in themselves, often by the help of the smallest insects and of the least plants, that we raise ourselves to Him. Content with these words let us offer our thanks, I to Him who has given me the ministry of the Word, you to Him who feeds you with spiritual food; Who, even at this moment, makes you find in my weak voice the strength of barley bread. May He feed you for ever, and in proportion to your faith grant you the manifestation of the Spirit in Jesus Christ our Lord, to whom be glory and power for ever and ever. Amen.

## Homily 7
### The creation of moving creatures.

1. "And God said, Let the waters bring forth abundantly the moving creature that has life" after their kind, "and fowl that may fly above the earth" after their kind. Genesis 1:20 After the creation of the luminaries the waters are now filled with living beings and its own adornment is given to this part of the world. Earth had received hers from her own plants, the heavens had received the flowers of the stars, and, like two eyes, the great luminaries beautified them in concert. It still remained for the waters to receive their adornment. The command was given, and immediately

the rivers and lakes becoming fruitful brought forth their natural broods; the sea travailed with all kinds of swimming creatures; not even in mud and marshes did the water remain idle; it took its part in creation. Everywhere from its ebullition frogs, gnats and flies came forth. For that which we see today is the sign of the past. Thus everywhere the water hastened to obey the Creator's command. Who could count the species which the great and ineffable power of God caused to be suddenly seen living and moving, when this command had empowered the waters to bring forth life? Let the waters bring forth moving creatures that have life. Then for the first time is made a being with life and feeling. For though plants and trees be said to live, seeing that they share the power of being nourished and growing; nevertheless they are neither living beings, nor have they life. To create these last God said, "Let the water produce moving creatures."

Every creature that swims, whether it skims on the surface of the waters, or cleaves the depths, is of the nature of a moving creature, since it drags itself on the body of the water. Certain aquatic animals have feet and walk; especially amphibia, such as seals, crabs, crocodiles, river horses and frogs; but they are above all gifted with the power of swimming. Thus it is said, Let the waters produce moving creatures. In these few words what species is omitted? Which is not included in the command of the Creator? Do we not see viviparous animals, seals, dolphins, rays and all cartilaginous animals? Do we not see oviparous animals comprising every sort of fish, those which have a skin and those which have scales, those which have fins and those which have not? This command has only required one word, even less than a word, a sign, a motion of the divine will, and it has such a wide sense that it includes all the varieties and all the families of fish. To review them all would be to undertake to count the waves of the ocean or to measure its waters in the hollow of the hand. "Let the waters produce moving creatures." That is to say, those which people the high seas and those which love the shores; those which inhabit the depths and those which attach themselves to rocks; those which are gregarious and those which live dispersed, the cetaceous, the huge, and the tiny. It is from the same power, the same command, that all, small and great receive their existence. "Let the waters bring forth." These words show you the natural affinity of animals which swim in the water; thus, fish, when drawn out of the water, quickly die, because they have no respiration such as could attract our air and water is their element, as air is that of terrestrial animals. The reason for it is clear. With us the lung, that porous and spongy portion of the inward parts which receives air by the dilatation of the chest, disperses and cools interior warmth; in fish the motion of the gills, which open and shut by turns to take in and to eject the water, takes the place of respiration. Fish have a peculiar lot, a special nature, a nourishment of their own, a life apart. Thus they cannot be tamed and cannot bear the touch of a man's hand.

2. "Let the waters bring forth moving creatures after their kind." God caused to be born the firstlings of each species to serve as seeds for nature. Their multitudinous numbers are kept up in subsequent succession, when it is necessary for them to grow and multiply. Of another kind is the species of testacea, as muscles, scallops, sea snails, conches, and the infinite variety of oysters. Another kind is that of the crustacea, as crabs and lobsters; another of fish without shells, with soft and tender flesh, like polypi and cuttle fish. And amidst these last what an innumerable variety! There are weevers, lampreys and eels, produced in the mud of rivers and ponds, which more resemble venomous reptiles than fish in their nature. Of another kind is the species of the ovipara; of another, that of the vivipara. Among the latter are sword-fish, cod,

211

in one word, all cartilaginous fish, and even the greater part of the cetacea, as dolphins, seals, which, it is said, if they see their little ones, still quite young, frightened, take them back into their belly to protect them.

Let the waters bring forth after their kind. The species of the cetacean is one; another is that of small fish. What infinite variety in the different kinds! All have their own names, different food, different form, shape, and quality of flesh. All present infinite variety, and are divided into innumerable classes. Is there a tunny fisher who can enumerate to us the different varieties of that fish? And yet they tell us that at the sight of great swarms of fish they can almost tell the number of the individual ones which compose it. What man is there of all that have spent their long lives by coasts and shores, who can inform us with exactness of the history of all fish?

Some are known to the fishermen of the Indian ocean, others to the toilers of the Egyptian gulf, others to the islanders, others to the men of Mauretania. Great and small were all alike created by this first command, by this ineffable power. What a difference in their food! What a variety in the manner in which each species reproduces itself! Most fish do not hatch eggs like birds; they do not build nests; they do not feed their young with toil; it is the water which receives and vivifies the egg dropped into it. With them the reproduction of each species is invariable, and natures are not mixed. There are none of those unions which, on the earth, produce mules and certain birds contrary to the nature of their species. With fish there is no variety which, like the ox and the sheep, is armed with a half-equipment of teeth, none which ruminates except, according to certain writers, the scar. All have serried and very sharp teeth, for fear their food should escape them if they masticate it for too long a time. In fact, if it were not crushed and swallowed as soon as divided, it would be carried away by the water.

3. The food of fish differs according to their species. Some feed on mud; others eat sea weed; others content themselves with the herbs that grow in water. But the greater part devour each other, and the smaller is food for the larger, and if one which has possessed itself of a fish weaker than itself becomes a prey to another, the conqueror and the conquered are both swallowed up in the belly of the last. And we mortals, do we act otherwise when we press our inferiors? What difference is there between the last fish and the man who, impelled by devouring greed, swallows the weak in the folds of his insatiable avarice? Yon fellow possessed the goods of the poor; you caught him and made him a part of your abundance. You have shown yourself more unjust than the unjust, and more miserly than the miser. Look to it lest you end like the fish, by hook, by weel, or by net. Surely we too, when we have done the deeds of the wicked, shall not escape punishment at the last.

Now see what tricks, what cunning, are to be found in a weak animal, and learn not to imitate wicked doers. The crab loves the flesh of the oyster; but, sheltered by its shell, a solid rampart with which nature has furnished its soft and delicate flesh, it is a difficult prey to seize. Thus they call the oyster "sherd-hide." Thanks to the two shells with which it is enveloped, and which adapt themselves perfectly the one to the other, the claws of the crab are quite powerless. What does he do? When he sees it, sheltered from the wind, warming itself with pleasure, and half opening its shells to the sun, he secretly throws in a pebble, prevents them from closing, and takes by cunning what force had lost. Such is the malice of these animals, deprived as they are of reason and of speech. But I would that you should at once rival the crab in cunning and industry, and abstain from harming your neighbour; this animal is the image of him who craftily approaches his brother, takes advantage of his neighbour's misfortunes, and finds his delight in other men's troubles. O copy not the damned! Content yourself with your own lot. Poverty, with what is necessary, is of more value in the eyes of the wise than all pleasures.

I will not pass in silence the cunning and trickery of the squid, which takes the colour of the rock to which it attaches itself. Most fish swim idly up to the squid as they might to a rock, and become themselves the prey of the crafty creature. Such are men who court ruling powers, bending themselves to all circumstances and not remaining for a moment in the same purpose; who praise self-restraint in the company of the self-restrained, and license in that of the licentious, accommodating their feelings to the pleasure of each. It is difficult to escape them and to put ourselves on guard against their mischief; because it is under the mask of friendship that they hide their clever wickedness. Men like this are ravening wolves covered with sheep's clothing, as the Lord calls them. Flee then fickleness and pliability; seek truth, sincerity, simplicity. The serpent is shifty; so he has been condemned to crawl. The just is an honest man, like Job. Wherefore God sets the solitary in families. So is this great and wide sea, wherein are things creeping innumerable, both small and great beasts. Yet a wise and marvellous order reigns among these animals. Fish do not always deserve our reproaches; often they offer us useful examples. How is it that each sort of fish, content with the region that has been assigned to it, never travels over its own limits to pass into foreign seas? No surveyor has ever distributed to them their habitations, nor enclosed them in walls, nor assigned limits to them; each kind has been naturally assigned its own home. One gulf nourishes one kind of fish, another other sorts; those which swarm here are absent elsewhere. No mountain raises its sharp peaks between them; no rivers bar the passage to them; it is a law of nature, which according to the needs of each kind, has allotted to them their dwelling places with equality and justice.

4. It is not thus with us. Why? Because we incessantly move the ancient landmarks which our fathers have set. We encroach, we add house to house, field to field, to enrich ourselves at the expense of our neighbour. The great fish know the sojourning place that nature has assigned to them; they occupy the sea far from the haunts of men, where no islands lie, and where are no continents rising to confront them, because it has never been crossed and neither curiosity nor need has persuaded sailors to tempt it. The monsters that dwell in this sea are in size like high mountains, so witnesses who have seen tell us, and never cross their boundaries to ravage islands and seaboard towns. Thus each kind is as if it were stationed in towns, in villages, in an ancient country, and has for its dwelling place the regions of the sea which have been assigned to it.

Instances have, however, been known of migratory fish, who, as if common deliberation transported them into strange regions, all start on their march at a given sign. When the time marked for breeding arrives, they, as if awakened by a common law of nature, migrate from gulf to gulf, directing their course toward the North Sea. And at the epoch of their return you may see all these fish streaming like a torrent across the Propontis towards the Euxine Sea. Who puts them in marching array? Where is the prince's order? Has an edict affixed in the public place indicated to them their day of departure? Who serves them as a guide? See how the divine order embraces all and extends to the smallest object. A fish does not resist God's law, and we men cannot endure His precepts of salvation! Do not despise fish because they are dumb and quite unreasoning; rather fear lest, in your resistance to the disposition of the Creator, you have even less reason than they. Listen to the fish, who by their actions all but speak and say: it is for the perpetuation of our race that we undertake this long voyage. They have not the gift of reason, but they have the law of nature firmly seated within them, to show them what they have to do. Let us go, they say, to the North Sea. Its water is sweeter than that of the rest of the sea; for the sun does not remain long there, and its rays do not draw up all the drinkable portions. Even sea creatures love fresh water. Thus one often sees them enter into rivers and swim far up them from the sea. This is the reason which makes them prefer the Euxine Sea to other gulfs, as the most fit for breeding and for bringing up their young. When they have obtained their object the whole tribe returns home. Let us hear these dumb creatures tell us the reason. The Northern sea, they say, is shallow and its surface is exposed to the violence of the wind, and it has few shores and retreats. Thus the winds easily agitate it to its bottom and mingle the sands of its bed with its waves. Besides, it is cold in winter, filled as it is from all directions by large rivers. Wherefore after a moderate enjoyment of its waters, during the summer, when the winter comes they hasten to reach warmer depths and places heated by the sun, and after fleeing from the stormy tracts of the North, they seek a haven in less agitated seas.

5. I myself have seen these marvels, and I have admired the wisdom of God in all things. If beings deprived of reason are capable of thinking and of providing for their own preservation; if a fish knows what it ought to seek and what to shun, what shall we say, who are honoured with reason, instructed by law, encouraged by the promises, made wise by the Spirit, and are nevertheless less reasonable about our own affairs than the fish? They know how to provide for the future, but we renounce our hope of the future and spend our life in brutal indulgence. A fish traverses the extent of

the sea to find what is good for it; what will you say then— you who live in idleness, the mother of all vices? Do not let any one make his ignorance an excuse. There has been implanted in us natural reason which tells us to identify ourselves with good, and to avoid all that is harmful. I need not go far from the sea to find examples, as that is the object of our researches. I have heard it said by one living near the sea, that the sea urchin, a little contemptible creature, often foretells calm and tempest to sailors. When it foresees a disturbance of the winds, it gets under a great pebble, and clinging to it as to an anchor, it tosses about in safety, retained by the weight which prevents it from becoming the plaything of the waves. It is a certain sign for sailors that they are threatened with a violent agitation of the winds. No astrologer, no Chaldæan, reading in the rising of the stars the disturbances of the air, has ever communicated his secret to the urchin: it is the Lord of the sea and of the winds who has impressed on this little animal a manifest proof of His great wisdom. God has foreseen all, He has neglected nothing. His eye, which never sleeps, watches over all. He is present everywhere and gives to each being the means of preservation. If God has not left the sea urchin outside His providence, is He without care for you?

"Husbands love your wives." Ephesians 5:25 Although formed of two bodies you are united to live in the communion of wedlock. May this natural link, may this yoke imposed by the blessing, reunite those who are divided. The viper, the cruelest of reptiles, unites itself with the sea lamprey, and, announcing its presence by a hiss, it calls it from the depths to conjugal union. The lamprey obeys, and is united to this venomous animal. What does this mean? However hard, however fierce a husband may be, the wife ought to bear with him, and not wish to find any pretext for breaking the union. He strikes you, but he is your husband. He is a drunkard, but he is united to you by nature. He is brutal and cross, but he is henceforth one of your members, and the most precious of all.

6. Let husbands listen as well: here is a lesson for them. The viper vomits forth its venom in respect for marriage; and you, will you not put aside the barbarity and the inhumanity of your soul, out of respect for your union? Perhaps the example of the viper contains another meaning. The union of the viper and of the lamprey is an adulterous violation of nature. You, who are plotting against other men's wedlock, learn what creeping creature you are like. I have only one object, to make all I say turn to the edification of the Church. Let then libertines put a restraint on their passions, for they are taught by the examples set by creatures of earth and sea.

My bodily infirmity and the lateness of the hour force me to end my discourse. However, I have still many observations to make on the products of the sea, for the admiration of my attentive audience. To speak of the sea itself, how does its water change into salt? How is it that coral, a stone so much esteemed, is a plant in the midst of the sea, and when once exposed to the air becomes hard as a rock? Why has nature enclosed in the meanest of animals, in an oyster, so precious an object as a pearl? For these pearls, which are coveted by the caskets of kings, are cast upon the shores, upon the coasts, upon sharp rocks, and enclosed in oyster shells. How can the sea pinna produce her fleece of gold, which no dye has ever imitated? How can shells give kings purple of a brilliancy not surpassed by the flowers of the field?

"Let the waters bring forth." What necessary object was there that did not immediately appear? What object of luxury was not given to man? Some to supply his needs, some to make him contemplate the marvels of creation. Some are terrible, so as to take our idleness to school. "God created great whales." Genesis 1:21 Scripture gives them the name of "great" not because they are greater than a shrimp and a sprat, but because the size of their bodies equals that of great hills. Thus when they swim on the surface of the waters one often sees them appear like islands. But these monstrous creatures do not frequent our coasts and shores; they inhabit the Atlantic ocean. Such are these animals created to strike us with terror and awe. If now you hear say that the greatest vessels, sailing with full sails, are easily stopped by a very small fish, by the remora, and so forcibly that the ship remains motionless for a long time, as if it had taken root in the middle of the sea, do you not see in this little creature a like proof of the power of the Creator? Sword fish, saw fish, dog fish, whales, and sharks, are not therefore the only things to be dreaded; we have to fear no less the spike of the stingray even after its death, and the sea-hare, whose mortal blows are as rapid as they are inevitable. Thus the Creator wishes that all may keep you awake, so that full of hope in Him you may avoid the evils with which all these creatures threaten you.

But let us come out of the depths of the sea and take refuge upon the shore. For the marvels of creation, coming one after the other in constant succession like the waves, have submerged my discourse. However, I should not be surprised if, after finding greater wonders upon the earth, my spirit seeks like Jonah's to flee to the sea. But it seems to me, that meeting with these innumerable marvels has made me forget all measure, and experience the fate of those who navigate the high seas without a fixed point to mark their progress, and are often ignorant of the space which they have traversed. This is what has happened to me; while my words glanced at creation, I have not been sensible of the multitude of beings of which I spoke to you. But although this honourable assembly is pleased by my speech, and the recital of the marvels of the Master is grateful to the ears of His servants, let me here bring the ship of my discourse to anchor, and await the day to deliver you the rest. Let us, therefore, all arise, and, giving thanks for what has been said, let us ask for strength to hear the rest. Whilst taking your food may the conversation at your table turn upon what has occupied us this morning and this evening. Filled with these thoughts may you, even in sleep, enjoy the pleasure of the day, so that you may be permitted to say, "I sleep but my heart wakes," Song of Songs 5:2 meditating day and night upon the law of the Lord, to Whom be glory and power world without end. Amen.

## Homily 8
## The creation of fowl and water animals.

1. And God said "Let the earth bring forth the living creature after his kind, cattle and creeping things, and beast of the earth after his kind; and it was so." Genesis 1:24 The command of God advanced step by step and earth thus received her adornment. Yesterday it was said, "Let the waters produce moving things," and today "let the earth bring forth the living creature." Is the earth then alive? And are the mad-minded Manichæans right in giving it a soul? At these words "Let the earth bring forth," it did not produce a germ contained in it, but He who gave the order at the same time gifted it with the grace and power to bring forth. When the earth had heard this command "Let the earth bring forth grass and the tree yielding fruit," it was not grass that it had hidden in it that it caused to spring forth, it did not bring to the surface a palm tree, an oak, a cypress, hitherto kept back in its depths. It is the word of God which forms the nature of things created. "Let the earth bring forth;" that is to say not that she may bring forth that which she has but that she may acquire that which she lacks, when God gives her the power. Even so now, "Let the earth bring forth the living creature," not the living creature that is contained in herself, but

that which the command of God gives her. Further, the Manichæans contradict themselves, because if the earth has brought forth the life, she has left herself despoiled of life. Their execrable doctrine needs no demonstration.

But why did the waters receive the command to bring forth the moving creature that has life and the earth to bring forth the living creature? We conclude that, by their nature, swimming creatures appear only to have an imperfect life, because they live in the thick element of water. They are hard of hearing, and their sight is dull because they see through the water; they have no memory, no imagination, no idea of social intercourse. Thus divine language appears to indicate that, in aquatic animals, the carnal life originates their psychic movements, while in terrestrial animals, gifted with a more perfect life, the soul enjoys supreme authority. In fact the greater part of quadrupeds have more power of penetration in their senses; their apprehension of present objects is keen, and they keep all exact remembrance of the past. It seems therefore, that God, after the command given to the waters to bring forth moving creatures that have life, created simply living bodies for aquatic animals, while for terrestrial animals He commanded the soul to exist and to direct the body, showing thus that the inhabitants of the earth are gifted with greater vital force. Without doubt terrestrial animals are devoid of reason. At the same time how many affections of the soul each one of them expresses by the voice of nature! They express by cries their joy and sadness, recognition of what is familiar to them, the need of food, regret at being separated from their companions, and numberless emotions. Aquatic animals, on the contrary, are not only dumb; it is impossible to tame them, to teach them, to train them for man's society. "The ox knows his owner, and the ass his master's crib." Isaiah 1:3 But the fish does not know who feeds him. The ass knows a familiar voice, he knows the road which he has often trodden, and even, if man loses his way, he sometimes serves him as a guide. His hearing is more acute than that of any other terrestrial animal. What animal of the sea can show so much rancour and resentment as the camel? The camel conceals its resentment for a long time after it has been struck, until it finds an opportunity, and then repays the wrong. Listen, you whose heart does not pardon, you who practise vengeance as a virtue; see what you resemble when you keep your anger for so long against your neighbour like a spark, hidden in the ashes, and only waiting for fuel to set your heart ablaze!

2. "Let the earth bring forth a living soul." Why did the earth produce a living soul? So that you may make a difference between the soul of cattle and that of man. You will soon learn how the human soul was formed; hear now about the soul of creatures devoid of reason. Since, according to Scripture, "the life of every creature is in the blood," as the blood when thickened changes into flesh, and flesh when corrupted decomposes into earth, so the soul of beasts is naturally an earthy substance. "Let the earth bring forth a living soul." See the affinity of the soul with blood, of blood with flesh, of flesh with earth; and remounting in an inverse sense from the earth to the flesh, from the flesh to the blood, from the blood to the soul, you will find that the soul of beasts is earth. Do not suppose that it is older than the essence of their body, nor that it survives the dissolution of the flesh; avoid the nonsense of those arrogant philosophers who do not blush to liken their soul to that of a dog; who say that they have been formerly themselves women, shrubs, fish. Have they ever been fish? I do not know; but I do not fear to affirm that in their writings they show less sense than fish. "Let the earth bring forth the living creature." Perhaps many of you ask why there is such a long silence in the middle of the rapid rush

of my discourse. The more studious among my auditors will not be ignorant of the reason why words fail me. What! Have I not seen them look at each other, and make signs to make me look at them, and to remind me of what I have passed over? I have forgotten a part of the creation, and that one of the most considerable, and my discourse was almost finished without touching upon it. "Let the waters bring forth abundantly the moving creature that has life and fowl that may fly above the earth in the open firmament, of heaven." Genesis 1:20 I spoke of fish as long as eventide allowed: today we have passed to the examination of terrestrial animals; between the two, birds have escaped us. We are forgetful like travellers who unmindful of some important object, are obliged, although they be far on their road, to retrace their steps, punished for their negligence by the weariness of the journey. So we have to turn back. That which we have omitted is not to be despised. It is the third part of the animal creation, if indeed there are three kinds of animals, land, winged and water.

"Let the waters" it is said "bring forth abundantly moving creature that has life and fowl that may fly above the earth in the open firmament of heaven." Why do the waters give birth also to birds? Because there is, so to say, a family link between the creatures that fly and those that swim. In the same way that fish cut the waters, using their fins to carry them forward and their tails to direct their movements round and round and straightforward, so we see birds float in the air by the help of their wings. Both endowed with the property of swimming, their common derivation from the waters has made them of one family. At the same time no bird is without feet, because finding all its food upon the earth it cannot do without their service. Rapacious birds have pointed claws to enable them to close on their prey; to the rest has been given the indispensable ministry of feet to seek their food and to provide for the other needs of life. There are a few who walk badly, whose feet are neither suitable for walking nor for preying. Among this number are swallows, incapable of walking and seeking their prey, and the birds called swifts who live on little insects carried about by the air. As to the swallow, its flight, which grazes the earth, fulfils the function of feet.

3. There are also innumerable kinds of birds. If we review them all, as we have partly done the fish, we shall find that under one name, the creatures which fly differ infinitely in size, form and colour; that in their life, their actions and their manners, they present a variety equally beyond the power of description. Thus some have tried to imagine names for them of which the singularity and the strangeness might, like brands, mark the distinctive character of each kind known. Some, as eagles, have been called Schizoptera, others Dermoptera, as the bats, others Ptilota, as wasps, others Coleoptera, as beetles and all those insects which brought forth in cases and coverings, break their prison to fly away in liberty. But we have enough words of common usage to characterise each species and to mark the distinction which Scripture sets up between clean and unclean birds. Thus the species of carnivora is of one sort and of one constitution which suits their manner of living, sharp talons, curved beak, swift wings, allowing them to swoop easily upon their prey and to tear it up after having seized it. The constitution of those who pick up seeds is different, and again that of those who live on all they come across. What a variety in all these creatures! Some are gregarious, except the birds of prey who know no other society than conjugal union; but innumerable kinds, doves, cranes, starlings, jackdaws, like a common life. Among them some live without a chief and in a sort of independence; others, as cranes, do not refuse to submit themselves to a leader. And a fresh difference between them is that some are stationary and non-migratory; others

undertake long voyages and the greater part of them migrate at the approach of winter. Nearly all birds can be tamed and are capable of training, except the weakest, who through fear and timidity cannot bear the constant and annoying contact of the hand. Some like the society of man and inhabit our dwellings; others delight in mountains and in desert places. There is a great difference too in their peculiar notes. Some twitter and chatter, others are silent, some have a melodious and sonorous voice, some are wholly inharmonious and incapable of song; some imitate the voice of man, taught their mimicry either by nature or training; others always give forth the same monotonous cry. The cock is proud; the peacock is vain of his beauty; doves and fowls are amorous, always seeking each other's society. The partridge is deceitful and jealous, lending perfidious help to the huntsmen to seize their prey.

4. What a variety, I have said, in the actions and lives of flying creatures. Some of these unreasoning creatures even have a government, if the feature of government is to make the activity of all the individuals centre in one common end. This may be observed in bees. They have a common dwelling place; they fly in the air together, they work at the same work together; and what is still more extraordinary is that they give themselves to these labours under the guidance of a king and superintendent, and that they do not allow themselves to fly to the meadows without seeing if the king is flying at their head. As to this king, it is not election that gives him this authority; ignorance on the part of the people often puts the worst man in power; it is not fate; the blind decisions of fate often give authority to the most unworthy. It is not heredity that places him on the throne; it is only too common to see the children of kings, corrupted by luxury and flattery, living in ignorance of all virtue. It is nature which makes the king of the bees, for nature gives him superior size, beauty, and sweetness of

character. He has a sting like the others, but he does not use it to revenge himself. It is a principle of natural and unwritten law, that those who are raised to high office, ought to be lenient in punishing. Even bees who do not follow the example of their king, repent without delay of their imprudence, since they lose their lives with their sting. Listen, Christians, you to whom it is forbidden to "recompense evil for evil" and commanded "to overcome evil with good." Take the bee for your model, which constructs its cells without injuring any one and without interfering with the goods of others. It gathers openly wax from the flowers with its mouth, drawing in the honey scattered over them like dew, and injects it into the hollow of its cells. Thus at first honey is liquid; time thickens it and gives it its sweetness. The book of Proverbs has given the bee the most honourable and the best praise by calling her wise and industrious. How much activity she exerts in gathering this precious nourishment, by which both kings and men of low degree are brought to health! How great is the art and cunning she displays in the construction of the store houses which are destined to receive the honey! After having spread the wax like a thin membrane, she distributes it in contiguous compartments which, weak though they are, by their number and by their mass, sustain the whole edifice. Each cell in fact holds to the one next to it, and is separated by a thin partition; we thus see two or three galleries of cells built one upon the other. The bee takes care not to make one vast cavity, for fear it might break under the weight of the liquid, and allow it to escape. See how the discoveries of geometry are mere by-works to the wise bee!

The rows of honey-comb are all hexagonal with equal sides. They do not bear on each other in straight lines, lest the supports should press on empty spaces between and give way; but the angles of the lower hexagons serve as foundations and bases to those which rise above, so as to furnish a sure support to the lower mass, and so that each cell may securely keep the liquid honey.

5. How shall we make an exact review of all the peculiarities of the life of birds? During the night cranes keep watch in turn; some sleep, others make the rounds and procure a quiet slumber for their companions. After having finished his duty, the sentry utters a cry, and goes to sleep, and the one who awakes, in his turn, repays the security which he has enjoyed. You will see the same order reign in their flight. One leads the way, and when it has guided the flight of the flock for a certain time, it passes to the rear, leaving to the one who comes after the care of directing the march.

The conduct of storks comes very near intelligent reason. In these regions the same season sees them all migrate. They all start at one given signal. And it seems to me that our crows, serving them as escort, go to bring them back, and to help them against the attacks of hostile birds. The proof is that in this season not a single crow appears, and that they return with wounds, evident marks of the help and of the assistance that they have lent. Who has explained to them the laws of hospitality? Who has threatened them with the penalties of desertion? For not one is missing from the company. Listen, all inhospitable hearts, you who shut your doors, whose house is never open either in the winter or in the night to travellers. The solicitude of storks for their old would be sufficient, if our children would reflect upon it, to make them love their parents; because there is no one so failing in good sense, as not to deem it a shame to be surpassed in virtue by birds devoid of reason. The storks surround their father, when old age makes his feathers drop off, warm him with their wings, and provide abundantly for his support, and even in their flight they help him as much as they are able, raising him gently on each side upon their wings, a conduct so notorious that it has given to gratitude the name of "antipelargosis." Let no one lament poverty; let not the man whose house is bare despair of his life, when he considers the industry of the swallow. To build her nest, she brings bits of straw in her beak; and, as she cannot raise the mud in her claws, she moistens the end of her wings in water and then rolls in very fine dust and thus procures mud. After having united, little by little, the bits of straw with this mud, as with glue, she feeds her young; and if any one of them has its eyes injured, she has a natural remedy to heal the sight of her little ones.

This sight ought to warn you not to take to evil ways on account of poverty; and, even if you are reduced to the last extremity, not to lose all hope; not to abandon yourself to inaction and idleness, but to have recourse to God. If He is so bountiful to the swallow, what will He not do for those who call upon Him with all their heart?

The halcyon is a sea bird, which lays its eggs along the shore, or deposits them in the sand. And it lays in the middle of winter, when the violence of the winds dashes the sea against the land. Yet all winds are hushed, and the wave of the sea grows calm, during the seven days that the halcyon sits.

For it only takes seven days to hatch the young. Then, as they are in need of food so that they may grow, God, in His munificence, grants another seven days to this tiny animal. All sailors know this, and call these days halcyon days. If divine Providence has established these marvellous laws in favour of creatures devoid of reason, it is to induce you to ask for your salvation from God. Is there a wonder which He will not perform for you— you have been made in His image, when for so little a bird, the great, the fearful sea is held in check and is commanded in the midst of winter to be calm.

6. It is said that the turtle-dove, once separated from her mate, does not contract a new union, but remains in widowhood, in remembrance of her first alliance. Listen, O women! What veneration for widowhood, even in these creatures devoid of reason, how they prefer it to an unbecoming multiplicity of marriages. The eagle shows the greatest injustice in the education which she gives to her young. When she has hatched two little ones, she throws one on the ground, thrusting it out with blows from her wings, and only acknowledges the remaining one. It is the difficulty of finding food which has made her repulse the offspring she has brought forth. But the osprey, it is said, will not allow it to perish, she carries it away and brings it up with her young ones. Such are parents who, under the plea of poverty, expose their children; such are again those who, in the distribution of their inheritance, make unequal divisions. Since they have given existence equally to each of their children, it is just that they should equally and without preference furnish them with the means of livelihood. Beware of imitating the cruelty of birds with hooked talons. When they see their young are from henceforth capable of encountering the air in their flight, they throw them out of the nest, striking them and pushing them with their wings, and do not take the least care of them. The love of the crow for its young is laudable! When they begin to fly, she follows them, gives them food, and for a very long time provides for their nourishment. Many birds have no need of union with males to conceive. But their eggs are unfruitful, except those of vultures, who more often, it is said, bring forth without coupling: and this although they have a very long life, which often reaches its hundredth year. Note and retain, I pray you, this point in the history of birds; and if ever you see any one laugh at our mystery, as if it were impossible and contrary to nature that a virgin should become a mother without losing the purity of her virginity, bethink you that He who would

save the faithful by the foolishness of preaching, has given us beforehand in nature a thousand reasons for believing in the marvellous.

7. "Let the waters bring forth the moving creatures that have life, and fowl that may fly above the earth in the open firmament of heaven." They received the command to fly above the earth because earth provides them with nourishment. "In the firmament of heaven," that is to say, as we have said before, in that part of the air called οὐρανός, heaven, from the word ὁ ῥᾶν, which means to see; called firmament, because the air which extends over our heads, compared to the æther, has greater density, and is thickened by the vapours which exhale from the earth. You have then heaven adorned, earth beautified, the sea peopled with its own creatures, the air filled with birds which scour it in every direction. Studious listener, think of all these creations which God has drawn out of nothing, think of all those which my speech has left out, to avoid tediousness, and not to exceed my limits; recognise everywhere the wisdom of God; never cease to wonder, and, through every creature, to glorify the Creator.

There are some kinds of birds which live by night in the midst of darkness; others which fly by day in full light. Bats, owls, night-ravens are birds of night: if by chance you cannot sleep, reflect on these nocturnal birds and their peculiarities and glorify their Maker. How is it that the nightingale is always awake when sitting on her eggs, passing the night in a continual melody? How is it that one animal, the bat, is at the same time quadruped and fowl? That it is the only one of the birds to have teeth? That it is viviparous like quadrupeds, and traverses the air, raising itself not upon wings, but upon a kind of membrane? What natural love bats have for each other! How they interlace like a chain and hang the one upon the other! A very rare spectacle among men, who for the greater part prefer individual and private life to the union of common life. Have not those who give themselves up to vain science the eyes of owls? The sight of the owl, piercing during the night time, is dazzled by the splendour of the sun; thus the intelligence of these men, so keen to contemplate vanities, is blind in presence of the true light.

During the day, also, how easy it is for you to admire the Creator everywhere! See how the domestic cock calls you to work with his shrill cry, and how, forerunner of the sun, and early as the traveller, he sends forth labourers to the harvest! What vigilance in geese! With what sagacity they divine secret dangers! Did they not once upon a time save the imperial city? When enemies were advancing by subterranean passages to possess themselves of the capitol of Rome, did not geese announce the danger? Is there any kind of bird whose nature offers nothing for our admiration? Who announces to the vultures that there will be carnage when men march in battle array against one another? You may see flocks of vultures following armies and calculating the result of warlike preparations; a calculation very nearly approaching to human reasoning. How can I describe to you the fearful invasions of locusts, which rise everywhere at a given signal, and pitch their camps all over a country? They do not attack crops until they have received the divine command. Or shall I describe how the remedy for this curse, the thrush, follows them with its insatiable appetite, and the devouring nature that the loving God has given it in His kindness for men? How does the grasshopper modulate its song? Why is it more melodious at midday owing to the air that it breathes in dilating its chest?

But it appears to me that in wishing to describe the marvels of winged creatures, I remain further behind than I should if my feet had tried to match the rapidity of their flight. When you see bees, wasps, in short all those flying creatures called insects, because they have an incision all around, reflect that they have neither respiration nor lungs, and that they are supported by air through all parts of their bodies. Thus they perish, if they are covered with oil, because it stops up their pores. Wash them with vinegar, the pores reopen and the animal returns to life. Our God has created nothing unnecessarily and has omitted nothing that is necessary. If now you cast your eyes upon aquatic creatures, you will find that their organization is quite different. Their feet are not split like those of the crow, nor hooked like those of the carnivora, but large and membraneous; therefore they can easily swim, pushing the water with the membranes of their feet as with oars. Notice how the swan plunges his neck into the depths of the water to draw his food from it, and you will understand the wisdom of the Creator in giving this creature a neck longer than his feet, so that he may throw it like a line, and take the food hidden at the bottom of the water.

8. If we simply read the words of Scripture we find only a few short syllables. "Let the waters bring forth fowl that may fly above the earth in the open firmament of heaven," but if we enquire into the meaning of these words, then the great wonder of the wisdom of the Creator appears. What a difference He has foreseen among winged creatures! How He has divided them by kinds! How He has characterized each one of them by distinct qualities! But the day will not suffice me to recount the wonders of the air. Earth is calling me to describe wild beasts, reptiles and cattle, ready to show us in her turn sights rivalling those of plants, fish, and birds. "Let the earth bring forth the living soul" of domestic animals, of wild beasts, and of reptiles after their kind. What have you to say, you who do not believe in the change that Paul promises you in the resurrection, when you see so many metamorphoses among creatures of the air? What are we not told of the horned worm of

India! First it changes into a caterpillar, then becomes a buzzing insect, and not content with this form, it clothes itself, instead of wings, with loose, broad plates. Thus, O women, when you are seated busy with your weaving, I mean of the silk which is sent you by the Chinese to make your delicate dresses, remember the metamorphoses of this creature, conceive a clear idea of the resurrection, and do not refuse to believe in the change that Paul announces for all men.

But I am ashamed to see that my discourse oversteps the accustomed limits; if I consider the abundance of matters on which I have just discoursed to you, I feel that I am being borne beyond bounds; but when I reflect upon the inexhaustible wisdom which is displayed in the works of creation, I seem to be but at the beginning of my story. Nevertheless, I have not detained you so long without profit. For what would you have done until the evening? You are not pressed by guests, nor expected at banquets. Let me then employ this bodily fast to rejoice your souls. You have often served the flesh for pleasure, today persevere in the ministry of the soul. "Delight yourself also in the Lord and he shall give you the desire of your heart." Do you love riches? Here are spiritual riches. "The judgments of the Lord are true and righteous altogether. More to be desired are they than gold and precious stones." Do you love enjoyment and pleasures? Behold the oracles of the Lord, which, for a healthy soul, are "sweeter than honey and the honey-comb." If I let you go, and if I dismiss this assembly, some will run to the dice, where they will find bad language, sad quarrels and the pangs of avarice. There stands the devil, inflaming the fury of the players with the dotted bones, transporting the same sums of money from one side of the table to the other, now exalting one with victory and throwing the other into despair, now swelling the first with boasting and covering his rival with confusion. Of what use is bodily fasting and filling the soul with innumerable evils? He who does not play spends his leisure elsewhere. What frivolities come from his mouth! What follies strike his ears! Leisure without the fear of the Lord is, for those who do not know the value of time, a school of vice. I hope that my words will be profitable; at least by occupying you here they have prevented you from sinning. Thus the longer I keep you, the longer you are out of the way of evil.

An equitable judge will deem that I have said enough, not if he considers the riches of creation, but if he thinks of our weakness and of the measure one ought to keep in that which tends to pleasure. Earth has welcomed you with its own plants, water with its fish, air with its birds; the continent in its turn is ready to offer you as rich treasures. But let us put an end to this morning banquet, for fear satiety may blunt your taste for the evening one. May He who has filled all with the works of His creation and has left everywhere visible memorials of His wonders, fill your hearts with all spiritual joys in Jesus Christ, our Lord, to whom belong glory and power, world without end. Amen.

**Homily 9**
**The creation of terrestrial animals.**

1. How did you like the fare of my morning's discourse? It seemed to me that I had the good intentions of a poor giver of a feast, who, ambitious of having the credit of keeping a good table saddens his guests by the poor supply of the more expensive dishes. In vain he lavishly covers his table with his mean fare; his ambition only shows his folly. It is for you to judge if I have shared the same fate. Yet, whatever my discourse may have been, take care lest you disregard it. No one refused to sit at the table of Elisha; and yet he only gave his friends wild vegetables. 2 Kings 4:39 I

know the laws of allegory, though less by myself than from the works of others. There are those truly, who do not admit the common sense of the Scriptures, for whom water is not water, but some other nature, who see in a plant, in a fish, what their fancy wishes, who change the nature of reptiles and of wild beasts to suit their allegories, like the interpreters of dreams who explain visions in sleep to make them serve their own ends. For me grass is grass; plant, fish, wild beast, domestic animal, I take all in the literal sense. "For I am not ashamed of the gospel." Romans 1:16 Those who have written about the nature of the universe have discussed at length the shape of the earth. If it be spherical or cylindrical, if it resemble a disc and is equally rounded in all parts, or if it has the forth of a winnowing basket and is hollow in the middle; all these conjectures have been suggested by cosmographers, each one upsetting that of his predecessor. It will not lead me to give less importance to the creation of the universe, that the servant of God, Moses, is silent as to shapes; he has not said that the earth is a hundred and eighty thousand furlongs in circumference; he has not measured into what extent of air its shadow projects itself while the sun revolves around it, nor stated how this shadow, casting itself upon the moon, produces eclipses. He has passed over in silence, as useless, all that is unimportant for us. Shall I then prefer foolish wisdom to the oracles of the Holy Spirit? Shall I not rather exalt Him who, not wishing to fill our minds with these vanities, has regulated all the economy of Scripture in view of the edification and the making perfect of our souls? It is this which those seem to me not to have understood, who, giving themselves up to the distorted meaning of allegory, have undertaken to give a majesty of their own invention to Scripture. It is to believe themselves wiser than the Holy Spirit, and to bring forth their own ideas under a pretext of exegesis. Let us hear Scripture as it has been written.

2. "Let the earth bring forth the living creature." Genesis 1:24
Behold the word of God pervading creation, beginning even then
the efficacy which is seen displayed today, and will be displayed to
the end of the world! As a ball, which one pushes, if it meet a
declivity, descends, carried by its form and the nature of the ground
and does not stop until it has reached a level surface; so nature,
once put in motion by the Divine command, traverses creation
with an equal step, through birth and death, and keeps up the
succession of kinds through resemblance, to the last. Nature always
makes a horse succeed to a horse, a lion to a lion, an eagle to an
eagle, and preserving each animal by these uninterrupted
successions she transmits it to the end of all things. Animals do not
see their peculiarities destroyed or effaced by any length of time;
their nature, as though it had been just constituted, follows the
course of ages, for ever young. "Let the earth bring forth the living
creature." This command has continued and earth does not cease
to obey the Creator. For, if there are creatures which are
successively produced by their predecessors, there are others that
even today we see born from the earth itself. In wet weather she
brings forth grasshoppers and an immense number of insects
which fly in the air and have no names because they are so small;
she also produces mice and frogs. In the environs of Thebes in
Egypt, after abundant rain in hot weather, the country is covered
with field mice. We see mud alone produce eels; they do not
proceed from an egg, nor in any other manner; it is the earth alone
which gives them birth. Let the earth produce a living creature.

Cattle are terrestrial and bent towards the earth. Man, a celestial
growth, rises superior to them as much by the mould of his bodily
conformation as by the dignity of his soul. What is the form of
quadrupeds? Their head is bent towards the earth and looks
towards their belly, and only pursues their belly's good. Your head,

O man! Is turned towards heaven; your eyes look up. When therefore you degrade yourself by the passions of the flesh, slave of your belly, and your lowest parts, you approach animals without reason and becomest like one of them. You are called to more noble cares; "seek those things which are above where Christ sits." Colossians 3:1 Raise your soul above the earth; draw from its natural conformation the rule of your conduct; fix your conversation in heaven. Your true country is the heavenly Jerusalem; your fellow citizens and your compatriots are "the first-born which are written in heaven." Hebrews 12:23

3. "Let the earth bring forth the living creature." Thus when the soul of brutes appeared it was not concealed in the earth, but it was born by the command of God. Brutes have one and the same soul of which the common characteristic is absence of reason. But each animal is distinguished by peculiar qualities. The ox is steady, the ass is lazy, the horse has strong passions, the wolf cannot be tamed, the fox is deceitful, the stag timid, the ant industrious, the dog grateful and faithful in his friendships. As each animal was created the distinctive character of his nature appeared in him in due measure; in the lion spirit, taste for solitary life, an unsociable character. True tyrant of animals, he, in his natural arrogance, admits but few to share his honours. He disdains his yesterday's food and never returns to the remains of the prey. Nature has provided his organs of voice with such great force that often much swifter animals are caught by his roaring alone. The panther, violent and impetuous in his leaps, has a body fitted for his activity and lightness, in accord with the movements of his soul. The bear has a sluggish nature, ways of its own, a sly character, and is very secret; therefore it has an analogous body, heavy, thick, without articulations such as are necessary for a cold dweller in dens.

When we consider the natural and innate care that these creatures without reason take of their lives we shall be induced to watch over ourselves and to think of the salvation of our souls; or rather we shall be the more condemned when we are found falling short even of the imitation of brutes. The bear, which often gets severely wounded, cares for himself and cleverly fills the wounds with mullein, a plant whose nature is very astringent. You will also see the fox heal his wounds with droppings from the pine tree; the tortoise, gorged with the flesh of the viper, finds in the virtue of marjoram a specific against this venomous animal and the serpent heals sore eyes by eating fennel.

And is not reasoning intelligence eclipsed by animals in their provision for atmospheric changes? Do we not see sheep, when winter is approaching, devouring grass with avidity as if to make provision for future scarcity? Do we not also see oxen, long confined in the winter season, recognise the return of spring by a natural sensation, and look to the end of their stables towards the doors, all turning their heads there by common consent? Studious observers have remarked that the hedgehog makes an opening at the two extremities of his hole. If the wind from the north is going to blow he shuts up the aperture which looks towards the north; if the south wind succeeds it the animal passes to the northern door. What lesson do these animals teach man? They not only show us in our Creator a care which extends to all beings, but a certain presentiment of future even in brutes. Then we ought not to attach ourselves to this present life and ought to give all heed to that which is to come. Will you not be industrious for yourself, O man? And will you not lay up in the present age rest in that which is to come, after having seen the example of the ant? The ant during summer collects treasures for winter. Far from giving itself up to idleness, before this season has made it feel its severity, it hastens to work with an invincible zeal until it has abundantly filled its storehouses. Here again, how far it is from being negligent! With what wise foresight it manages so as to keep its provisions as long as possible! With its pincers it cuts the grains in half, for fear lest they should germinate and not serve for its food. If they are damp it dries them; and it does not spread them out in all weathers, but when it feels that the air will keep of a mild temperature. Be sure that you will never see rain fall from the clouds so long as the ant has left the grain out.

What language can attain to the marvels of the Creator? What ear could understand them? And what time would be sufficient to relate them? Let us say, then, with the prophet, "O Lord, how manifold are your works! In wisdom have you made them all." We shall not be able to say in self-justification, that we have learned useful knowledge in books, since the untaught law of nature makes us choose that which is advantageous to us. Do you know what good you ought to do your neighbour? The good that you expect from him yourself. Do you know what is evil? That which you would not wish another to do to you. Neither botanical researches nor the experience of simples have made animals discover those which are useful to them; but each knows naturally what is salutary and marvellously appropriates what suits its nature.

4. Virtues exist in us also by nature, and the soul has affinity with them not by education, but by nature herself. We do not need lessons to hate illness, but by ourselves we repel what afflicts us, the soul has no need of a master to teach us to avoid vice. Now all vice is a sickness of the soul as virtue is its health. Thus those have defined health well who have called it a regularity in the discharge of natural functions; a definition that can be applied without fear to the good condition of the soul. Thus, without having need of lessons, the soul can attain by herself to what is fit and

conformable to nature. Hence it comes that temperance everywhere is praised, justice is in honour, courage admired, and prudence the object of all aims; virtues which concern the soul more than health concerns the body. Children love your parents, and you, "parents provoke not your children to wrath." Does not nature say the same? Paul teaches us nothing new; he only tightens the links of nature. If the lioness loves her cubs, if the she wolf fights to defend her little ones, what shall man say who is unfaithful to the precept and violates nature herself; or the son who insults the old age of his father; or the father whose second marriage has made him forget his first children?

With animals invincible affection unites parents with children. It is the Creator, God Himself, who substitutes the strength of feeling for reason in them. From whence it comes that a lamb as it bounds from the fold, in the midst of a thousand sheep recognises the colour and the voice of its mother, runs to her, and seeks its own sources of milk. If its mother's udders are dry, it is content, and, without stopping, passes by more abundant ones. And how does the mother recognise it among the many lambs? All have the same voice, the same colour, the same smell, as far at least as regards our sense of smell. Yet there is in these animals a more subtle sense than our perception which makes them recognise their own. The little dog has as yet no teeth, nevertheless he defends himself with his mouth against any one who teases him. The calf has as yet no horns, nevertheless he already knows where his weapons will grow. Here we have evident proof that the instinct of animals is innate, and that in all beings there is nothing disorderly, nothing unforeseen. All bear the marks of the wisdom of the Creator, and show that they have come to life with the means of assuring their preservation.

The dog is not gifted with a share of reason; but with him instinct has the power of reason. The dog has learned by nature the secret of elaborate inferences, which sages of the world, after long years of study, have hardly been able to disentangle. When the dog is on the track of game, if he sees it divide in different directions, he examines these different paths, and speech alone fails him to announce his reasoning. The creature, he says, is gone here or there or in another direction. It is neither here nor there; it is therefore in the third direction. And thus, neglecting the false tracks, he discovers the true one. What more is done by those who, gravely occupied in demonstrating theories, trace lines upon the dust and reject two propositions to show that the third is the true one?

Does not the gratitude of the dog shame all who are ungrateful to their benefactors? Many are said to have fallen dead by their murdered masters in lonely places. Others, when a crime has just been committed, have led those who were searching for the murderers, and have caused the criminals to be brought to justice. What will those say who, not content with not loving the Master who has created them and nourished them, have for their friends men whose mouth attacks the Lord, sitting at the same table with them, and, while partaking of their food, blaspheme Him who has given it to them?

5. But let us return to the spectacle of creation. The easiest animals to catch are the most productive. It is on account of this that hares and wild goats produce many little ones, and that wild sheep have twins, for fear lest these species should disappear, consumed by carnivorous animals. Beasts of prey, on the contrary, produce only a few and a lioness with difficulty gives birth to one lion; because, if they say truly, the cub issues from its mother by tearing her with its claws; and vipers are only born by gnawing through the womb, inflicting a proper punishment on their mother. Thus in nature all

has been foreseen, all is the object of continual care. If you examine the members even of animals, you will find that the Creator has given them nothing superfluous, that He has omitted nothing that is necessary. To carnivorous animals He has given pointed teeth which their nature requires for their support. Those that are only half furnished with teeth have received several distinct receptacles for their food. As it is not broken up enough in the first, they are gifted with the power of returning it after it has been swallowed, and it does not assimilate until it has been crushed by rumination. The first, second, third, and fourth stomachs of ruminating animals do not remain idle; each one of them fulfils a necessary function. The neck of the camel is long so that it may lower it to its feet and reach the grass on which it feeds. Bears, lions, tigers, all animals of this sort, have short necks buried in their shoulders; it is because they do not live upon grass and have no need to bend down to the earth; they are carnivorous and eat the animals upon whom they prey.

Why has the elephant a trunk? This enormous creature, the greatest of terrestrial animals, created for the terror of those who meet it, is naturally huge and fleshy. If its neck was large and in proportion to its feet it would be difficult to direct, and would be of such an excessive weight that it would make it lean towards the earth. As it is, its head is attached to the spine of the back by short vertebrae and it has its trunk to take the place of a neck, and with it it picks up its food and draws up its drink. Its feet, without joints, like united columns, support the weight of its body. If it were supported on lax and flexible legs, its joints would constantly give way, equally incapable of supporting its weight, should it wish either to kneel or rise. But it has under the foot a little ankle joint which takes the place of the leg and knee joints whose mobility would never have resisted this enormous and swaying mass. Thus it had need of this nose which nearly touches its feet. Have you seen them in war marching at the head of the phalanx, like living towers, or breaking the enemies' battalions like mountains of flesh with their irresistible charge? If their lower parts were not in accordance with their size they would never have been able to hold their own. Now we are told that the elephant lives three hundred years and more, another reason for him to have solid and unjointed feet. But, as we have said, his trunk, which has the form and the flexibility of a serpent, takes its food from the earth and raises it up. Thus we are right in saying that it is impossible to find anything superfluous or wanting in creation. Well! God has subdued this monstrous animal to us to such a point that he understands the lessons and endures the blows we give him; a manifest proof that the Creator has submitted all to our rule, because we have been made in His image. It is not in great animals only that we see unapproachable wisdom; no less wonders are seen in the smallest. The high tops of the mountains which, near to the clouds and continually beaten by the winds, keep up a perpetual winter, do not arouse more admiration in me than the hollow valleys, which escape the storms of lofty peaks and preserve a constant mild temperature. In the same way in the constitution of animals I am not more astonished at the size of the elephant, than at the mouse, who is feared by the elephant, or at the scorpion's delicate sting, which has been hollowed like a pipe by the supreme artificer to throw venom into the wounds it makes. And let nobody accuse the Creator of having produced venomous animals, destroyers and enemies of our life. Else let them consider it a crime in the schoolmaster when he disciplines the restlessness of youth by the use of the rod and whip to maintain order.

6. Beasts bear witness to the faith. Have you confidence in the Lord? "Thou shall walk upon the asp and the basilisk and you shall

trample under feet the lion and the dragon." With faith you have the power to walk upon serpents and scorpions. Do you not see that the viper which attached itself to the hand of Paul, while he gathered sticks, did not injure him, because it found the saint full of faith? If you have not faith, do not fear beasts so much as your faithlessness, which renders you susceptible of all corruption. But I see that for a long time you have been asking me for an account of the creation of man, and I think I can hear you all cry in your hearts, We are being taught the nature of our belongings, but we are ignorant of ourselves. Let me then speak of it, since it is necessary, and let me put an end to my hesitation. In truth the most difficult of sciences is to know one's self. Not only our eye, from which nothing outside us escapes, cannot see itself; but our mind, so piercing to discover the sins of others, is slow to recognise its own faults. Thus my speech, after eagerly investigating what is external to myself, is slow and hesitating in exploring my own nature. Yet the beholding of heaven and earth does not make us know God better than the attentive study of our being does; I am, says the Prophet, fearfully and wonderfully made; that is to say, in observing myself I have known Your infinite wisdom. And God said "Let us make man." Genesis 1:26 Does not the light of theology shine, in these words, as through windows; and does not the second Person show Himself in a mystical way, without yet manifesting Himself until the great day? Where is the Jew who resisted the truth and pretended that God was speaking to Himself? It is He who spoke, it is said, and it is He who made. "Let there be light and there was light." But then their words contain a manifest absurdity. Where is the smith, the carpenter, the shoemaker, who, without help and alone before the instruments of his trade, would say to himself; let us make the sword, let us put together the plough, let us make the boot? Does he not perform the work of his craft in silence? Strange folly, to say that any one has seated himself to command himself, to watch over himself, to constrain himself, to hurry himself, with the tones of a master! But the unhappy creatures are not afraid to calumniate the Lord Himself. What will they not say with a tongue so well practised in lying? Here, however, words stop their mouth; "And God said let us make man." Tell me; is there then only one Person? It is not written "Let man be made," but, "Let us make man." The preaching of theology remains enveloped in shadow before the appearance of him who was to be instructed, but, now, the creation of man is expected, that faith unveils herself and the dogma of truth appears in all its light. "Let us make man." O enemy of Christ, hear God speaking to His Co-operator, to Him by Whom also He made the worlds, Who upholds all things by the word of His power. But He does not leave the voice of true religion without answer. Thus the Jews, race hostile to truth, when they find themselves pressed, act like beasts enraged against man, who roar at the bars of their cage and show the cruelty and the ferocity of their nature, without being able to assuage their fury. God, they say, addresses Himself to several persons; it is to the angels before Him that He says, "Let us make man." Jewish fiction! A fable whose frivolity shows whence it has come. To reject one person, they admit many. To reject the Son, they raise servants to the dignity of counsellors; they make of our fellow slaves the agents in our creation. The perfect man attains the dignity of an angel; but what creature can be like the Creator? Listen to the continuation. "In our image." What have you to reply? Is there one image of God and the angels? Father and Son have by absolute necessity the same form, but the form is here understood as becomes the divine, not in bodily shape, but in the proper qualities of Godhead. Hear also, you who belong to the new concision Philippians 3:2 and who, under the appearance of Christianity, strengthen the error of the Jews. To Whom does He say, "in our image," to whom if it is not to Him who is "the brightness of His glory and the express image of His person," Hebrews 1:3 "the image of the invisible God"? Colossians 1:15 It is then to His living image, to Him Who has said "I and my Father are one," John 10:30 "He that has seen me has seen the Father," John 14:9 that God says "Let us make man in our image." Where is the unlikeness in these Beings who have only one image? "So God created man." Genesis 1:27 It is not "They made." Here Scripture avoids the plurality of the Persons. After having enlightened the Jew, it dissipates the error of the Gentiles in putting itself under the shelter of unity, to make you understand that the Son is with the Father, and guarding you from the danger of polytheism. He created him in the image of God. God still shows us His co-operator, because He does not say, in His image, but in the image of God.

If God permits, we will say later in what way man was created in the image of God, and how he shares this resemblance. Today we say but only one word. If there is one image, from whence comes the intolerable blasphemy of pretending that the Son is unlike the Father? What ingratitude! You have yourself received this likeness and you refuse it to your Benefactor! You pretend to keep personally that which is in you a gift of grace, and you do not wish that the Son should keep His natural likeness to Him who begot Him.

But evening, which long ago sent the sun to the west, imposes silence upon me. Here, then, let me be content with what I have said, and put my discourse to bed. I have told you enough up to this point to excite your zeal; with the help of the Holy Spirit I will make for you a deeper investigation into the truths which follow. Retire, then, I beg you, with joy, O Christ-loving congregation, and, instead of sumptuous dishes of various delicacies, adorn and sanctify your tables with the remembrance of my words. May the

Anomœan be confounded, the Jew covered with shame, the faithful exultant in the dogmas of truth, and the Lord glorified, the Lord to Whom be glory and power, world without end. Amen.